IMAGES
of America

MEXICAN AMERICANS IN LOS ANGELES

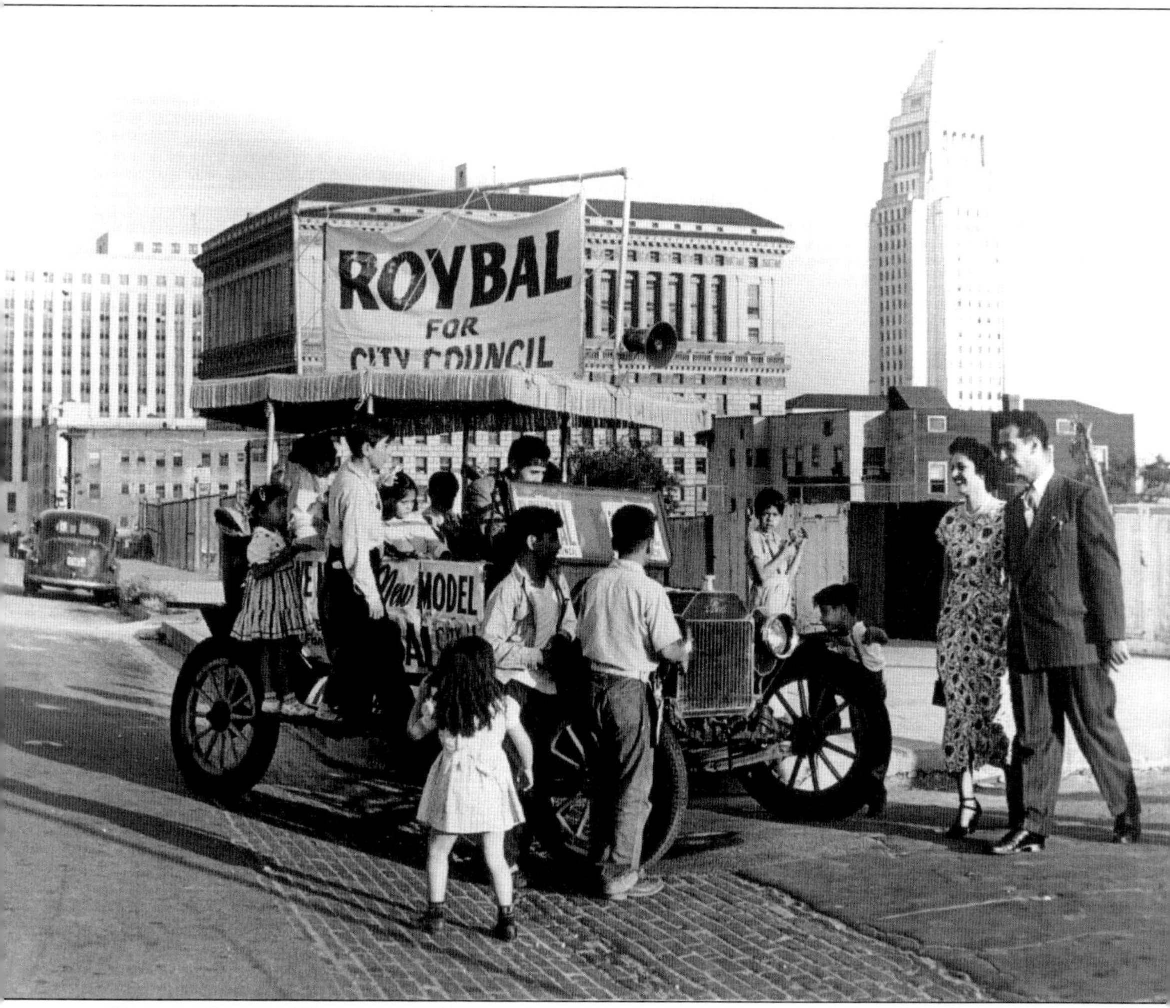

On the Cover: This image of Edward R. Roybal, far right, and his wife, Lucille, was taken in 1949 when he became a candidate for the Los Angeles City Council. Shown is an old model Ford convertible, used as a sound truck for the campaign. The children surround a sign saying, "We need a new model, vote Roybal for City Council." That year, he was elected and forever changed the face of Los Angeles politics. (The UCLA Chicano Studies Research Center and the Edward R. Roybal family.)

IMAGES
of America

MEXICAN AMERICANS IN LOS ANGELES

Alex Moreno Areyan

ARCADIA
PUBLISHING

ISBN 978-0-7385-8006-7

Published by Arcadia Publishing
Charleston, South Carolina

Printed in the United States of America

Library of Congress Control Number: 2009934031

For all general information contact Arcadia Publishing at:
Telephone 843-853-2070
Fax 843-853-0044
E-mail sales@arcadiapublishing.com
For customer service and orders:
Toll-Free 1-888-313-2665

Visit us on the Internet at www.arcadiapublishing.com

I dedicate this book to my parents Alejo Solorio Areyan (1907–1976) and Inez Moreno Areyan (1913–2007). Por haberme dado vida (for giving me life). And to my siblings Rudy, Carmen, Lupe, Julia, Mary, and Mike for picking the crops.

Contents

ACKNOWLEDGMENTS

I would like to express my heartfelt thanks to all those who assisted me while writing this book. They helped in more ways than I can mention. They were immeasurably generous in providing informational leads, connections, and encouragement to remain on course. This book would not have been possible without the help of the following: Rodolfo Acuna, Ph.D.; Ron Arias; Damian Areyan; Ryan Areyan; David Hayes-Bautista, Ph.D.; Connie Calderon; Barbara Carrasco; Sal Castro; Martin Chacon; Abelardo and "Cuca" De La Pena; Lucy Delgado; Victor Delgado; John Doyle; Louis Dominguez; Harry Gamboa; Ignacio and Imelda Gomez, Geree Gonzalez; Teri Griffin; Lizette Guerra; Gabriel Gutierrez, Ph.D.; Carlos Haro, Ph.D.; Ricardo Hong; David Jackson; Nicandro Juarez; Steve Kleinjan; Reynaldo Macias, Ph.D.; Ernie Martinez; Ken Melendez; Irene Mendoza; Eleanor Montano; Magdalena Morales; "Pancho" and Yolie Morales; Eddie Morin; Rosalio Munoz; John Olguin; Margarita Morales Padilla; Juan Gomez-Quinones, Ph.D.; Ramon Rodriguez; Liz Rollice; Chan Romero; Jose Ruiz; Irene Vasquez, Ph.D.; Arthur Verge, Ph.D.; Alex Villalobos; Tatiana Villalobos; Marc Wanamaker; and Diana Ybarra.

I owe a special debt of gratitude to my editor Jerry Roberts. An author could not wish to have a more supportive editor. The time he dedicated to helping me with his technical expertise and friendship is something I will not soon forget. To Mark Guerrero a huge thank you. I was looking for your father and found you. You are one of those true friends who opened the first doors for me, asking for nothing in return. Thank you to my *compadre* (godfather) Joe Ortiz and my *comadre* (godmother) Alycia Enciso. You will never know the depth of my gratitude for opening doors to obtain images that were impossible to find. To Sal Rodriguez, thank you for your unbridled enthusiasm, unflagging encouragement, and your photography. To my daughter Analisa Areyan, thank you for your superb editing skills and for tolerating my computer impairment. I promise to do better.

I am blessed to have had my wife, Linda, at my side during some very late nights. She gave up her valuable time to read, proofread, edit, and reread each word of text. She was also my chief wordsmith. All errors, however, are the sole responsibility of the author, who sometimes disregarded her always correct advice. No one had a more profound impact on this book than she. I could not have written this book without her. My thanks to her are insufficient, and I owe her more than she will ever know.

The abbreviation MAOF denotes, "The Mexican American Opportunities Foundation." The abbreviation UCLA archives denotes, "The Chicano Studies Research Center and Archives and the UCLA Special Collections Department, Charles Young Library."

INTRODUCTION

Greater Los Angeles and its harbor area, including the communities of Wilmington and San Pedro, are home to more than 2.5 million men and women of Mexican American heritage. They are a vital and growing force that, in the past 50 years, has changed the social, cultural, and political face of one of the most important cities of the world. After many decades of being overlooked as part of the geopolitical dynamics of the city, their presence is no longer unnoticed. They continue to reach outward to positions of political, educational, and economic leadership. Their presence is increasing across Los Angeles, and they are conquering barriers that once blocked their paths to success.

The Mexican American community consists of Americans who have made important contributions to the historical development of Los Angeles, although they have remained, for the most part, unsung heroes and heroines frequently ignored by conventional history. Their strengths include an exceptional work ethic, determined spirit, and resiliency to overcome daily impediments. They are entertainers, politicians, activists, educators, sports figures, journalists, artists, exceptional veterans, and entrepreneurs. No longer a subservient minority afraid to shape their own environment, they are, in fact, strong leaders in a city that embraces achievers. This book gives readers glimpses into the accomplishments of some exceptional Mexican Americans from East Los Angeles, Wilmington, San Pedro, and other Greater L.A. areas.

Selecting the individuals to include in this finite pictorial was extremely challenging. Several volumes would be required to include all the talented Mexican American contributors to the city's history. Constraints of space, time, and contacts in reaching some sources have made this book a beginning and not an end. The individuals mentioned here can serve as future role models. The author's hope is that Mexican Americans elsewhere might be motivated to express pride in their cultural heritage by creating similar histories. The adage, "Write your own history, or someone will write it for you," can be true enough.

Foreword

I met Alex Moreno Areyan through a mutual UCLA friend who had heard of the author while doing research on Chicano history. She invited me to listen to Alex as he presented his first book, *Mexican Americans in Redondo Beach and Hermosa Beach.* I was enthralled. Being a Chicano, born and raised in Boyle Heights, East Los Angeles, one of the city's major enclaves for Mexican Americans, it never occurred to me that other vibrant Chicano communities even existed outside of East Los Angeles, much less that they had such an extensive history. I was moved enough by his presentation that I bought his book, shook his hand, and offered him a tour of my old neighborhood if he ever decided to write a book about East Los Angeles.

That day came sooner than I expected. Alex got my number, and took me up on the offer. We spent time perusing some of the barrios of East Los Angeles: Boyle Heights, Estrada Courts, City Terrace, Whittier Boulevard, and visited some of the great cultural and historical landmarks that I remembered from my childhood. In the process, I discovered a kindred soul—a beach Chicano who might not have shared the inner city experience that I had growing up, but who shared the same cultural, religious, and family values that I had learned as a boy.

In his first book, Alex brought a story to life: what it was like to be Mexican American in a predominantly Anglo part of town. Through words and photographs the story is told of individuals and families with strong cultural values, making significant marks on their community as they struggled to find their place in it. Those communities continue to be served by the many contributions made in the past.

In this book, Alex captures the same essence and goes even further, by focusing on communities and barrios that are intrinsically defined by Mexican Americans. We all expect to hear that Mexican Americans live in East Los Angeles, in Wilmington, and in San Pedro. What we don't realize is how much our *gente* have shaped their neighborhoods and beyond, by creating and adding so many dimensions and stories to Los Angeles as a whole. In politics, in entertainment, in sports, and in the military service—we have so many stories to tell and share of individuals who made a lasting impression in these communities and beyond.

This book brings the Mexican American experience to life, and it communicates how powerful the values are that shape us as individuals and bind us as families. The basic values expressed in these pages—family, community, strong religious values, and the importance of our cultural heritage—are the essential building blocks we rely on in the struggle toward achievement and success.

Salvador Rodriguez
Proud former East Los Angeles resident and UCLA graduate

One

Entertainment and the Arts

Hollywood filmmakers and television networks have historically stereotyped Mexican Americans on the screen as subservient, unintelligent, lazy, and often as bandits, gardeners, maids, or sultry spitfires. Mexican Americans have not enjoyed many roles as doctors, lawyers, engineers, or any form of college-educated professional. Latinos are mostly portrayed as easygoing employees who are unable to think for themselves and cheerfully accept their fates. Latino males have often been cast as Latin lovers who are likely to steal away the white Caucasian daughters of wealthy ranchers with their supposed charm and dark handsome looks. Latinas are most often placed in roles of housekeepers, companions, tough widows of white ranchers trying to save the old homestead, or prostitutes. The result is that legitimate historical and artistic contributions of Latinos have almost never been accurately documented, appreciated, or respected. It can be safely said that Hollywood has not been kind or welcoming to Mexican Americans and that it is largely a disappointment to aspiring Mexican Americans and other Latino actors and directors.

Careers were forged in the 1910s of the silent film era by actors Antonio Moreno and Ramon Novarro, and in the 1920s by actresses Dolores Del Rio and Lupe Velez. Leo Carrillo, who also began acting in the 1920s, revitalized his career in the 1950s as Pancho, the companion in TV's *Cisco Kid* series. Gilbert Roland worked steadily from the 1920s into the 1980s. In the 1930s, Anthony Quinn and Rita Hayworth began long careers, Quinn's lasting from 1936 through *Avenging Angelo* (released in 2002, the year after his death). Ricardo Montalban, Katy Jurado, Carmen Zapata, and Elena Verdugo were also familiar actors of the mid- and late 20th century. The 1960s produced a number of strong supporting actors and actresses, but with the exception of Anthony Quinn, no one of star ranking. From the 1970s through the 1990s, Mexican American filmmakers such as Moctezuma Esparza, Luis Valdez, Edward James Olmos, and "Cheech" Marin began challenging the obstacles caused by long held prejudices. The exclusion and marginalization of Mexican Americans, which existed in the film industry for more that 75 years and in television for more than 50 years, has slowly begun to lessen. These, and other new Mexican American film professionals, have brought promise that the "celluloid curtain" blocking successful access to the entertainment world will be lifted for all Latinos.

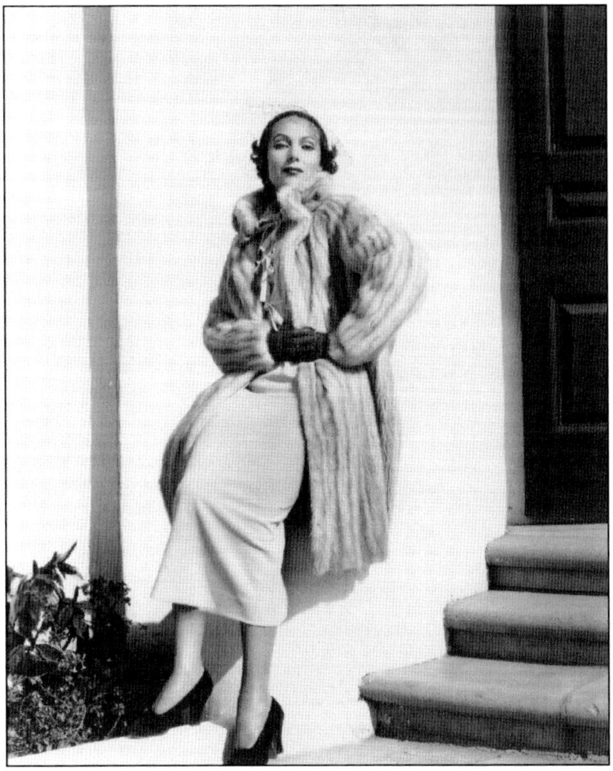

Dolores del Rio was born in Durango, Mexico, in 1905 and came to Hollywood in 1925 after being discovered at a party by the American film director Edwin Carewe. *Joanne* (1925) was her first of 15 films. This film earned $2 million. (Bison Archives.)

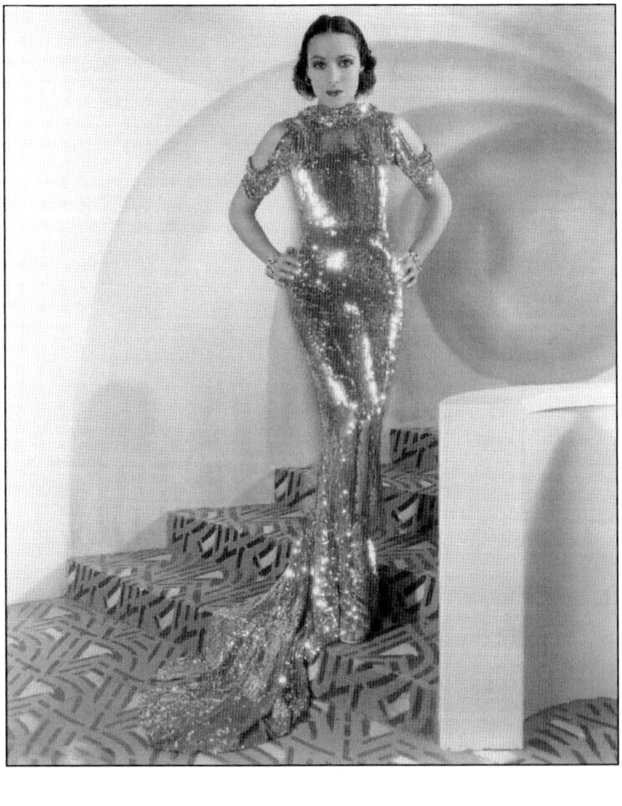

Dolores del Rio was considered one of the most beautiful women of the early movies. She later became one of Hollywood's top 10 moneymakers during the 1920s. The transition to sound film helped cause her to return to Mexico. (Bison Archives.)

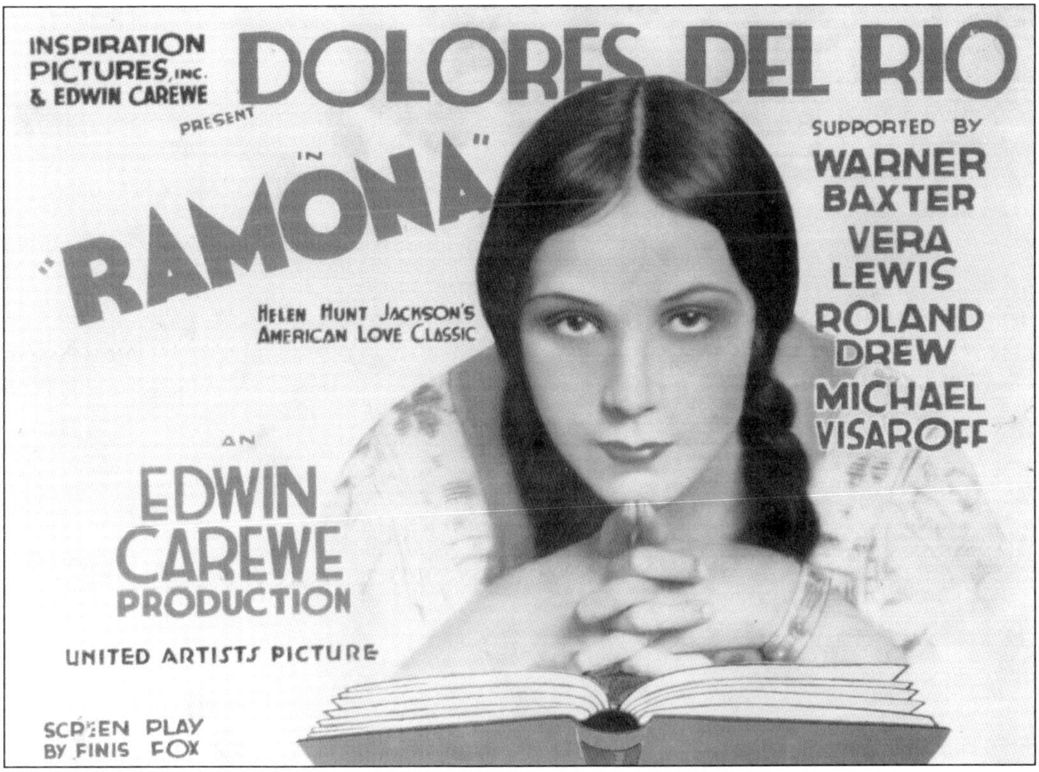

The movie poster above is an advertisement for the film *Ramona*, one of del Rio's important films between 1925 and 1929. In 1978, she returned to Hollywood and costarred with Anthony Quinn in *The Children of Sanchez*. The actress died in 1983 at her home in Newport Beach, California. (Bison Archives.)

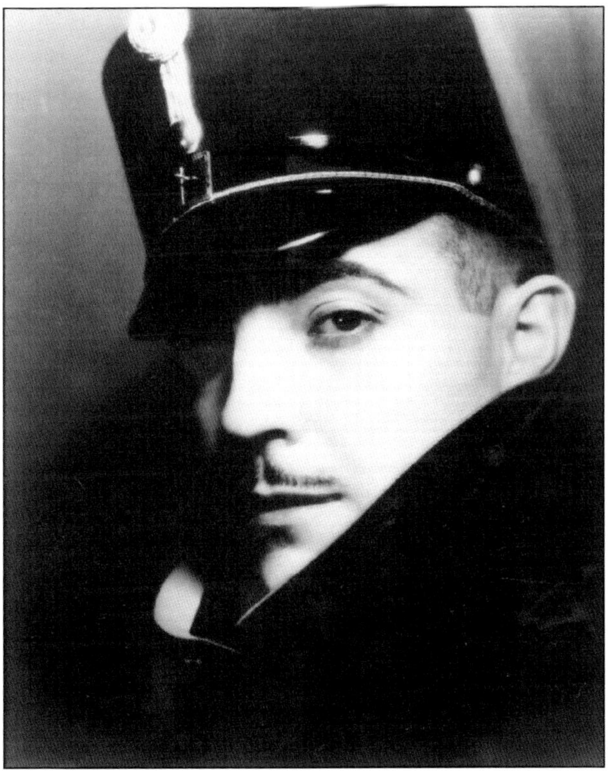

Ramon Novarro, an idol of silent movies in the 1920s and 1930s, is shown in this photograph from the 1931 film, *Daybreak*. He became the screen's first "Latin Lover." His career faltered with the introduction of "talkie" movies due to his Spanish accent. His voice was featured in the 1934 MGM musical *The Cat and the Fiddler*. His most famous role was in the 1926 film *Ben-Hur*. (Bison Archives.)

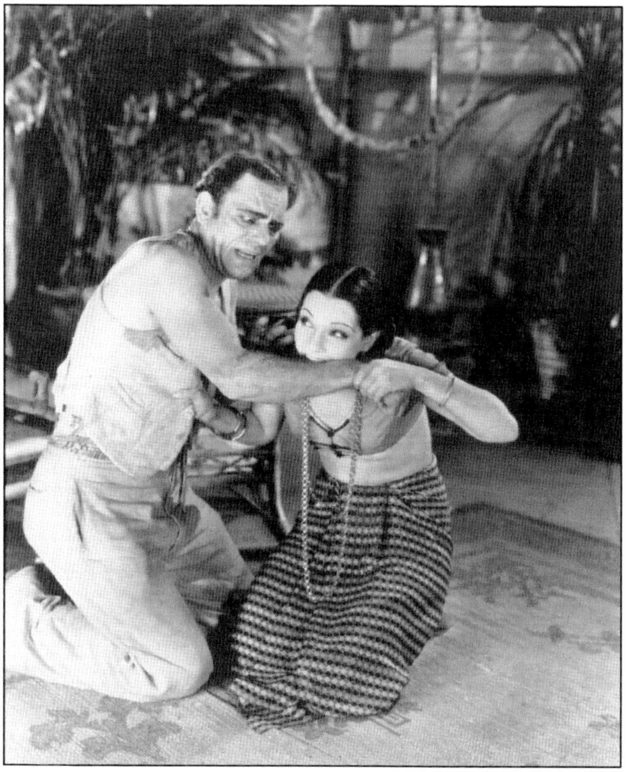

Lupe Velez was known as the "Mexican Spitfire of Hollywood." Between 1927 and 1944, she appeared in approximately 50 films, playing roles emphasizing strong personalities and an explosive temper. Her comic character was known for engaging in broken English with sudden bursts of angry Spanish. This c. 1929 photograph shows her pretending to bite the arm of her costar Lon Chaney in the movie, *Where East is East*. (Bison Archives.)

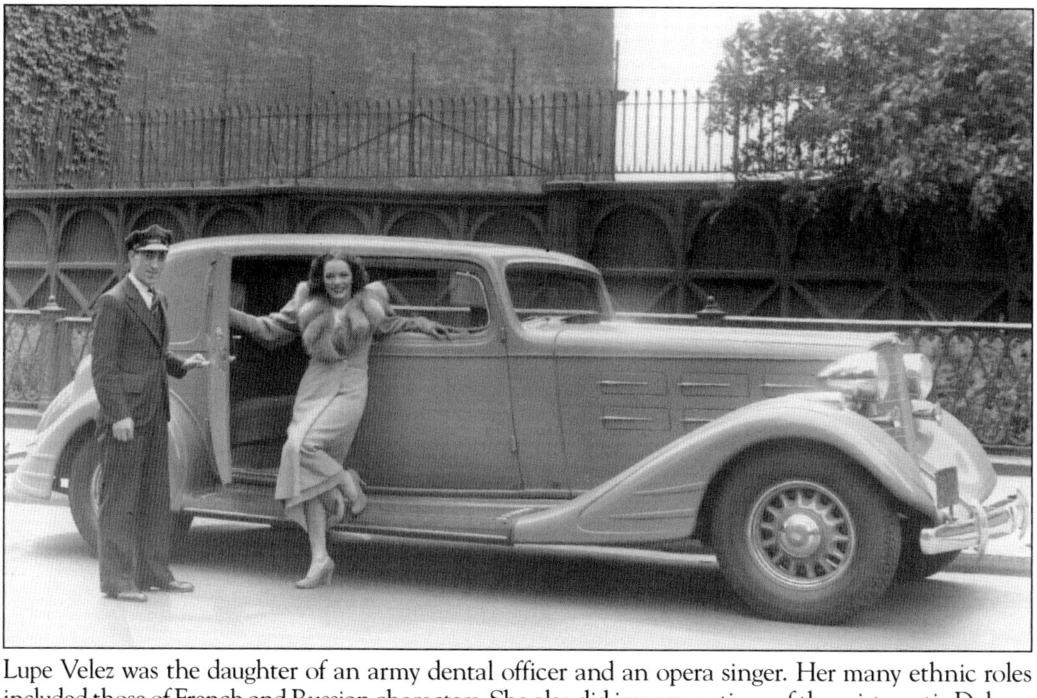

Lupe Velez was the daughter of an army dental officer and an opera singer. Her many ethnic roles included those of French and Russian characters. She also did impersonations of the aristocratic Dolores del Rio and Shirley Temple. Despite her unconventional roles, she was accorded star status as evidenced by this 1930s photograph showing her luxurious limousine and driver. (Bison Archives.)

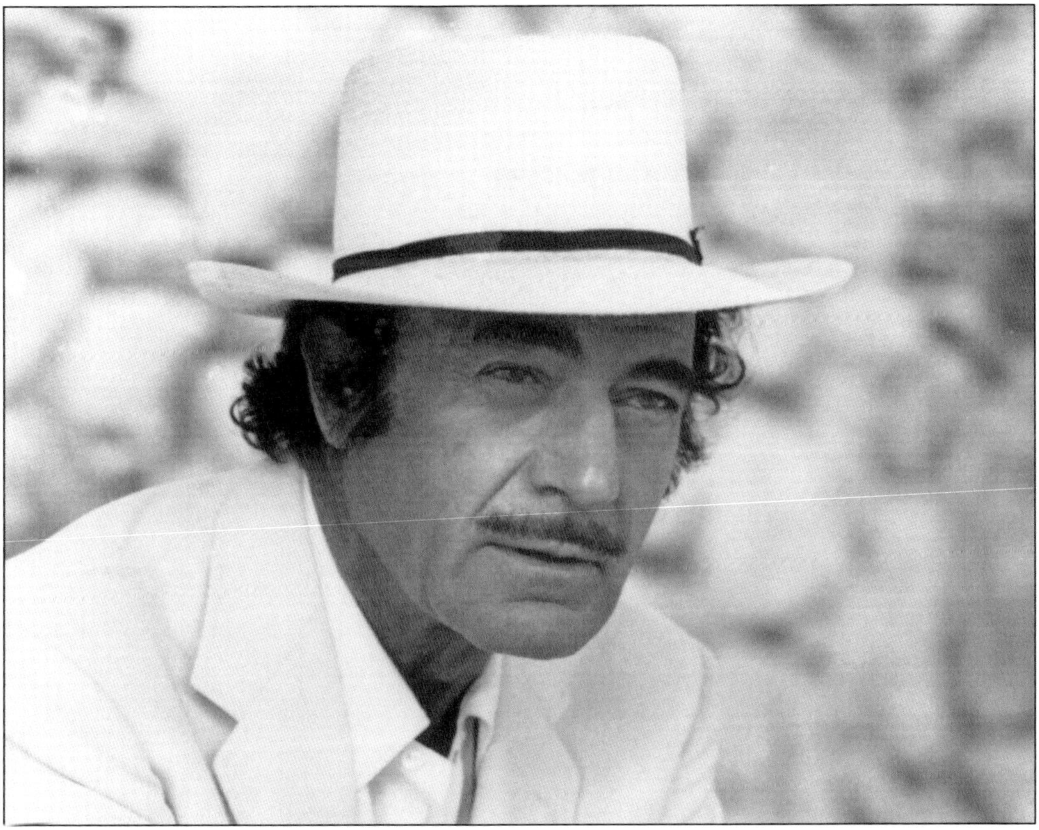

Born Luis Antonio Damaso Alonso, Gilbert Roland's career in films spanned more than 55 years. He started playing bit parts earning $2 a day in the early 1920s. In the 1940s, he was the first and only genuine Mexican American to portray the Cisco Kid in a movie series. Consigned to Latin lover roles, often in western movies, he later appeared in major films. (Bison Archives.)

Leo Carrillo was born in Los Angeles in 1880. A character actor from 1930 to 1964, he appeared in 90 motion pictures. A college graduate, he was also a political cartoonist. This 1950s photograph shows him grunion hunting in Santa Monica with California's chief justice Earl Warren and his family. Carrillo's father was the first mayor of Santa Monica, California. (Bill Beebe.)

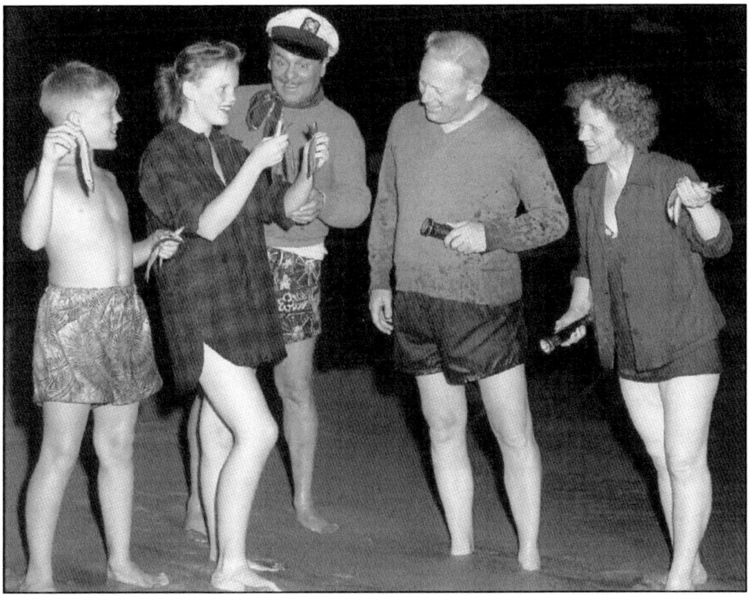

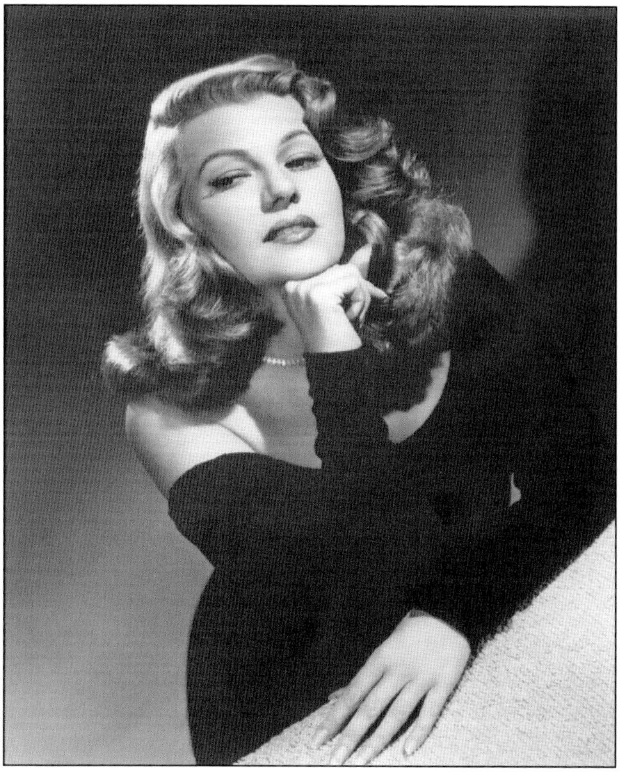

Born Margarita Cansino, Rita Hayworth was discovered in a nightclub act with her father, Eduardo Cansino, in Agua Caliente, Mexico. Dyeing her hair auburn and changing her name, she became one of the biggest movie stars in Hollywood and a favorite pinup of American servicemen in the 1940s. Although not Mexican American, she was identified as such, based on her Hispanic heritage and certain roles she played. (Bison Archives.)

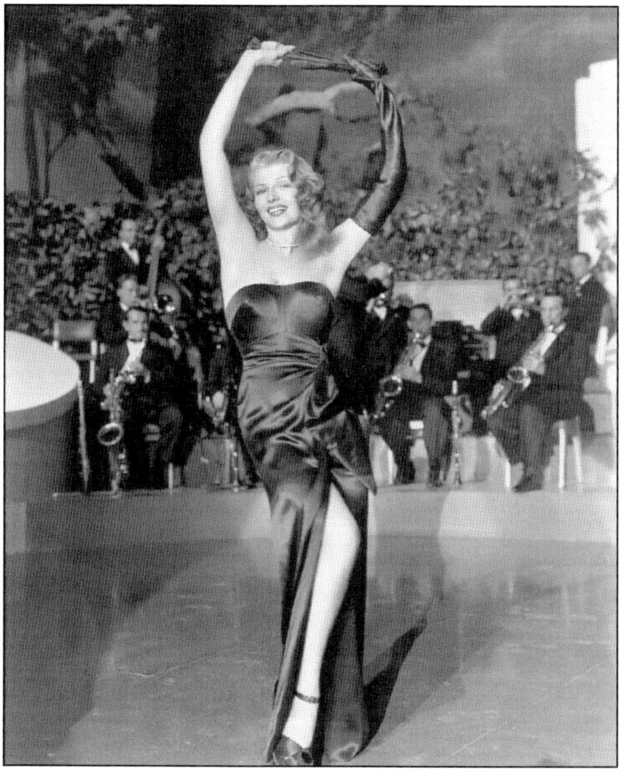

In this 1946 photograph from the movie *Gilda*, Rita Hayworth established herself as one of Hollywood's most glamorous screen stars. She is listed as one of the American Film Institute's greatest stars of all time. Early in her career, she and her father danced professionally on a gambling ship off the coast of California. In all, she appeared in 61 films over 37 years. (Bison Archives.)

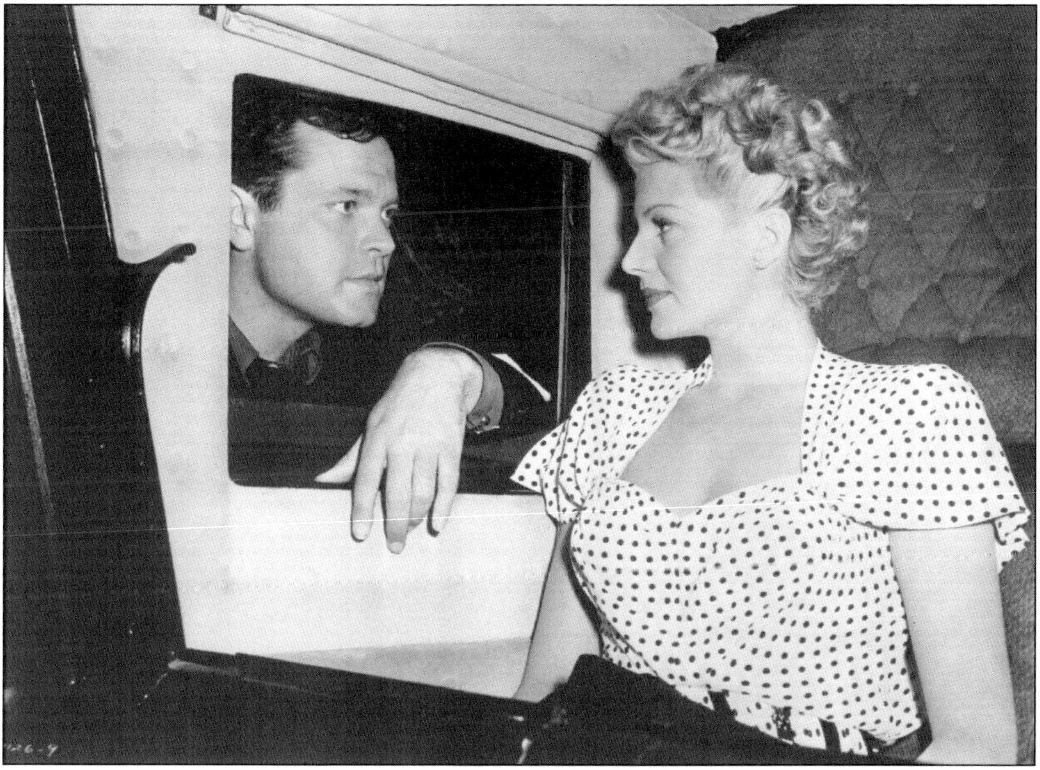

In this studio image, Rita Hayworth is shown with her husband, director Orson Welles, as a short-haired blonde in the 1948 film, *The Lady from Shanghai.* Her fans had difficulty accepting her radically changed look from that of a long-haired auburn star, and this is believed to have contributed to a decline in her image and status as a star. (Bison Archives.)

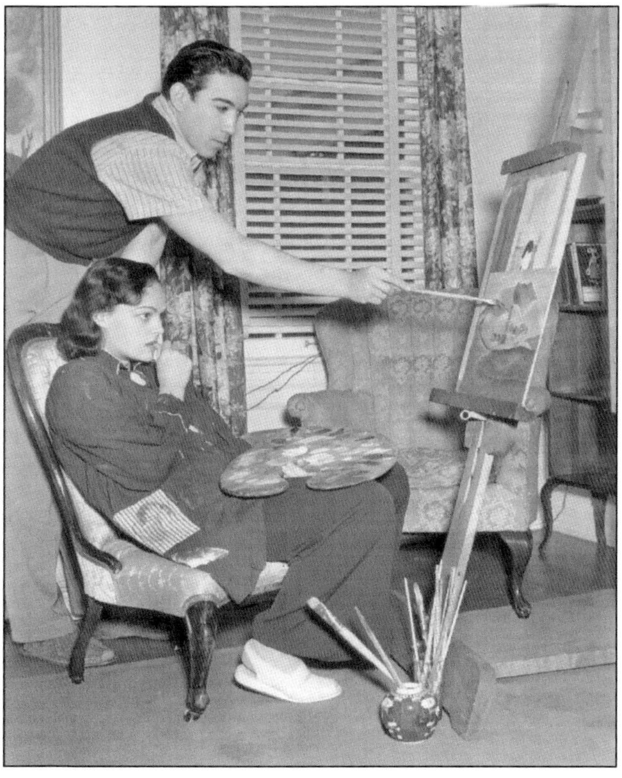

Anthony Rudolfo Oaxaca Quinn was born in 1915 in Chihuahua, Mexico, to an Irish Mexican father and a Mexican Indian mother. Raised in East Los Angeles, he drove taxis, preached, and boxed before acting. His career as a Hollywood actor and director spanned six decades, from 1936 to 1996. In this 1950s photograph, he demonstrates his artistic skills to his wife, Kathleen De Mille. (Bison Archives.)

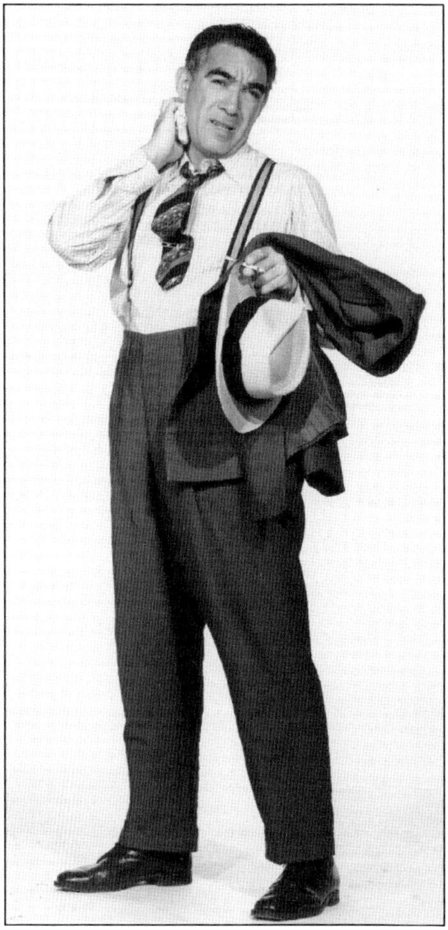

In 200 films as a lead and supporting actor, Quinn was the first Mexican American to receive two academy awards for best supporting actor—in 1952 for *Viva Zapata!* and in 1956 for *Lust for Life*. He is best remembered for the 1964 film, *Zorba the Greek*. In this photograph, his acting versatility is shown in the 1958 film, *Hot Spell*. (Bud Franker.)

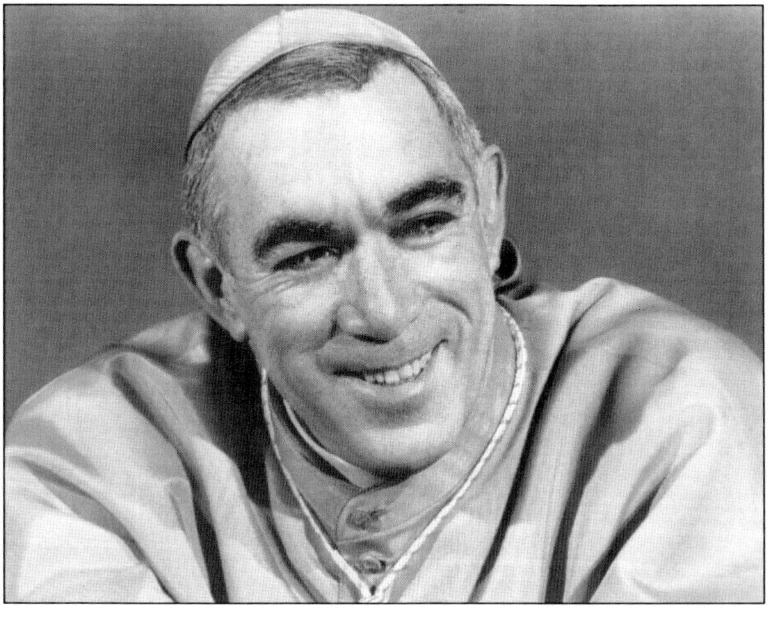

In the 1968 film *Shoes of the Fisherman*, Quinn portrays a Russian priest who becomes the first pope from a communist country. On May 5, 1982, a library on the site of his family's former home in East Los Angeles was renamed in his honor. He was an avid supporter of Cesar Chavez's United Farm Workers Union. He died in 2001 and is buried in Rhode Island. (Bison Archives.)

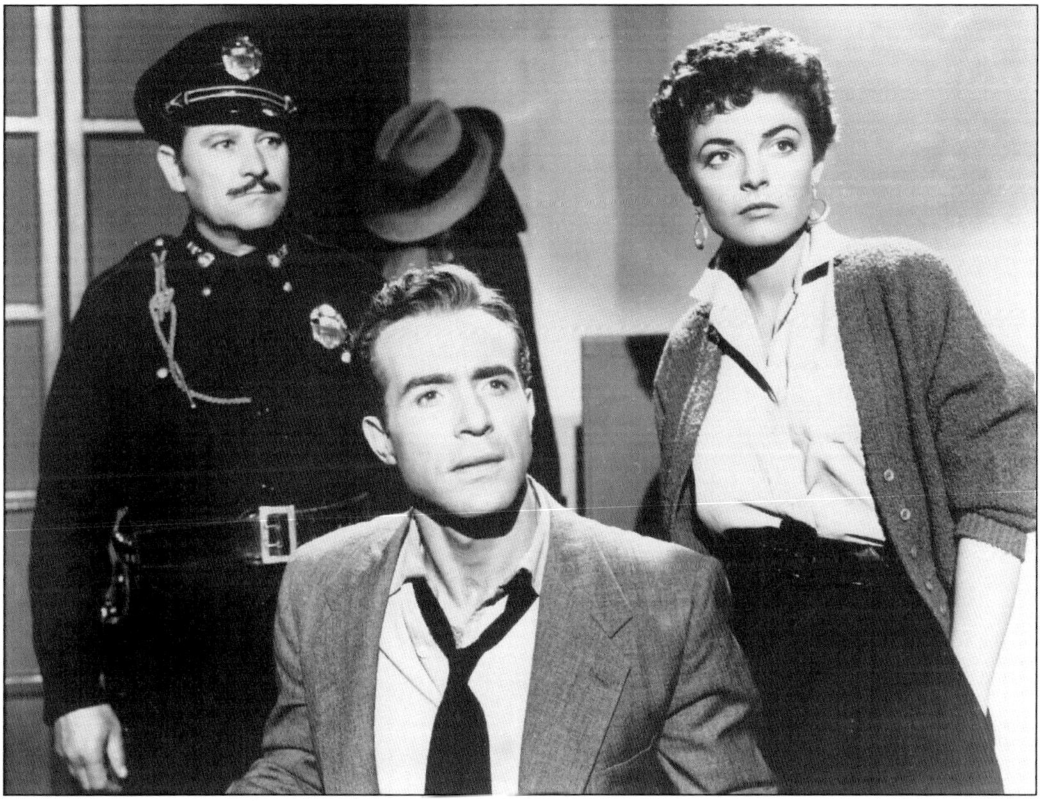

Ricardo Montalban, a Mexican American film icon, is shown in 1955 in the film *A life in the Balance*, with actress Anne Bancroft. Montalban starred in many film and television programs between 1941 -2006. He received an Emmy in 1978 as Mr. Roarke on the television series *Fantasy Island*. Montalban founded "Nosotros," an organization dedicated to more opportunities for Latinos. He died in January 2009. (Bison Archives.)

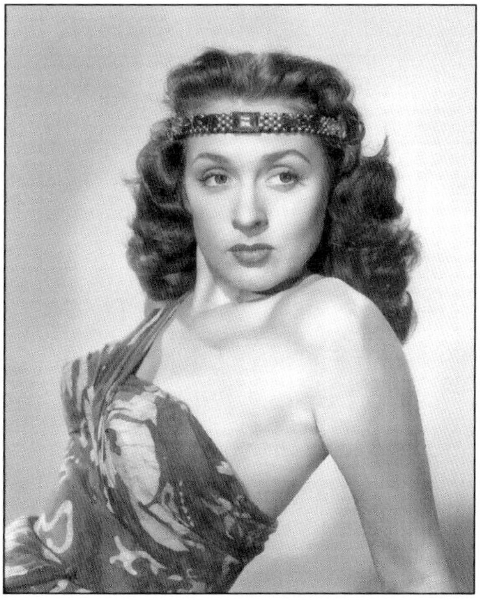

Emmy-nominated Elena Verdugo began her career in the film, *Cavalier Of The West*, in 1931, with a career spanning six decades in television and film. She starred in the 1942 film, *The Moon and Sixpence*. In 1952, she starred in the television series, *Meet Molly*. She is most remembered as nurse Consuelo Lopez in the 1969 television series, *Marcus Welby, M.D.* (MAOF.)

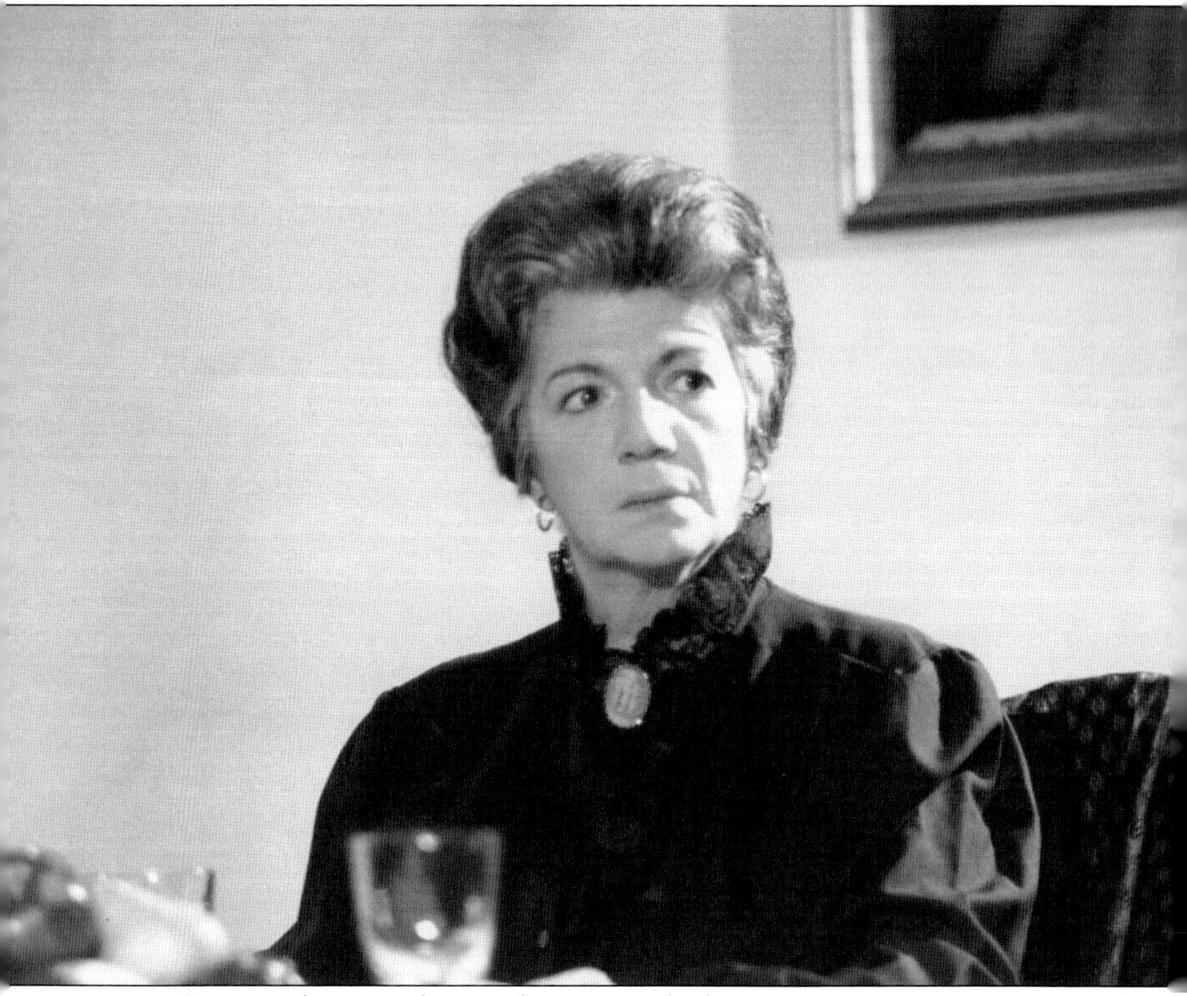

In 1967, actress, theater producer, and community leader Carmen Zapata came to Los Angeles from New York, where she began her career in 1946 on the Broadway stage. She is one of the most admired Hispanic women in the performing arts. This image from the 1997 production of Garcia-Lorca's *House of Bernardo Alba* manifests her versatility and commanding presence. (Carmen Zapata and the Bilingual Foundation of the Arts.)

Carmen Zapata is seen with Vito Scotti in the 1969 television series episode, "Love and Carmen Lopez." She is perhaps best known for her work in the 1973 bilingual television show, *Via Alegre*, on the Public Broadcasting System. She appeared with Anthony Quinn in *The Man and the City* in the 1970s and in *Flamingo Road* in 1981. (Carmen Zapata and the Bilingual Foundation of the Arts.)

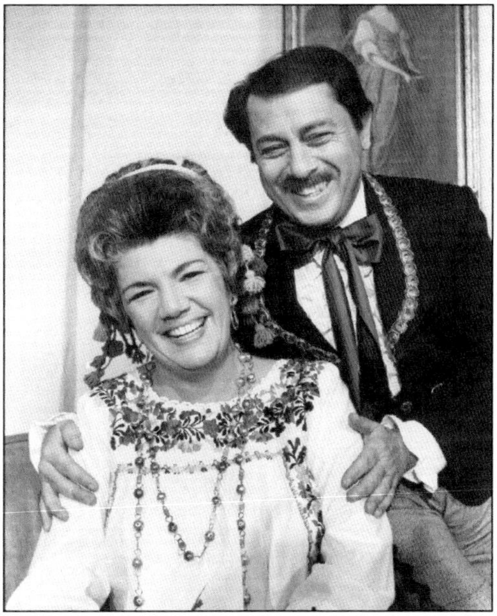

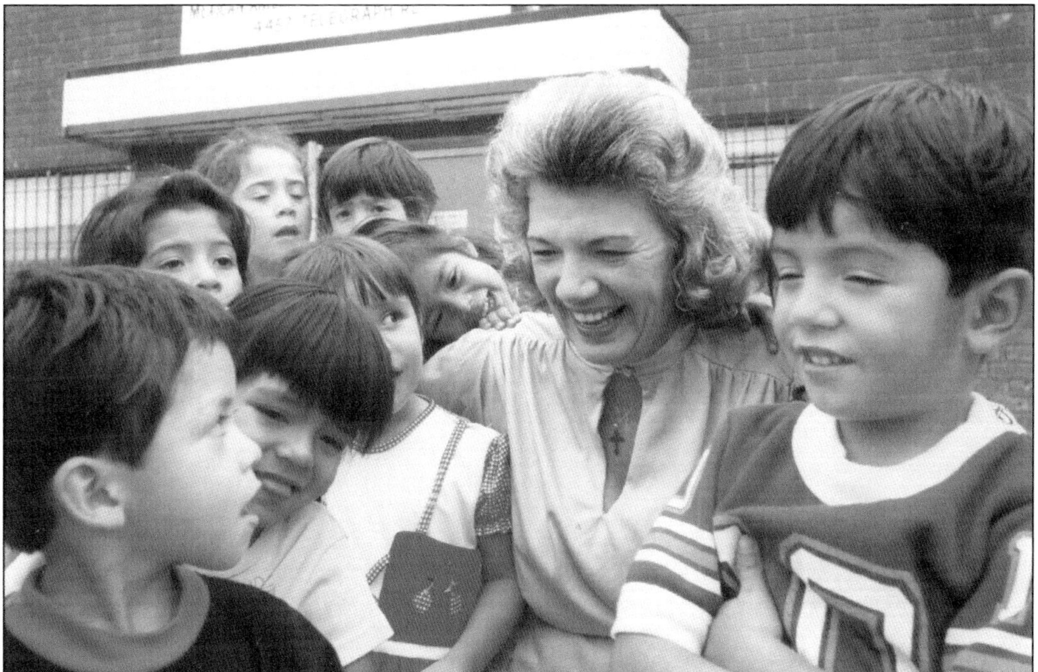

Together with the Los Angeles Unified School District, Zapata initiated a theater in education program designed to showcase the works of great Hispanic authors and provide performing arts exposure to underserved children of public schools. This allows Zapata to engage in two of her passions: theater and children. During the Christmas holidays, the foundation traditionally presents the holiday play, *Too Many Tamales*, based on Gary Soto's story, with stage adaptation by Margarita Galban and Lina Montalvo. In 1990, Zapata was knighted by King Juan Carlos of Spain for her unwavering support of Hispanic American culture. (Carmen Zapata and the Bilingual Foundation of the Arts.)

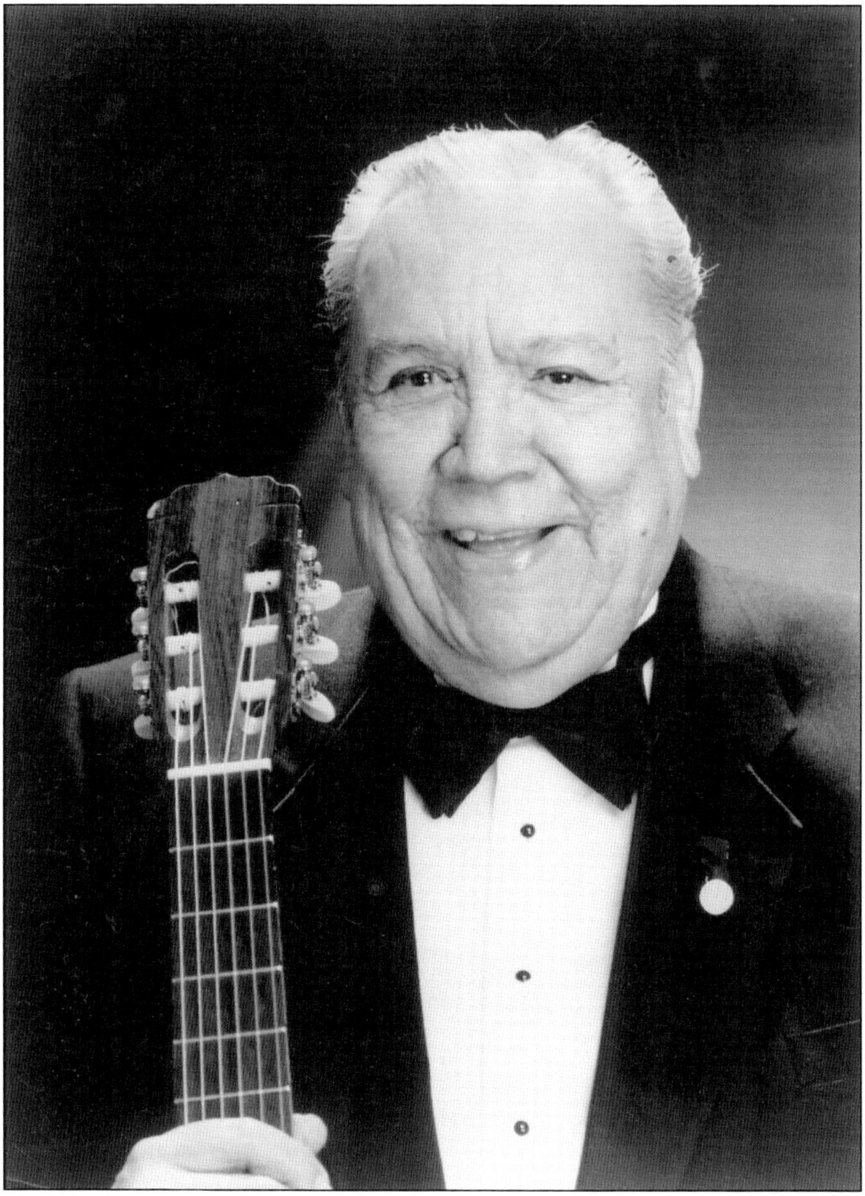

Regarded as the "Father of Chicano Music," Eduardo "Lalo" Guerrero was born Christmas eve in the old barrio of Tucson, Arizona. Coming to California in the 1940s, he created music that spanned more than 60 years and across two cultures. No other Mexican American artist ever came close to writing more memorable songs in all areas of Latin music including boleros, rancheras, corridos, swing, and musical parodies such as Pancho Claus and Elvis Perez, bringing laughter to Mexican and Anglo Americans alike. He performed around the world with his corridos and other music, chronicling the history of Mexico's past and the Mexican American/ Chicano experience that spoke of the hopes, disappointments, and triumphs of the Mexican American people. One of his countless awards included being declared a national folk treasure by the Smithsonian Institute in Washington, D.C. In 1992, at a tribute to Guerrero, the late labor leader Cesar Chavez said, "Lalo has chronicled the events of the Hispanic in this country better than anyone." (Mark Guerrero.)

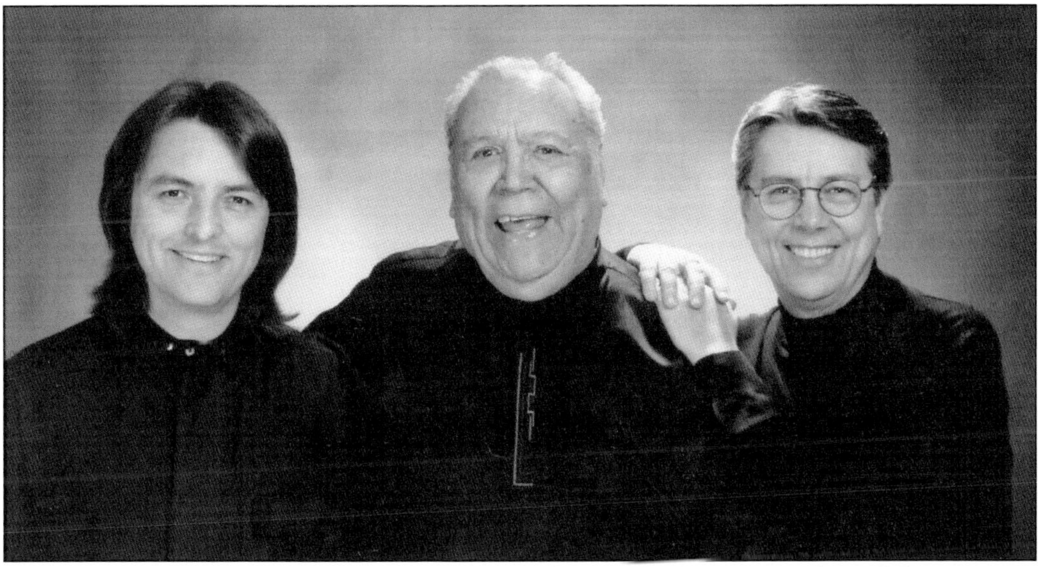

The 1997 photograph above shows the continuing legacy of Lalo Guerrero through his two sons, Dan and Mark. Mark, a singer-songwriter and stage artist continues to perform and compose. Mark has traveled worldwide and performed with numerous musicians, most recently in Liverpool, England, at the Cavern where the Beatles started. He's frequently called upon by museums and university directors for his expertise. Dan is an innovative producer of Latino-themed, English and Spanish productions for network and cable. He works to create more positive Latino images on the screen. (Mark and Dan Guerrero.)

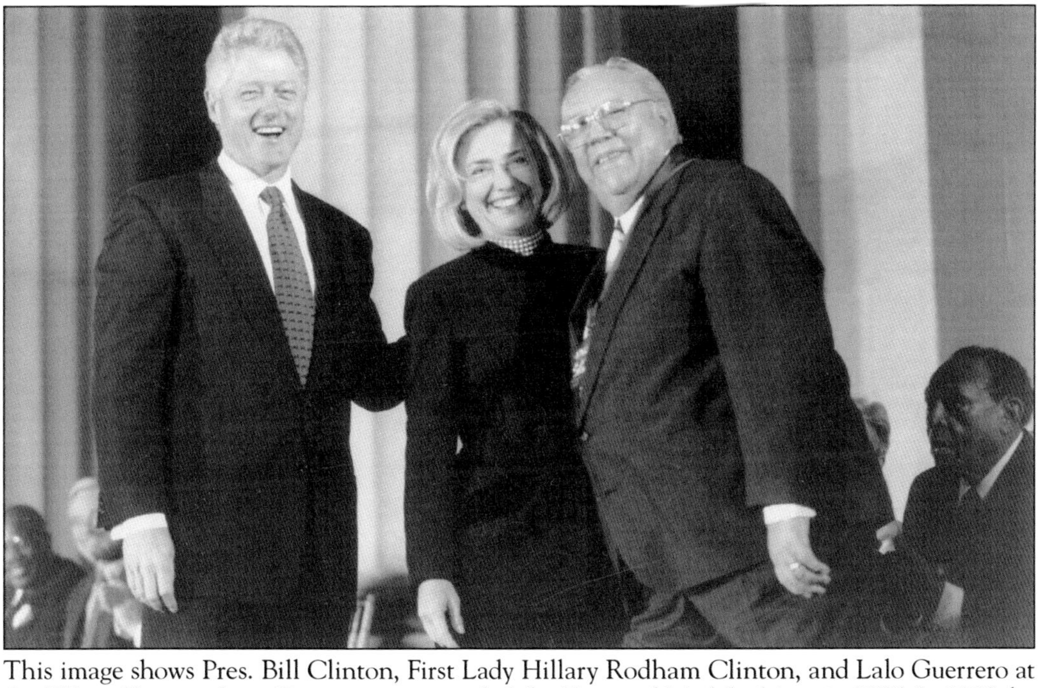

This image shows Pres. Bill Clinton, First Lady Hillary Rodham Clinton, and Lalo Guerrero at the White House, where Guerrero was awarded the National Medal of Arts in 1996. In 1992, he received the National Heritage Award from the National Endowment of the Arts. Guerrero died on St. Patrick's Day, March 17, 2005, in Rancho Mirage, California. (Mark Guerrero.)

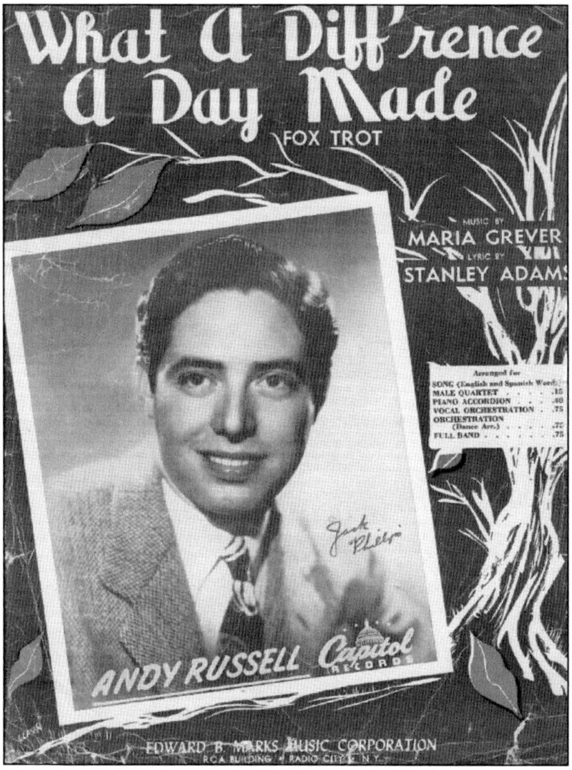

Andy Russell (Andres Rabago Perez) was born in East Los Angeles in 1919. He became internationally famous as a vocalist and drummer who sang in English and Spanish. His signature hits were, "Besame Mucho" and "Magic in the Moonlight." His big break came in 1947, when he replaced Frank Sinatra on a radio show. He changed his name to break into records. (MAOF.)

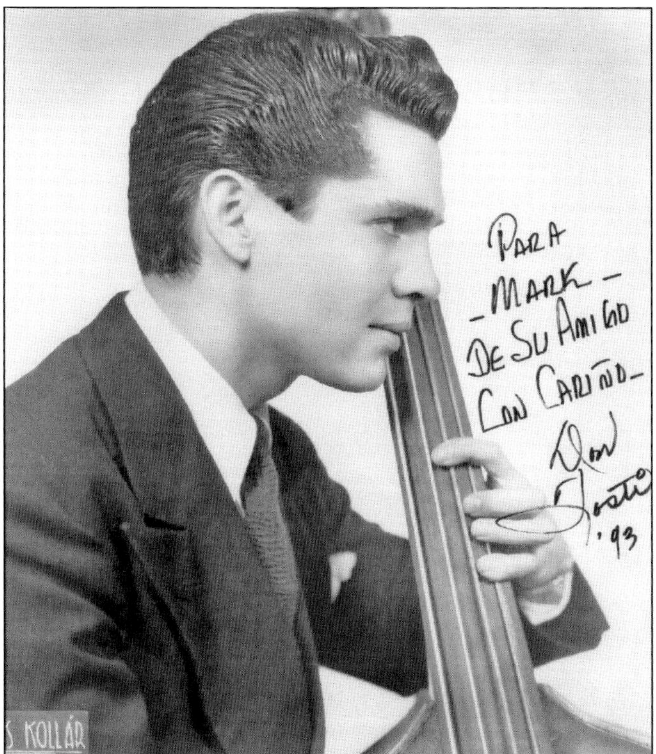

Born Edmundo Tostado, Don Tosti was a formally trained child prodigy. He played saxophone and bass and became concertmaster at Roosevelt High in East Los Angeles. This 1943 image shows him playing with the Charley Barnet band in 1943. He was one of the first Mexican Americans to play in the big bands of the 1940s and 1950s. He died in Palm Springs in 2004. (Mark Guerrero.)

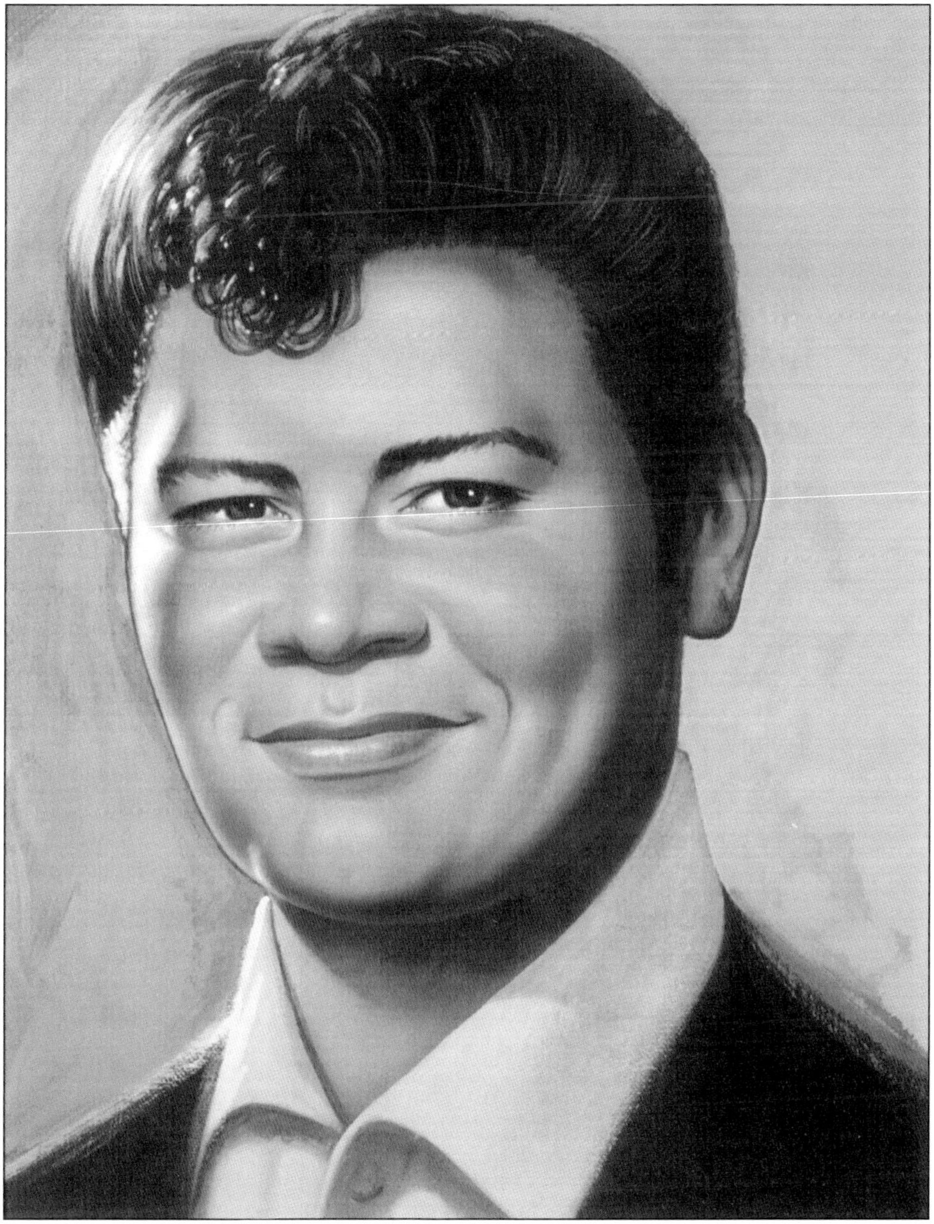

Richard Steven "Ritchie" Valens was born on May 31, 1941, in Pacoima, California, and perished in a plane crash after a 1959 Iowa concert. He was the father of the Chicano rock movement, a rock and roll pioneer, and the first Latino to successfully cross over into rock's mainstream. His first three records, *Come On Let's Go, Donna,* and *La Bamba,* were key rock and roll hits in the 1950s. In junior high school, he entertained friends by playing guitar in the stadium bleachers. He performed with the Silhouettes, a local band. He was called the "Little Richard of the Valley" for his high energy level. His career only lasted eight months, yet his name is alive after 50 years. As a Mexican American icon, he has been compared to James Dean. He was the first Latino rock star with a star on Hollywood's Walk of Fame, and in 1983, a postage stamp was issued in his honor. His mother, Consuelo, is buried next to him at the San Fernando Mission Cemetery. (Ignacio Gomez, artist.)

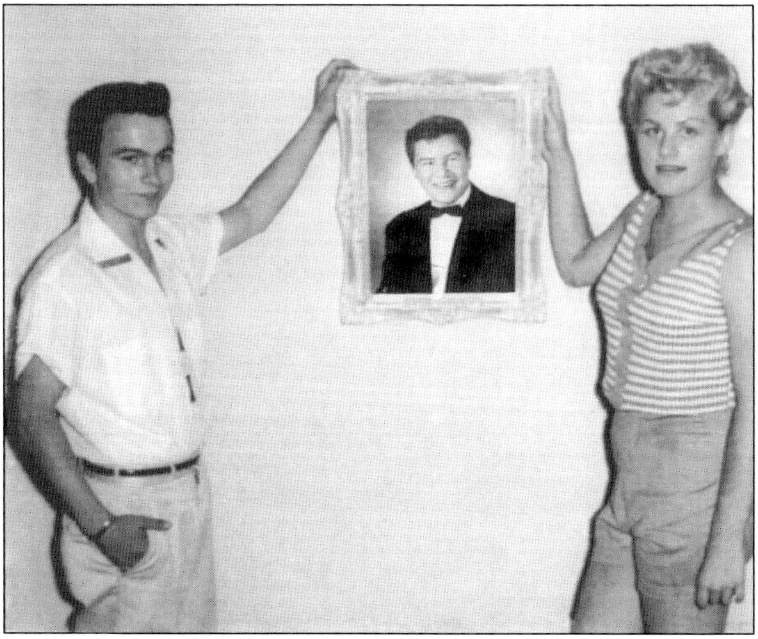

An image of singer Ritchie Valens is framed by Chan Romero and Donna Ludwig, Valens's sweetheart and inspiration for his record *Donna*. This photograph was a gift to Romero by Ritchie's mother, Consuelo, after Valens's death. Romero and Valens both recorded for producer Bob Keane. Romero lived with the family for a period of time. Ludwig's personalized license plate read, "ODONNA." (Chan Romero.)

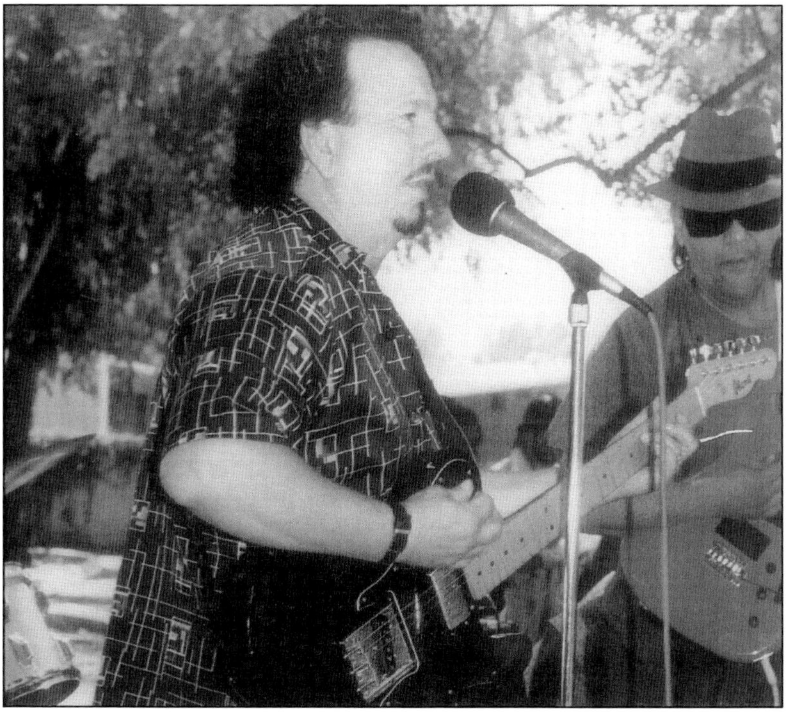

In this 1980s photograph, Chan Romero performs at a fund-raiser in Pacoima, California. Romero's voice and musical style emulated Ritchie Valens's brand of rock and roll in the years following the singer's death. He authored the song, "Hippy, Hippy, Shake," which was recorded by the Beatles. In 2007, he was the first Mexican American to be inducted into the Rockabilly Hall of Fame. (Chan Romero.)

The school hall of Saint Alphonsus, on Amalia Street in East Los Angeles, was a musical gathering place for many of the Eastside Sound's early bands. The hall provided a gathering place for groups to showcase their talent and start their careers. Other venues for these bands were Kennedy Hall and the Montebello Ballroom. (Author.)

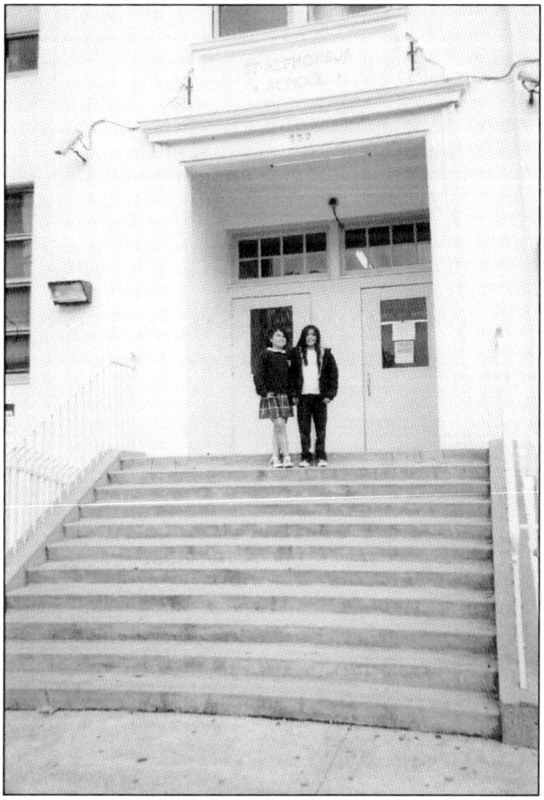

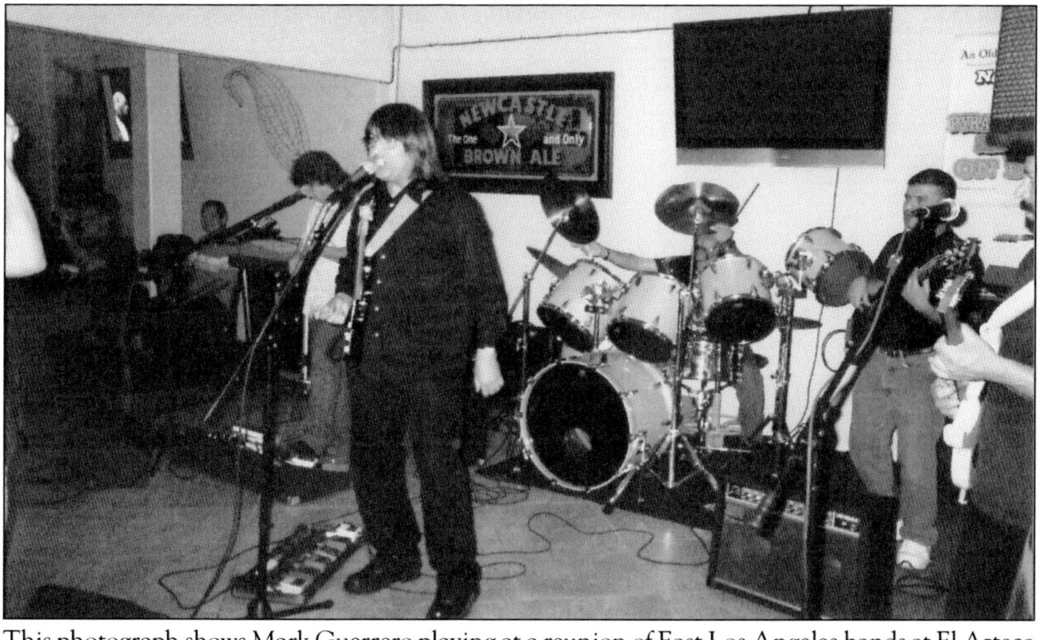

This photograph shows Mark Guerrero playing at a reunion of East Los Angeles bands at El Azteca restaurant in 2009. He is a performing artist who played at Saint Alphonsus with his first musical group, Mark and the Escorts. Guerrero founded and operates the world's largest Chicano rock and roll history Web site, www.markguerrero.com, based in Palm Springs, California. (Author.)

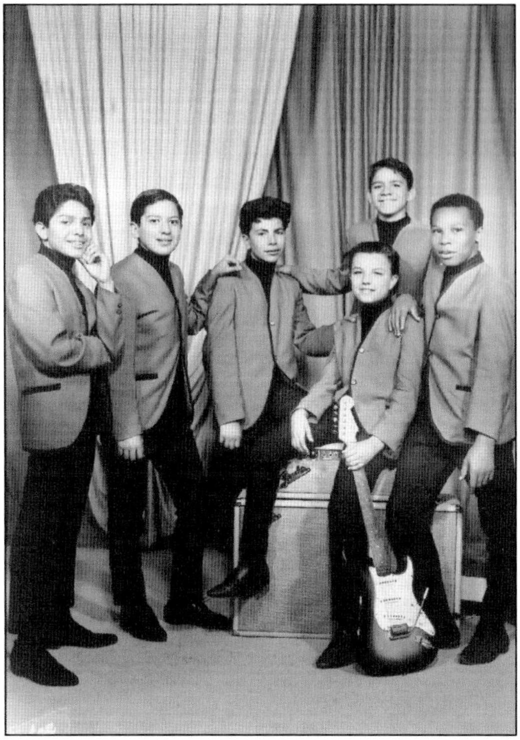

Mark Guerrero and the Escorts band are shown in 1964. Many of the 1960s musicians from East Los Angeles who created the East Los Angeles sound had their start in similar bands, later moving on to national prominence. Standing from left to right are Ricky Almaraz, Ernie Hernandez, Richard Rosas, Trini Basulto, and Robert Warren. Seated is Mark Guerrero. They recorded two singles, "Dance with Me" and "Get Your Baby." (Mark Guerrero.)

"Chico" Sesma is shown in this *c.* 1980 photograph at the Pasta House restaurant in East Los Angeles with prominent Los Angeles restaurateur Rudy Lopez, left, and at right, legendary Latin music band leader and percussionist Tito Puente. Sesma, an icon of Mexican American radio broadcasting, is still remembered by many friends. He makes periodic visits to Rudy's Baja Grill on the East side. (Lionel "Chico" Sesma.)

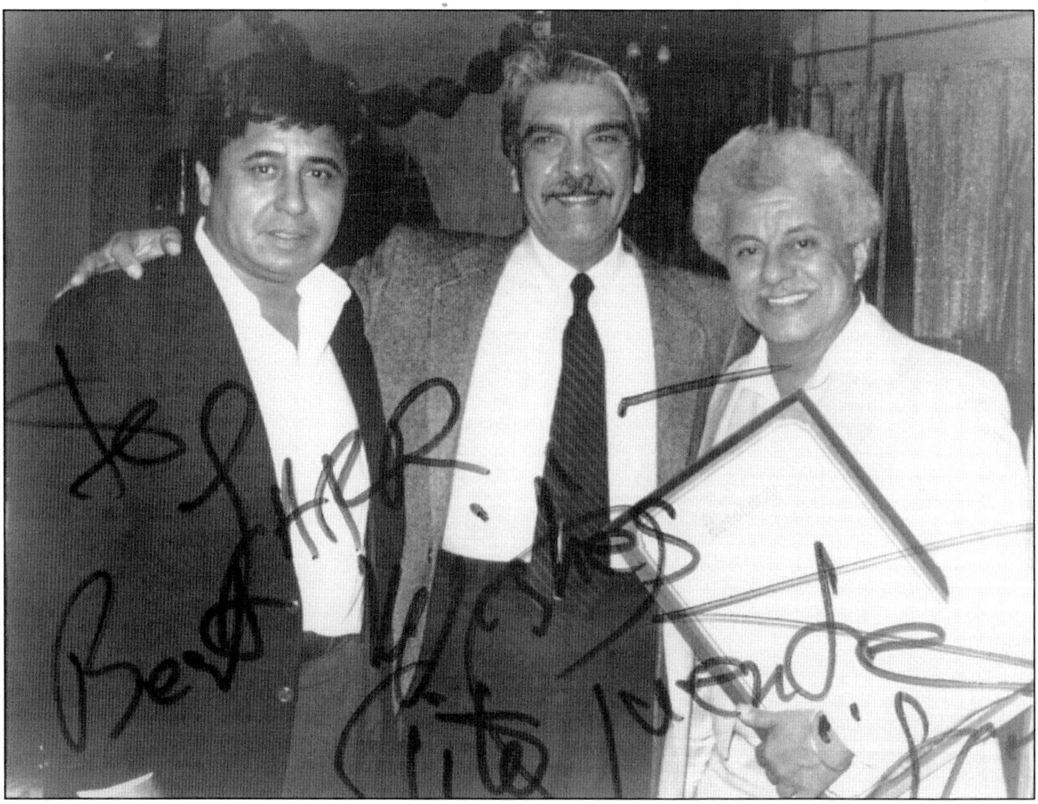

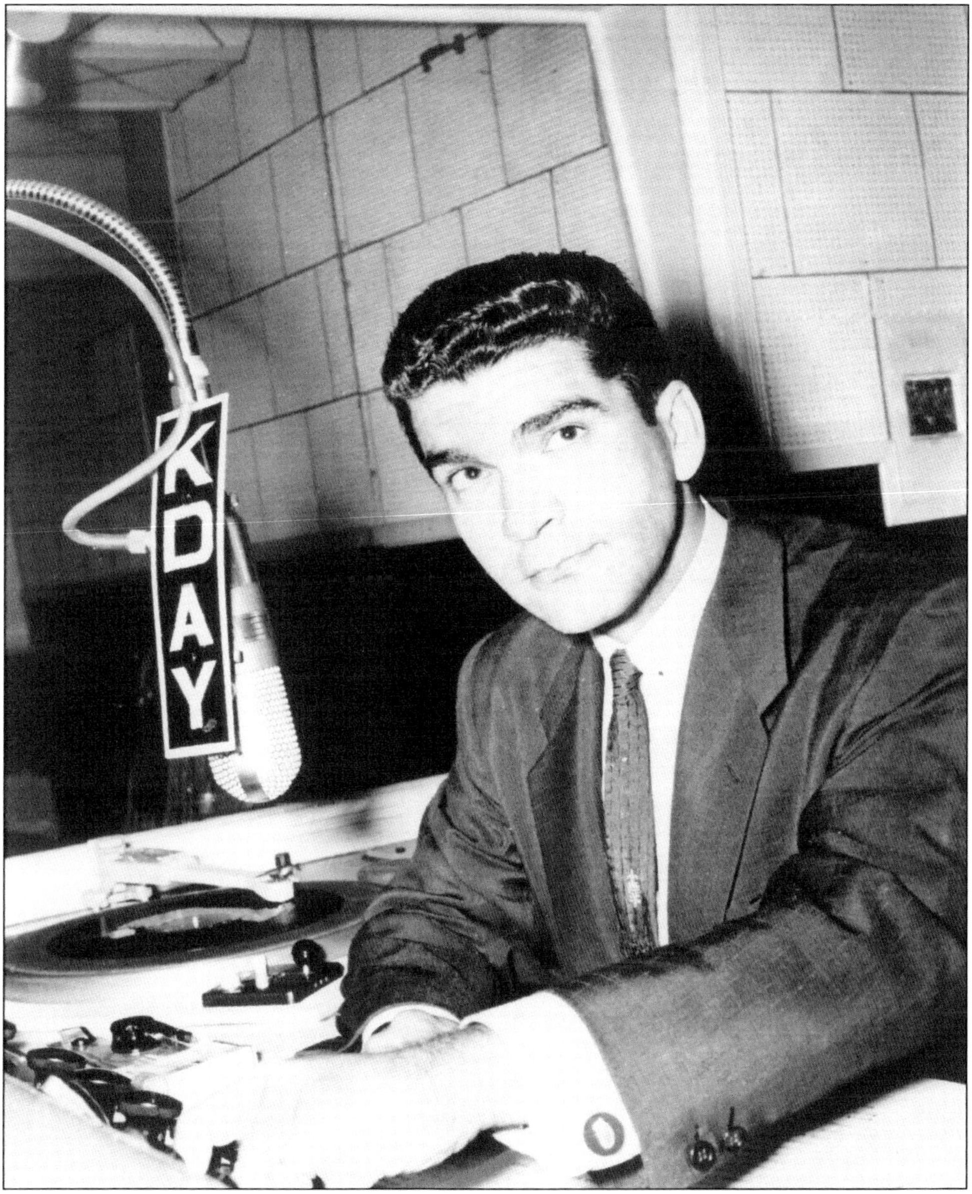

Lionel "Chico" Sesma, a native of East Los Angeles, was a true bridge-building pioneer of Los Angeles bilingual radio, who left a long-lasting impact on the broadcasting industry. In 1949, he hosted the first all-Latin-music format radio show in Los Angeles, bringing together the sounds of the west coast Latin bands with those of the east coast, introducing them to acculturated, second-generation Mexican Americans in their city. Perez Prado's and Tito Puente's bands were only two of the many groups introduced on his highly popular show. Sesma's early background as a formally trained trombonist in Tily Lopez and Phil Carreon's bands brought an advanced degree of musical knowledge to his radio programming. Another important impact left by Sesma, from 1954 to 1957, was his introduction of the "Latin Holiday" music programs at the Hollywood Palladium that enhanced the image of Mexican Americans through bilingual broadcasts. This c. 1953 image shows Sesma at the KDAY radio controls. Having retired from radio, he remains a resident of East Los Angeles. (Lionel "Chico" Sesma.)

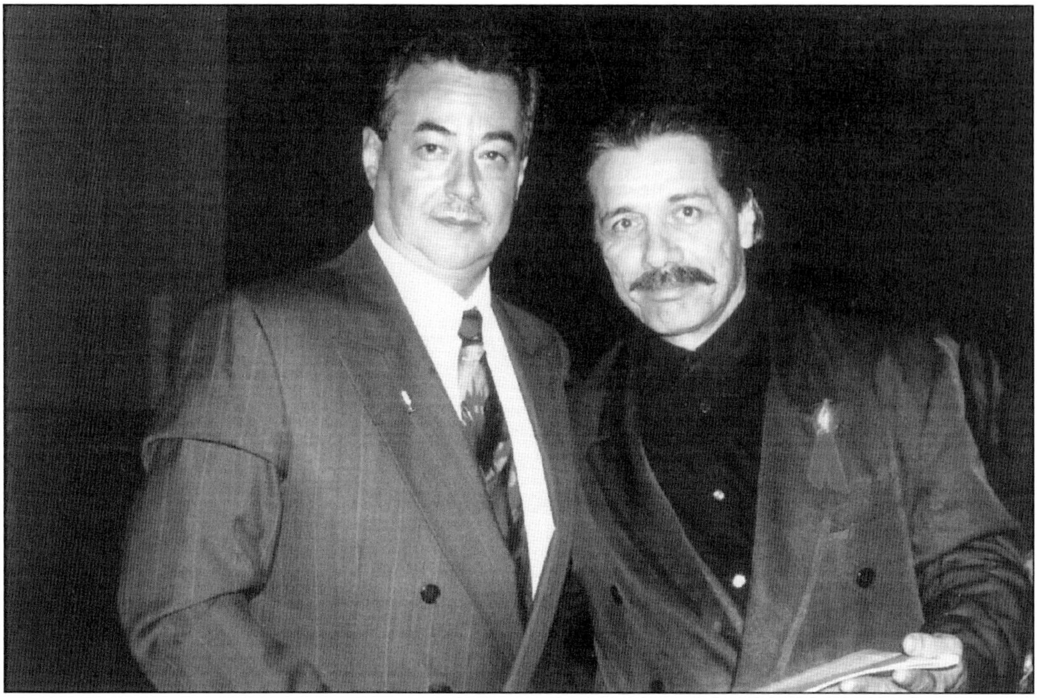

Joe Ortiz, a pioneer in the radio and television talk show industry, founded Joe Ortiz and Associates, a public relations firm in 1988. In 1971, he was the first Mexican American to host an English language talk show on a commercial radio station. Among many awards in broadcasting, he received a Golden Mike award from KPFK-FM radio. He was named one of the 100 most influential Hispanics in the United States for broadcasting excellence and community service. He developed and designed major publicity campaigns for celebrities and sports personalities such as Tom Flores, the former coach of the Los Angeles Rams football team. He is shown in this photograph with Academy Award–winning actor Edward James Olmos. (Joe Ortiz and Associates.)

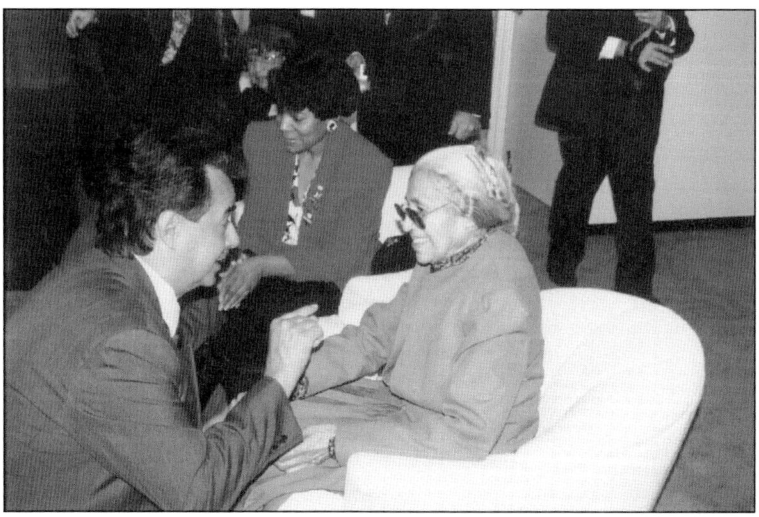

Los Angeles publicist Joe Ortiz's long career in radio and television broadcasting focused on bringing the newsmakers of the day to the public's attention. In this photograph, he is seen talking with civil rights icon Rosa Parks at a Los Angeles reception. (Joe Ortiz and Associates.)

Richard Anthony "Cheech" Marin is a Mexican American comedian, actor, director, and art collector. He is considered a cultural icon for his films such as *Born in East L.A*, and his many albums including Cheech and Chong. He's been honored for his work on behalf of Latinos by the IMAGEN Foundation and the National Council of La Raza. (MAOF.)

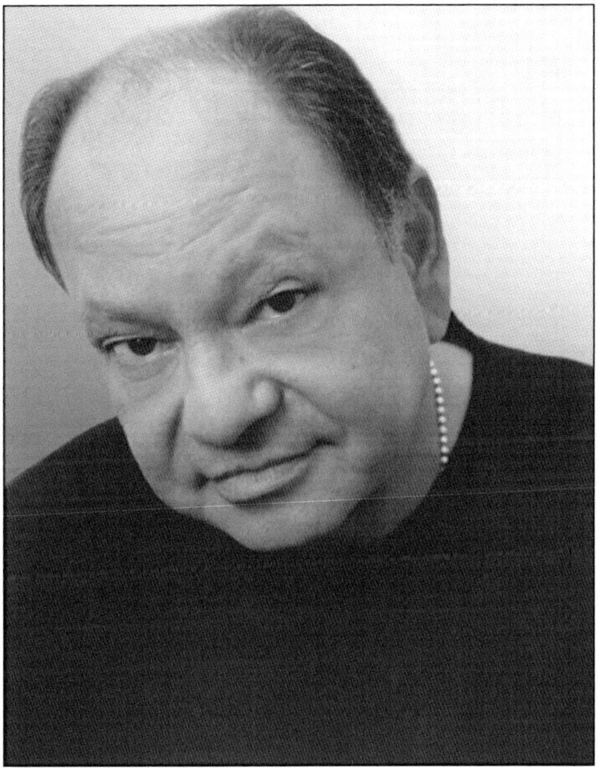

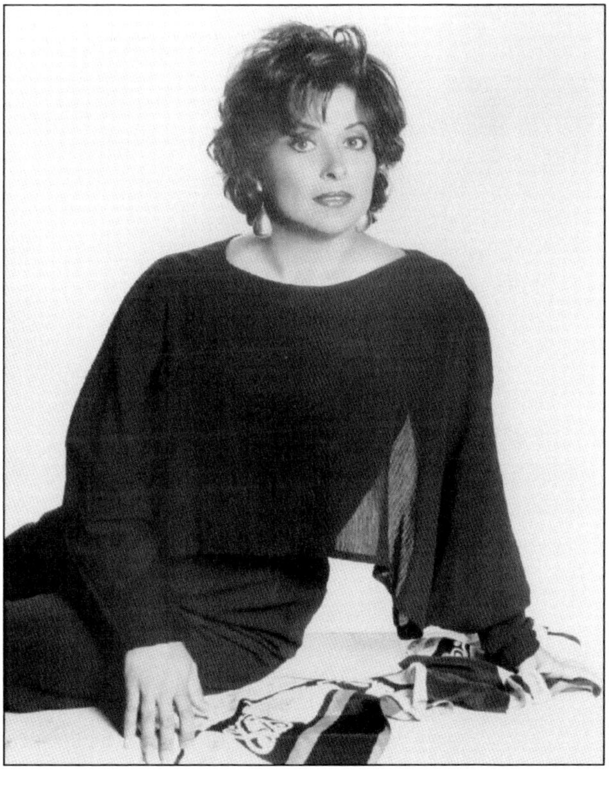

Los Angeles vocalist Geree Gonzalez has performed with bands such as El Chicano and Los Lobos. She toured the southwest and performed in Korea with Roger Clinton. In 1976, she recorded *Si Se Puede*, an album that benefited the United Farm Workers. Her sound is a mix between Donna Summer and Tina Turner. Her voice can be heard on many national commercials. (Geree Gonzalez.)

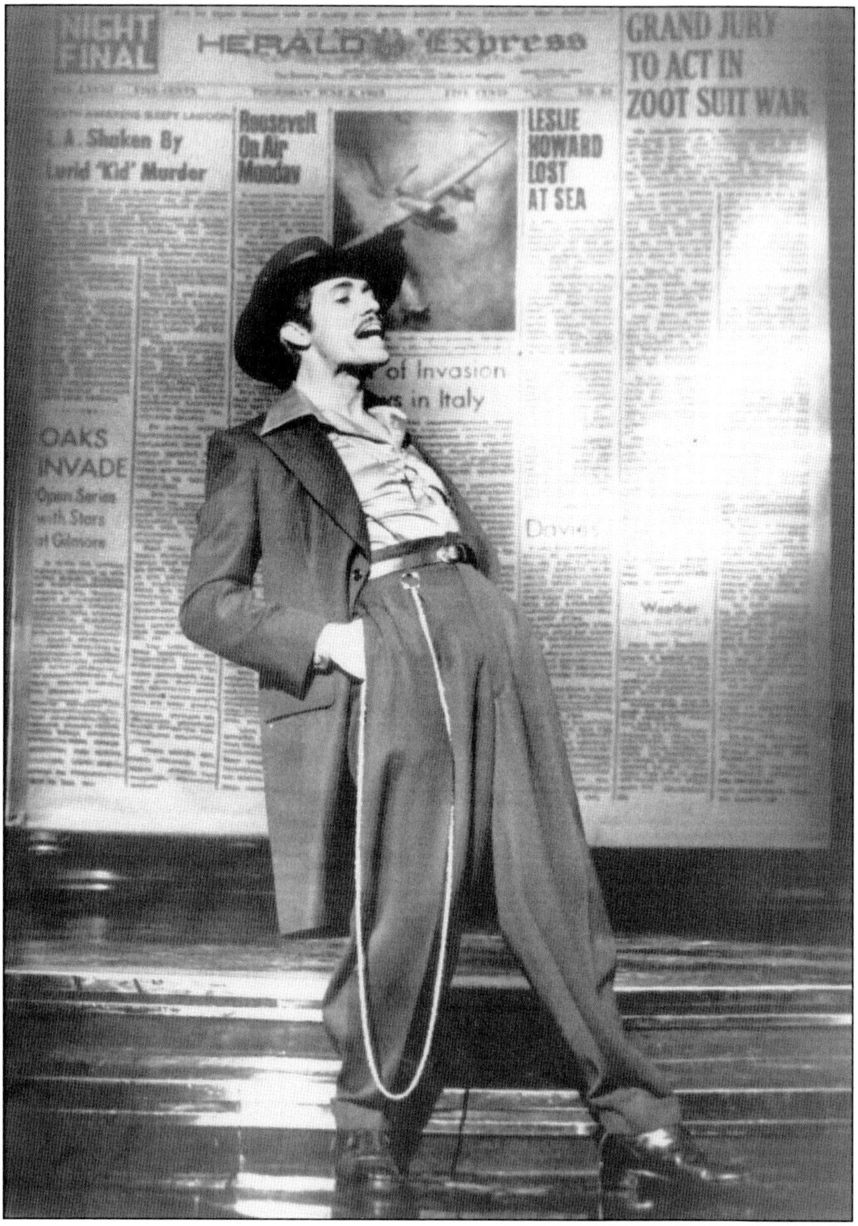

Edward James Olmos was born in 1947 in the East Los Angeles barrio of Boyle Heights. Today he is the most recognized Mexican American film and television star in Hollywood. In his youth, he sang and taught himself piano. An avid baseball fan, he credits the sport with teaching him discipline, a quality that later became important in his acting career. He earned an associate of arts degree at East Los Angeles College and later studied at California State University, Los Angeles. Initially, he played small parts on television series such as *Kojak* and *Medical Center*. By 1970, he appeared in his first stage presentation in the critically acclaimed role of El Pachuco, in *Zoot Suit*, Daniel Valdez's play. In 1984, he played police lieutenant Castillo in the television series *Miami Vice*, for which he received an Emmy Award, followed in 1986 by a Golden Globe Award. In the 1992 film *American Me*, he coproduced, directed, and played the lead in the film. In 1998, he was featured on a *Time* magazine cover. (Jerry Roberts.)

In this c. 1990 image, Edward James Olmos displays a pensive side. He sometimes contends that he would rather be known as an activist than an actor. He is known for having a profound social conscience. He is remembered for going into the streets with a broom in his hands after the chaos of the 1992 Los Angeles riots. (Jerry Roberts.)

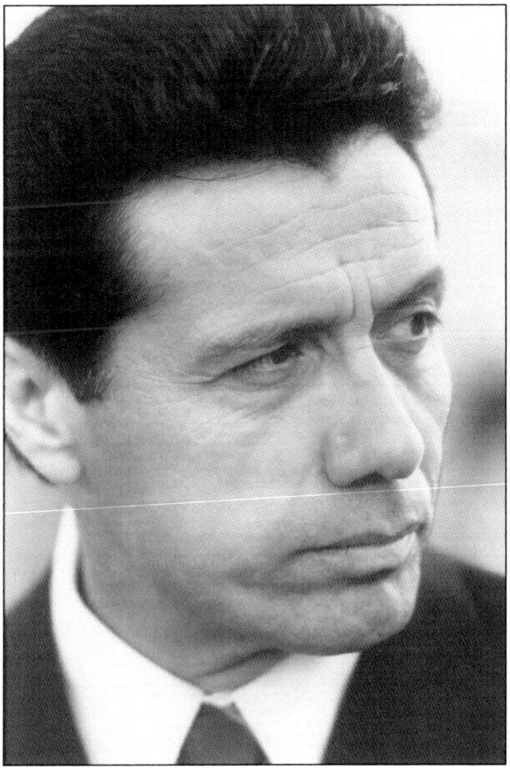

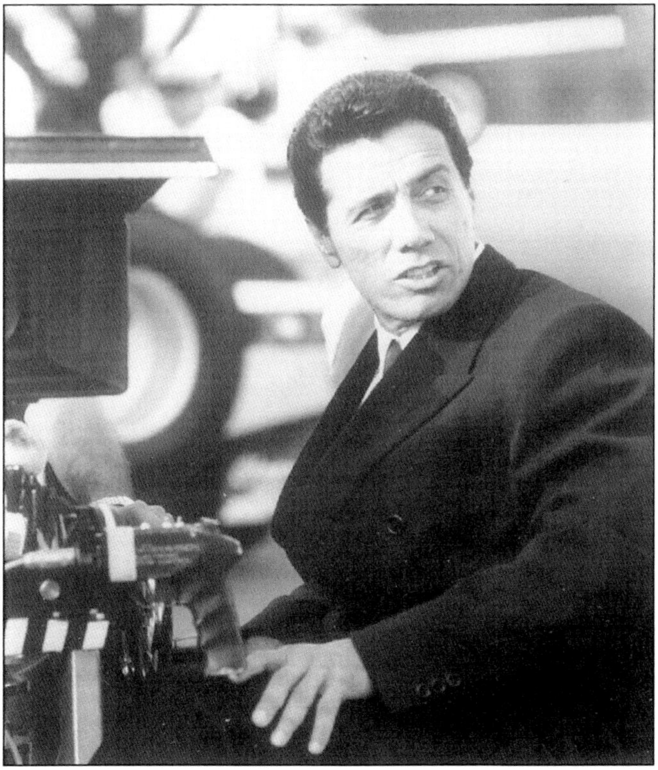

Edward James Olmos cofounded a film company, YOY, to produce films with a social message. He gives more than 100 speeches a year advising youth to take control of their own destinies through education. He has received five honorary doctorates from educational institutions for his work, and he is a goodwill ambassador for UNICEF. (Jerry Roberts.)

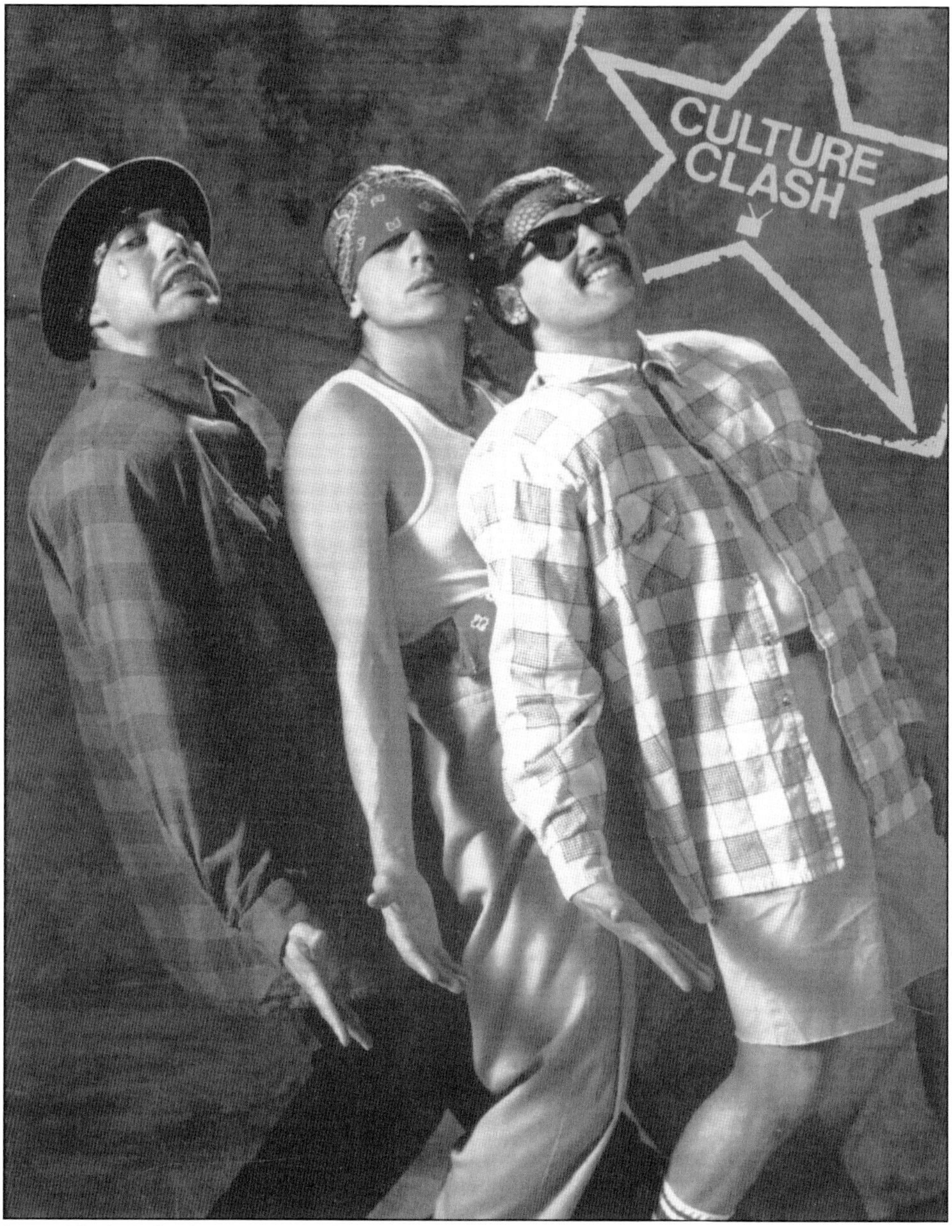

"Culture Clash," also known as Richard Montoya, Herbert Siguenza and Ric Salinas, is the most prominent Chicano and Latino performing troupe in the United States. The three write and perform their own material, which is sometimes described as a combination of ethnographic, political, and historical theater that looks at the clash of Mexican American and Latino and American cultures on their erratic journey towards coexistence. They look at America's racial history with satire and outrageous humor to expose the imperfections of that journey, while seeing American society for what it is. The group was founded on May 5, 1984, in San Francisco by Antonio Burciaga, Margo Gomez, Richard Montoya, Monica Palacios, Ric Salinas, and Herbert Siguenza as "Comedy Fiesta." Their work is sometimes viewed as a new vaudeville. They were influenced by Mexican tent circuses called Carpas, where the idol of Mexican comedy, Cantinflas, got his start, and by Charlie Chaplin, America's favorite mime. (Herbert Siguenza.)

Culture Clash's play, *Zorro in Hell,* deals with issues such as homeland security, Anglo-America's struggle with Mexican immigration, and American Indian casinos. Performed in 2007 at the Ricardo Montalban Theatre, its hero represents oppressed people everywhere, even west Los Angeles. Their work cuts across race, class, and culture to remind us that California was born from a clashing of cultures. The group's unique humor has earned them numerous awards. (Herbert Siguenza.)

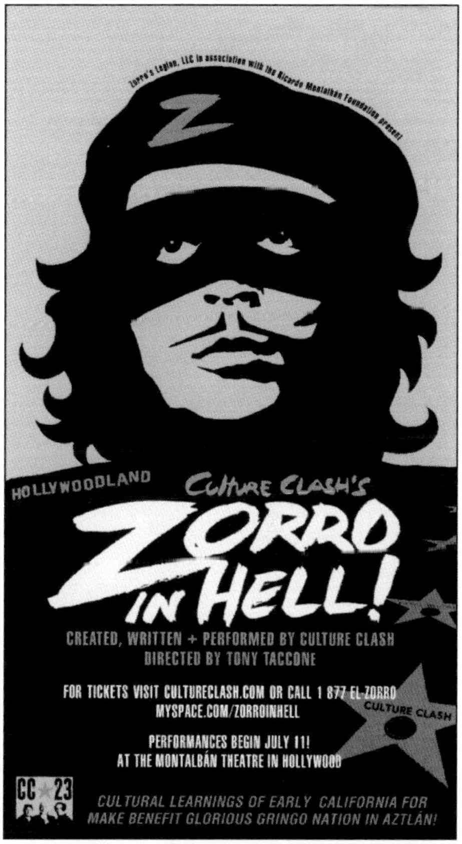

Moctezuma Esparza is the most prolific Mexican American filmmaker in the country. He has produced or directed more than 20 films and television productions including *Selena*, *Gettysburg*, and the *Milagro Beanfield War.* He has also worked on television's Sesame Street and Via Allegre. Possibly his greatest production was his family. Shown in this family portrait are, from left to right, (first row) Moctezuma Esparza (second row) his daughter, Tonantzin, and his wife, Esperanza; (third row) sons Tenoch, Tlacael, and Tovatiu. (Alycia Enciso.)

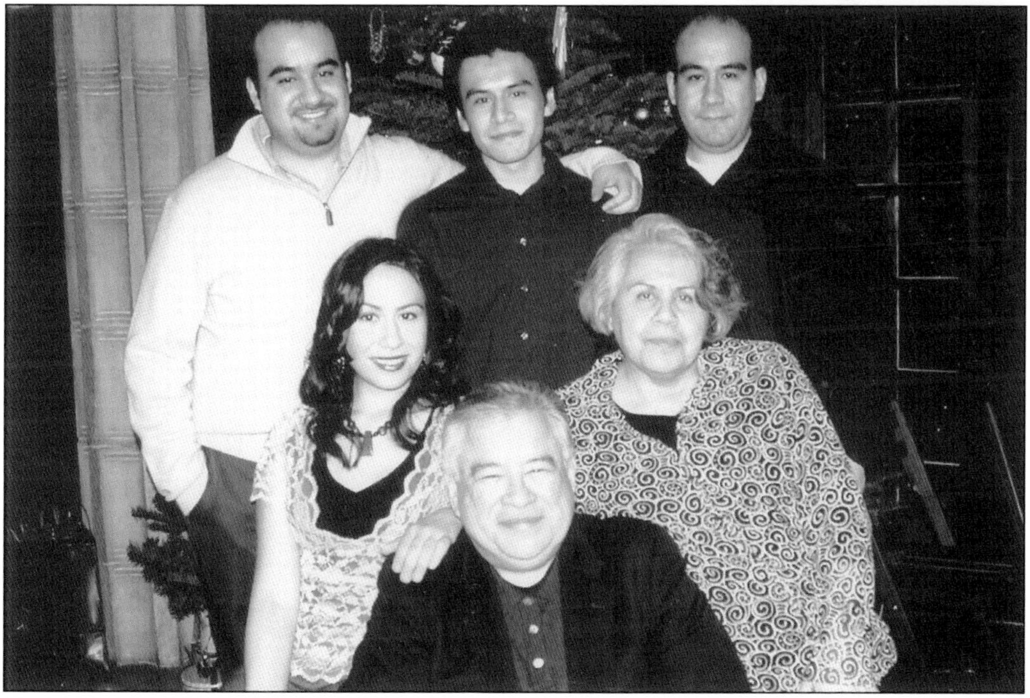

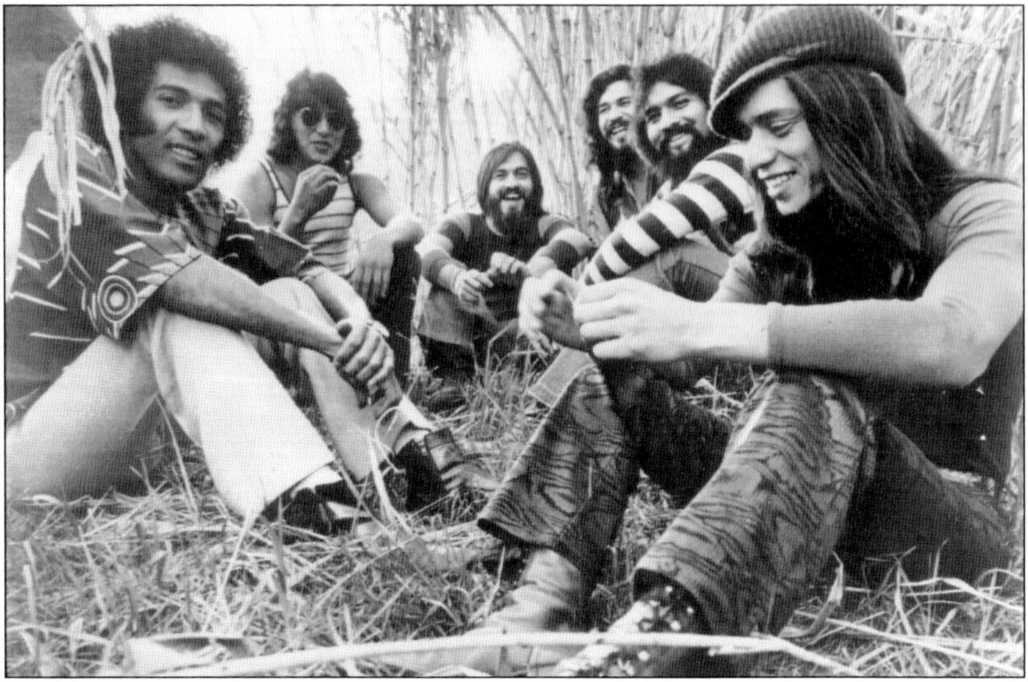

El Chicano, originally known as the V.I.P.'s, was founded by Fred Sanchez in the late 1960s. Their musical honesty and soulfulness comes from their exceptional ability to create original music by mixing traditional Mexican music, Latin jazz, and rock. Their unique sound does not come from classical training, but from an education born from the heart, as in "Viva Tirado," a tribute to Mexican bullfighter Jose Ramon Tirado, and "Tell Her She's Lovely." (Fred Sanchez.)

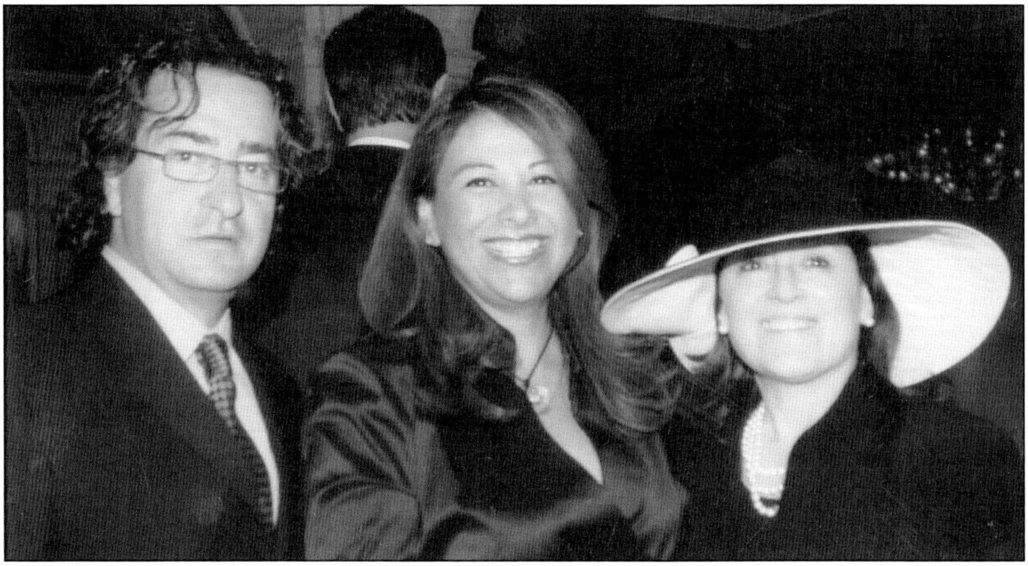

Jeff Valdez, left, cofounded Si TV, the first English language cable network that distributes English language programs directed at core Latino audiences. His syndicated shows capture the Latino experience, while appealing to diverse audiences. This 2008 photograph was taken at the Tomas Rivera Institute fund-raiser at the Biltmore Hotel in Los Angeles. At center is Ana Valdez, and at right is Alycia Enciso of A and E Designs. (Alycia Enciso.)

Two

Community Organizations and Activists

Mexican American community organizations and activists in Los Angeles represent one of the lasting legacies of the Chicano civil rights movement of the 1960s and 1970s. These groups continue the work of that period in a more local capacity, and they provide a place for activists to continue to promote change for the well-being of the Latino communities. While Mexican American political figures addressed the issues of discriminatory laws and public policies at the state and federal levels, community organizations and activists became spokespersons for the underserved members of the community at the local level. Community organizations became extensions of the activism practiced by students at the college level. In many cases, college students returned to their communities as entry-level professionals after graduation, and they continued to advocate for educational and social justice programs at the community level.

One extraordinary example of a local organization providing service to the community is the Mothers of East Los Angeles (MELA). Over the past four decades, they have served as neighborhood watchdogs protecting the living environment of the East Los Angeles residents by stopping the construction of a prison and a toxic waste incinerator plant in their neighborhood. In Wilmington, California, the Teen Post continues to provide important social services through outreach programs for at-risk youth, housing and educational assistance, and programs assisting Spanish-speaking residents and senior citizens.

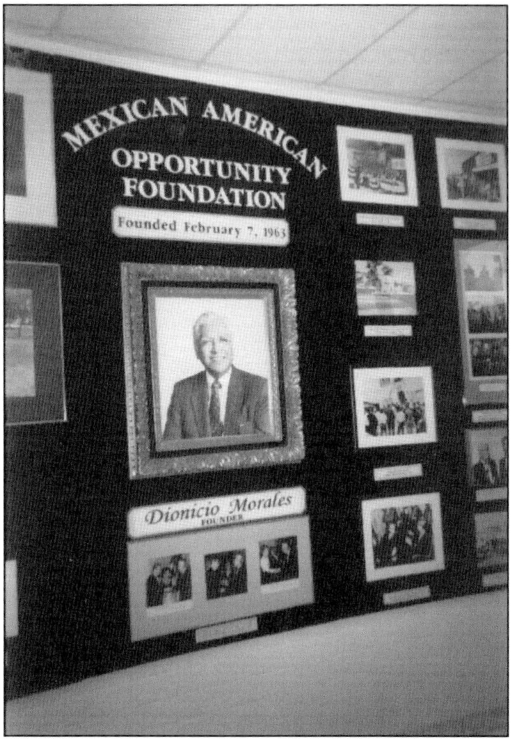

Dionicio Morales founded the Mexican American Opportunities Foundation (MAOF) in 1963 in a garage in Pico Rivera, California. He sought equality for all Americans after being denied admittance as a young man to a concert in Santa Monica and a theater in Moorpark, California. In 2008, California State University, Los Angeles bestowed on him an honorary doctorate of humanities. He is considered the urban Cesar Chavez. (Author.)

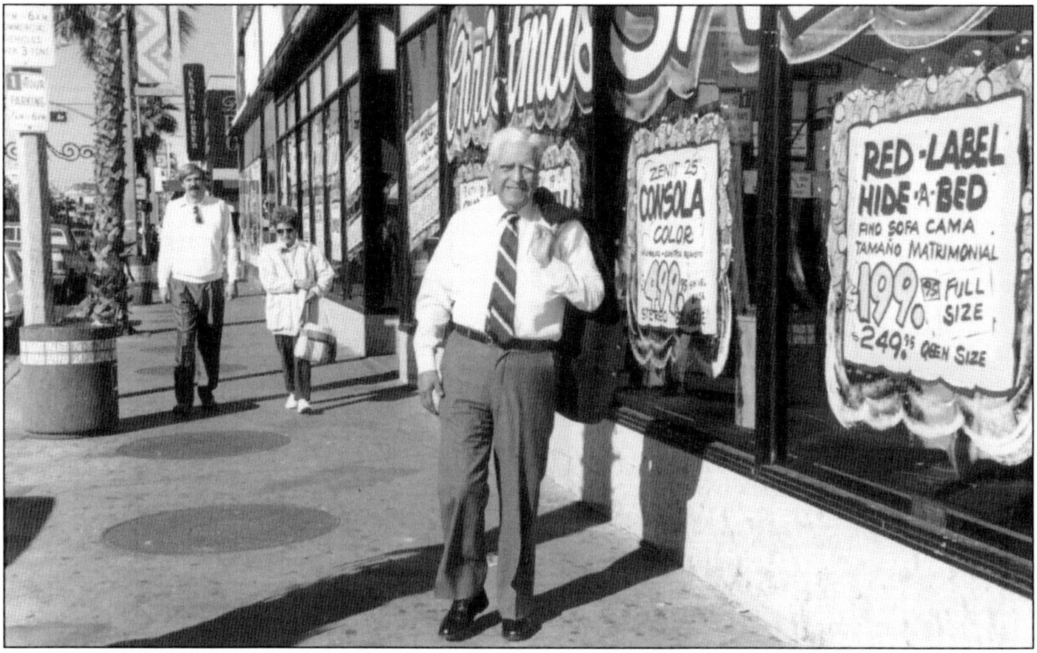

This c. 1990 image of Dionicio Morales on Whittier Boulevard in East Los Angeles captures the tireless energy he devoted to his work on behalf of the Mexican American community. Through the Mexican American Opportunities Foundation, he devoted his life to empowering Mexican Americans to obtain better jobs, educations, and better opportunities for themselves and their families. (UCLA archives and the Dionicio Morales family.)

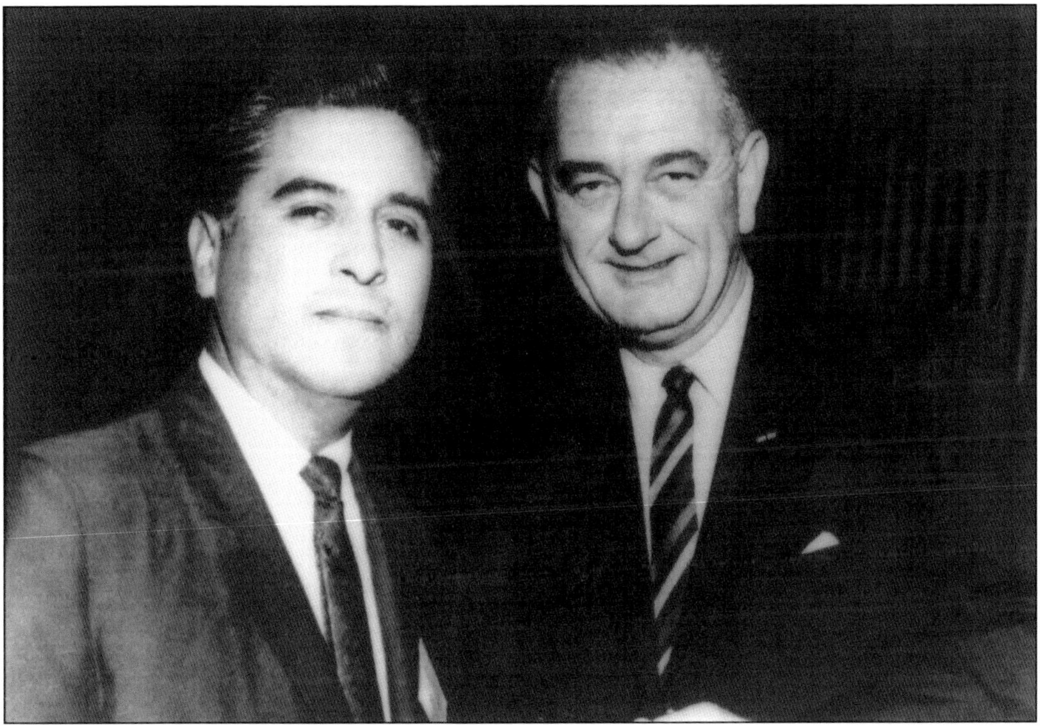

In 1963, Dionicio Morales achieved a major breakthrough when he met with Vice Pres. Lyndon Johnson and received federal funds to pursue equal-employment opportunities. Johnson later attended a MAOF employment conference in East Los Angeles, resulting in job partnerships with area employers. Morales was fearless in seeking out political figures that would help him improve the economic and social lives of all Americans. (Magdalena Morales.)

In this c. 2005 photograph, Dionicio Morales is shown with former Mexican president Vicente Fox. Morales has been internationally recognized as a spokesperson for underserved Mexican American communities across California. He proudly said, "I have only one political party, the brotherhood of man, and one agenda, equality and justice for all." He believed the brotherhood of man eclipsed political boundaries and national agendas. (Magdalena Morales.)

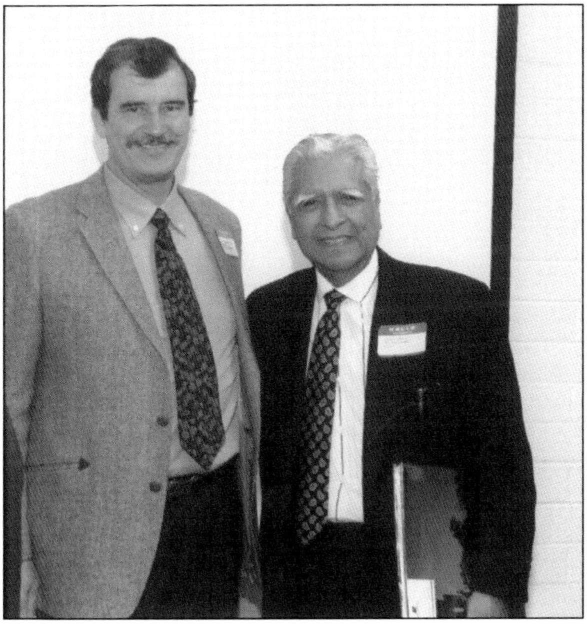

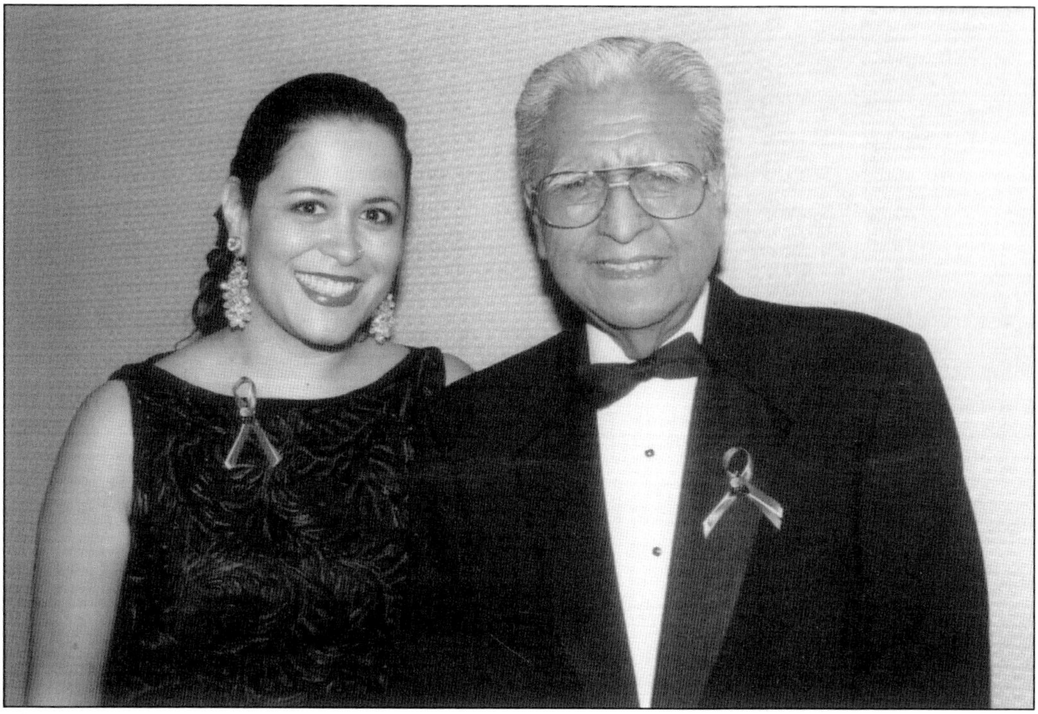

The 2001 MAOF Golden Aztec award dinner that Dionicio Morales attended with his daughter Magdalena is the setting for this image. The award honors individuals who have overcome adversity, have gone above and beyond, and have given back to the community. Today Magdalena actively continues her father's legacy through the work of the Dionicio Morales Foundation. (Photograph by George Rodriguez; courtesy of Magdalena Morales and the Dionicio Morales Foundation.)

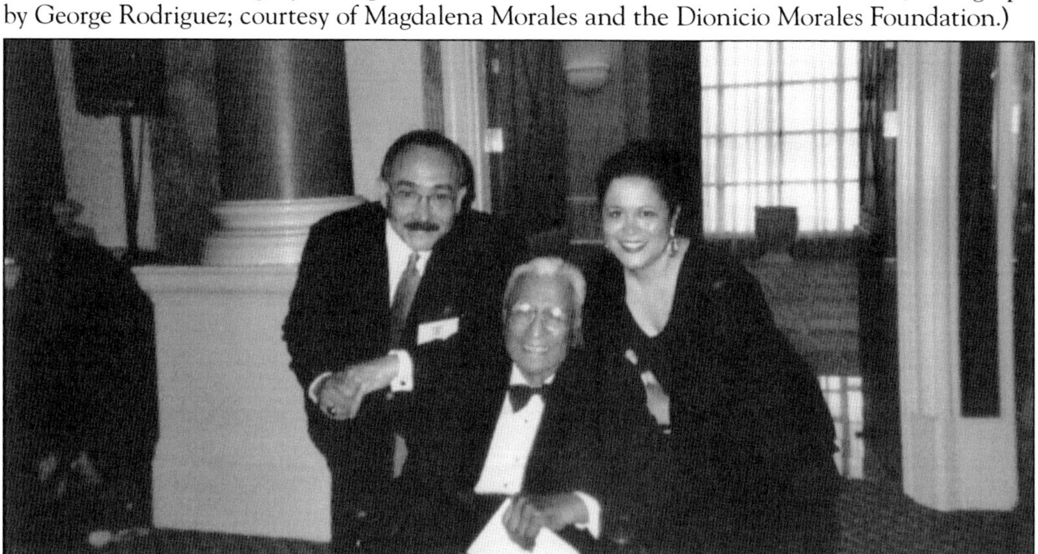

This 2006 photograph was taken at Caesar's Palace in Las Vegas at a Woman of the Year award dinner honoring Los Angeles county supervisor Gloria Molina. At left is *Hispanic Business* magazine publisher Jesus Chavarria, center is Dionicio Morales, and right is Magdalena Morales. In 2006, Morales was awarded *Hispanic* magazine's lifetime achievement award, one of hundreds over a 40-year period. (Magdalena Morales and the Dionicio Morales Foundation.)

Standing at the entrance to the MAOF headquarters in Montebello, California, are, left, Martin Castro—chief executive officer and president, and Margarita Morales Padilla—daughter of Dionicio Morales and a member of the foundation's board. MAOF is the nation's largest, nonprofit, social services organization, serving Latinos in seven California counties from Salinas to San Diego. They provide free or low-cost programs for child care, senior and disabled services, and youth programs. (Author.)

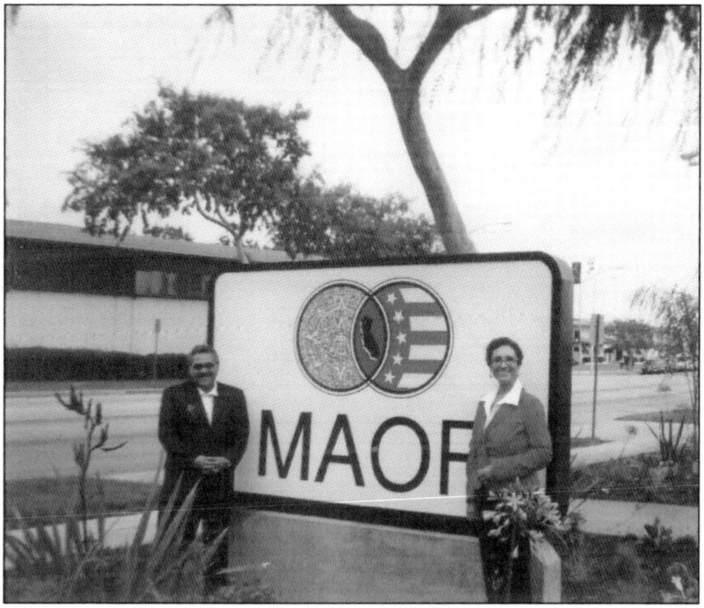

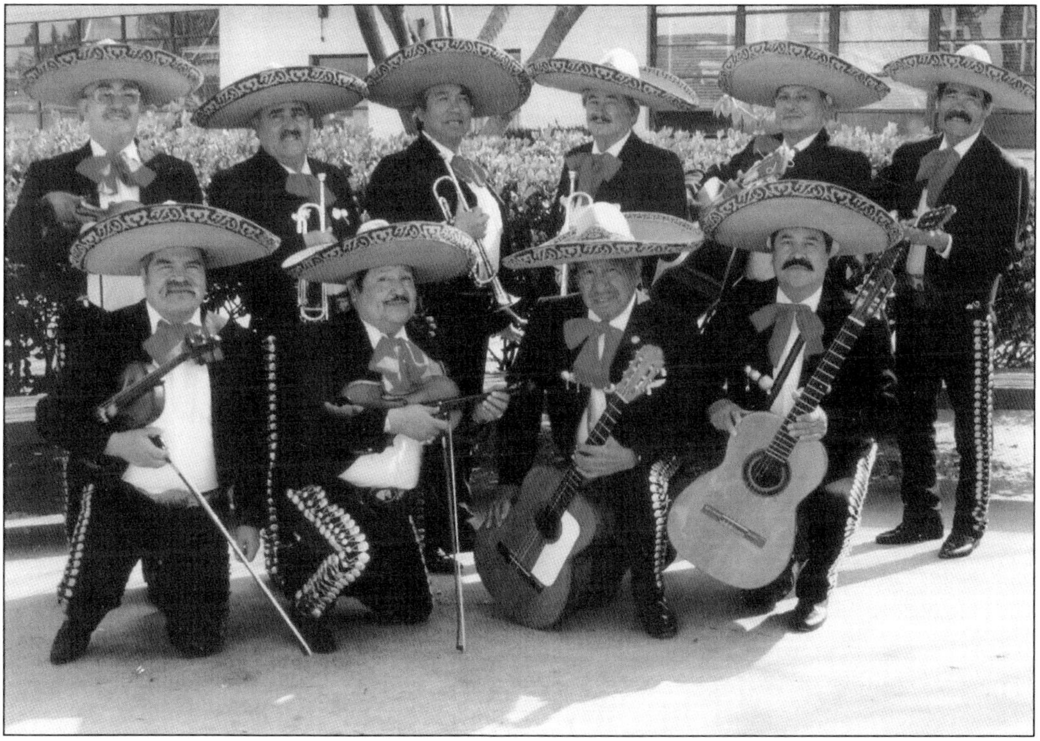

Dionicio Morales founded this mariachi group of senior aides of MAOF, who performed at events around Los Angeles. Morales believed mariachis represented the heart and soul of the Mexican American culture by creating music for important celebrations in life, such as weddings and funerals. Their music is a unique cultural and spiritual tradition. Morales played first trumpet in the Moorpark High School band. (Magdalena Morales and the Dionicio Morales Foundation.)

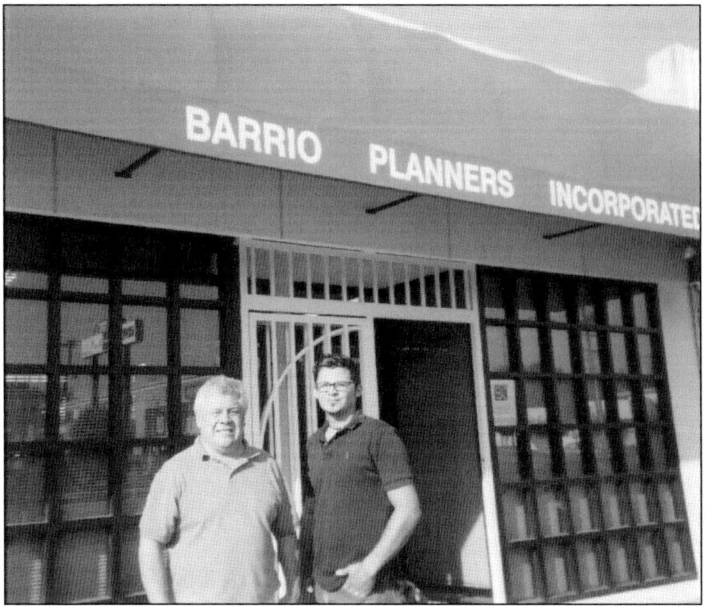

Frank Villalobos, FAIA, founder of Barrio Planners, is shown, at left, with his architectural designer son Alex. Villalobos founded the socially conscious East Los Angeles architectural firm in 1971, during a period of strong social and political growth. Over three decades, Villalobos has contributed substantially to the East Los Angeles community's prosperity by providing designs and advocacy planning services for many groups, including projects for migrant worker housing. (Author.)

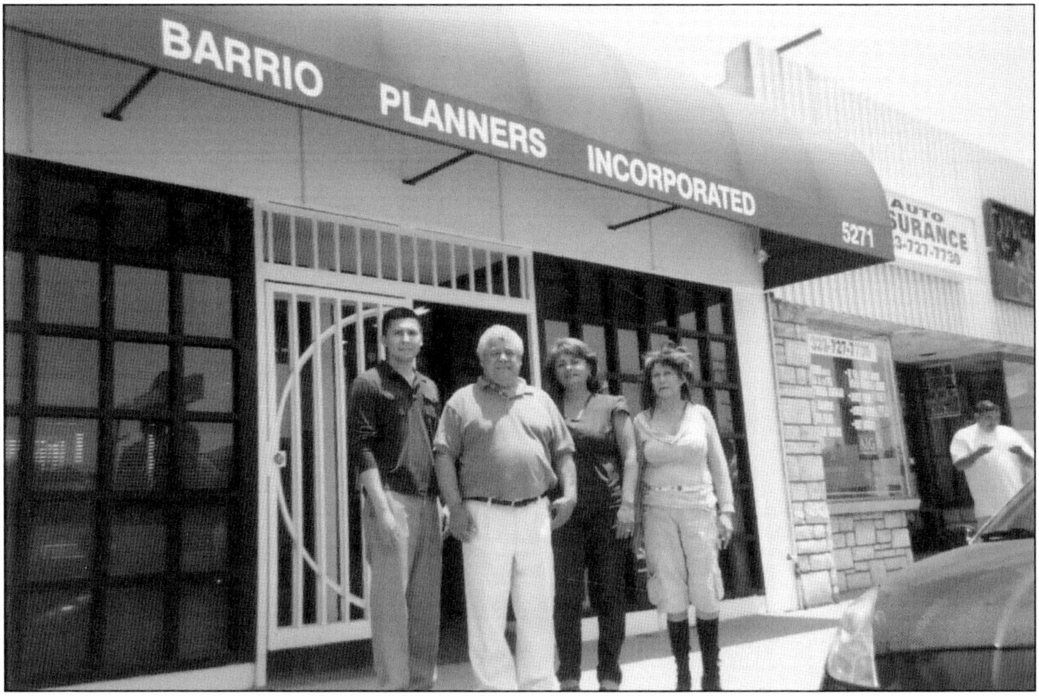

Barrio Planners' staff has a long history of social responsibility. They undertake environmental projects that positively impact residents of East Los Angeles. Pictured here are, from left to right, Luis Vazquez, president; Frank Villalobos, FAIA; Luz Maria Chavez; and controller Teri Griffin. Villalobos and Griffin are among the founders of the original MELA, a group originally organized to fight prison construction in their community. (Author.)

Architect Frank Villalobos, FAIA, stands on the platform of the Los Angeles Metro Rail Gold Line extension into East Los Angeles. His firm Barrio Planners conceived, designed, and constructed this station on Atlantic Avenue. White Memorial Hospital and the Mariachi Plaza are among many visible and successful projects Villalobos has undertaken. (Author.)

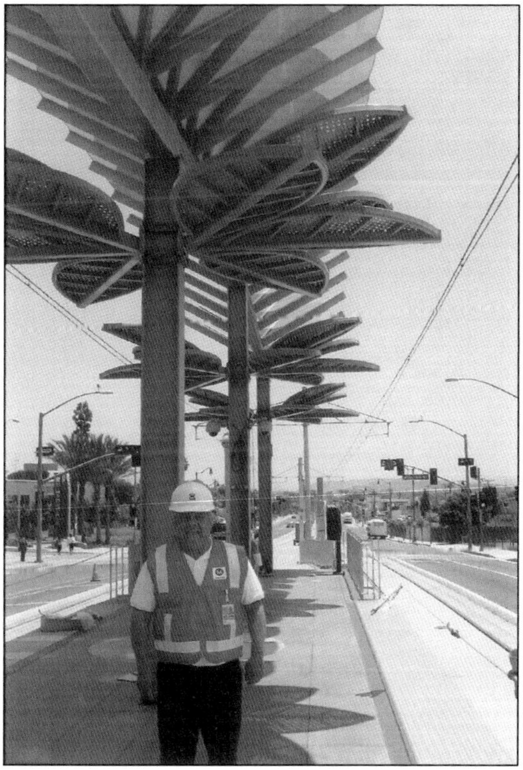

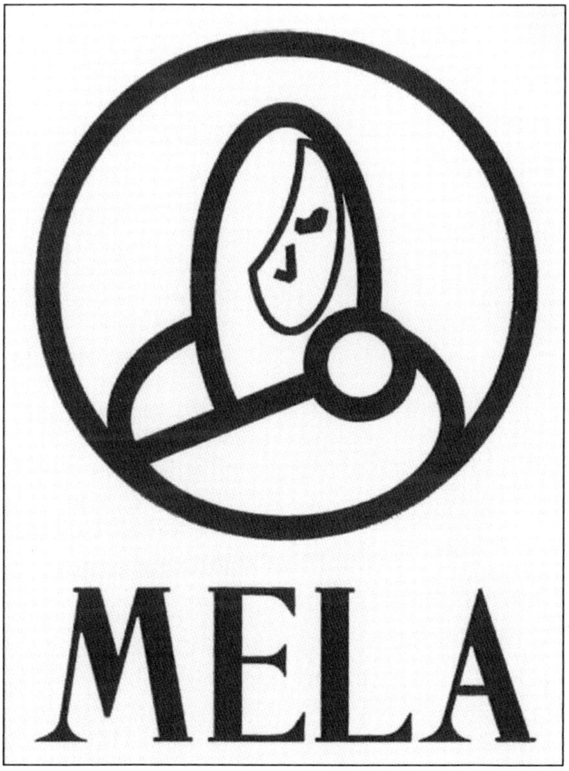

The MELA logo of a mother protecting her child was a powerful image used by the group in 1986 as they fought the building of a prison near 30 schools in the Boyle Heights neighborhood of the Eastside. MELA was founded at Resurrection Parish by Msgr. John Moretta. Later a second group, MELA-SI (Santa Isabel) was also formed. (Alex Villalobos and Barrio Planners.)

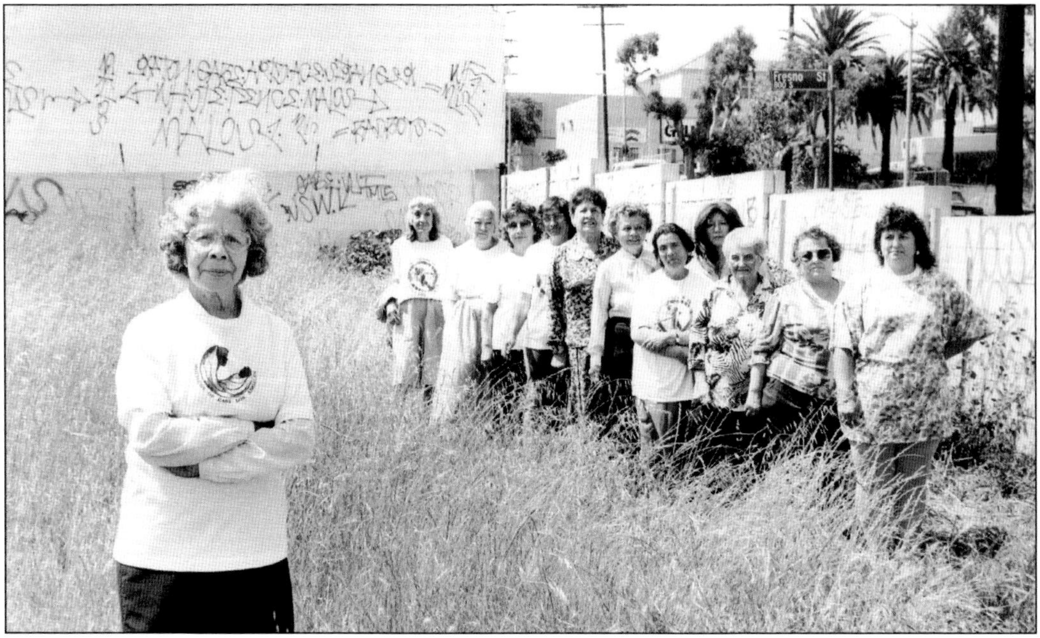

This 1980s photograph shows original members of MELA posing at a hazardous waste site at Whittier Boulevard and Lorena Street. At far left is Aurora Castillo, winner of the 1995 Goldman Award for environmental justice. At right rear are, from left to right, Josie Del Pozo, Lucy Delgado, Henrietta Castillo, Rosa Limon, Lucy Ramos, Lupe Lopez, Terri Griffin, Erlinda Robles, Stella Macias, and Irene Meras. (Alex Villalobos and Barrio Planners.)

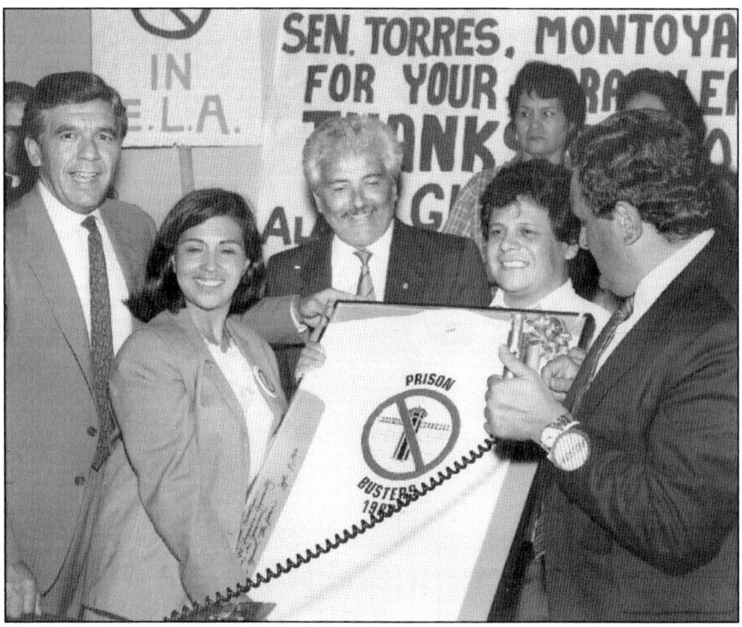

The 1986 defeat of California Senate Bill No. 904 by MELA to stop a prison in East Los Angeles is celebrated by, from left to right, (first row) supervisor Gloria Molina and state senate president pro tempore David Roberti; (second row) Frank Villalobos; (third row) state senator Art Torres and Carmine Boffo; (fourth row) Juana Gutierrez. Later MELA successfully defeated the building of a toxic waste incinerator and an oil pipeline. (Alex Villalobos and Barrio Planners.)

Eleanor Montano of Wilmington, California, 79 years young, has been giving back to her community for 63 years, and is still going strong. Her motto is: "I was brought up to pay back to my community," and she lives by those words every day. Montano spearheads social programs by assisting law enforcement with community efforts such as youth rehabilitation and uniting families against drugs and violence. (Eleanor Montano.)

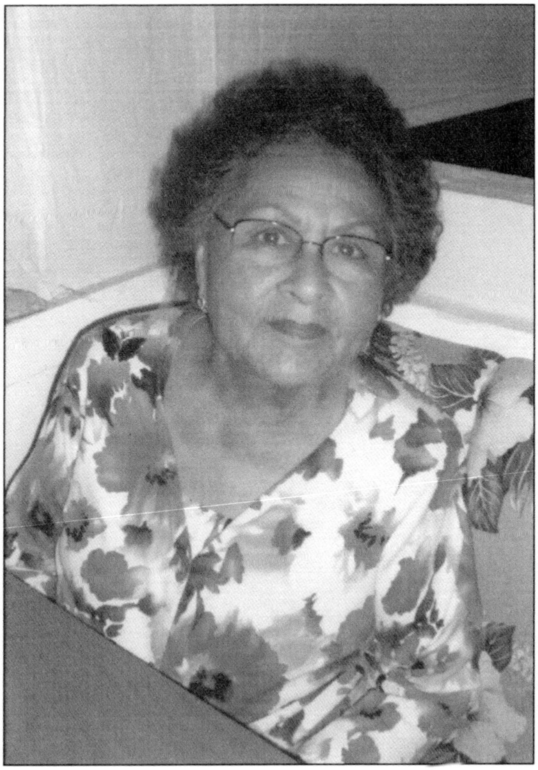

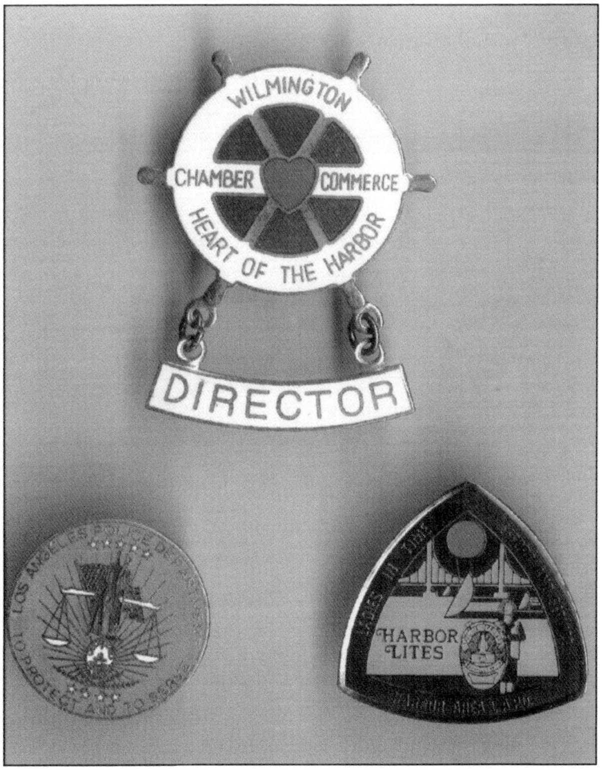

Eleanor Montano has served on committees, panels, and organizations for many years. This image shows three service pins from the City of Wilmington, the Los Angeles Police Department, and the Los Angeles Harbor "LITES" (Ladies in Time Effort and Service). LITES is a women's auxiliary program founded to assist Harbor division Police with such efforts as securing gas masks from the military after September 11, 2001. (Eleanor Montano.)

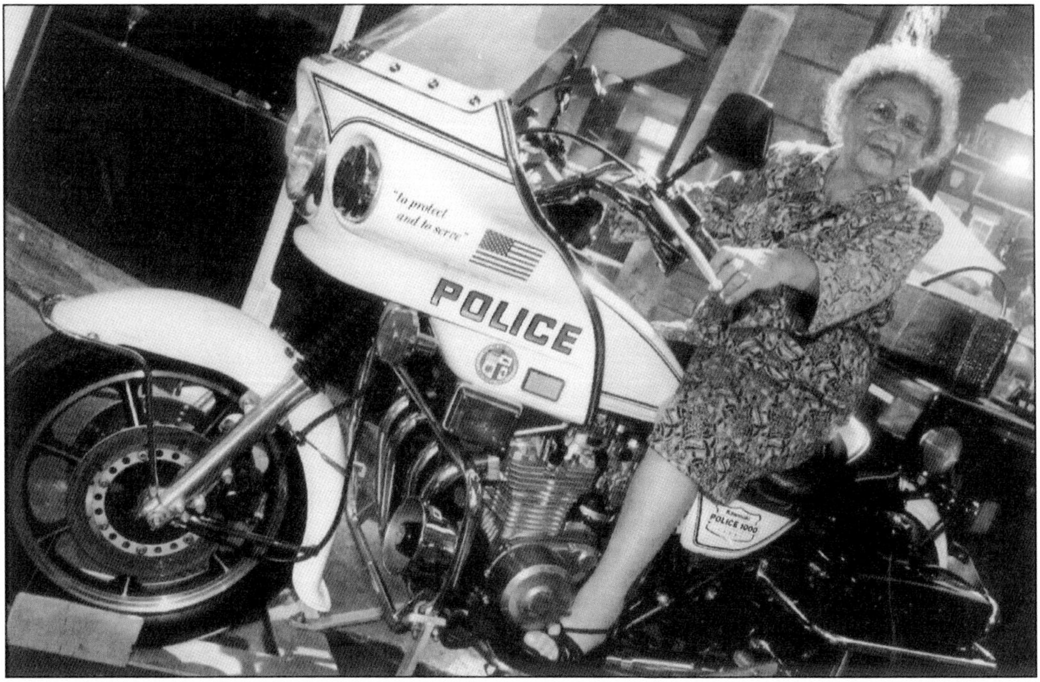

Eleanor Montano has served on the Los Angeles Police Department's board of rights since 1994. In 1995, she received the police department's commission medal and commendation. She currently serves as the chair of the Sybil Brand Institute's Commission for Institutional Inspection. Montano also served with the Selective Service department for 20 years. This motorcycle pose was taken at Paramount Studios in 2008. (Eleanor Montano.)

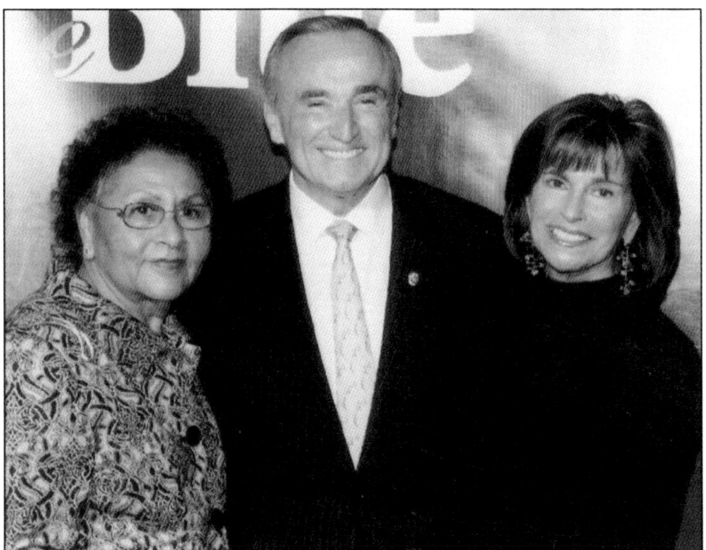

Honorary mayor of Wilmington, California, is one of many titles bestowed on Eleanor Montano. She was also on the governing board of Women Against Gun Violence (WAGV), until her leadership as an officer of the Los Angeles Commission on Human Relations. In this photograph, she is shown farthest left with Los Angeles police chief William Bratton and his wife, Rikki Klieman, at a police department function. (Eleanor Montano.)

Becoming a nun was Connie Calderon's first career choice. Unable to kneel for prayer with her bad knee, this changed, and she got a job at the Wilmington, California, Teen Post. She stayed for 40 years. This 1958 photograph shows her at age 15, planning activities with Ernie Paculba (left) and Johnny Mendez, then executive director (right). Mendez mentored Calderon for 17 years; then she became director. (Connie Calderon.)

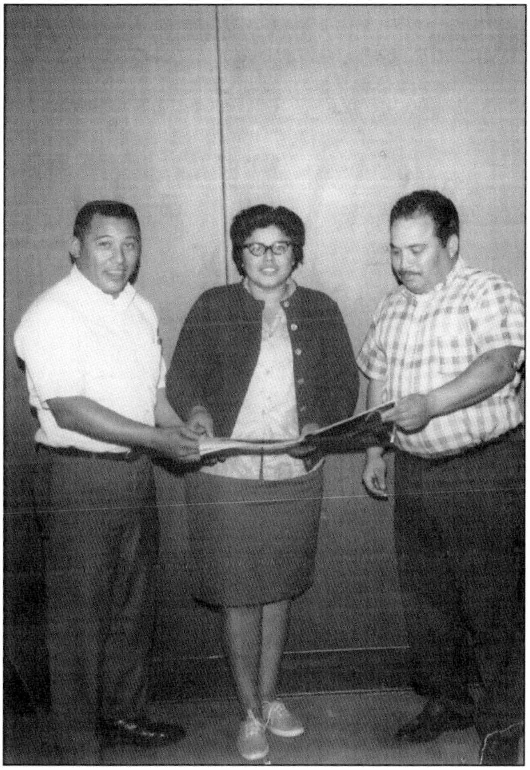

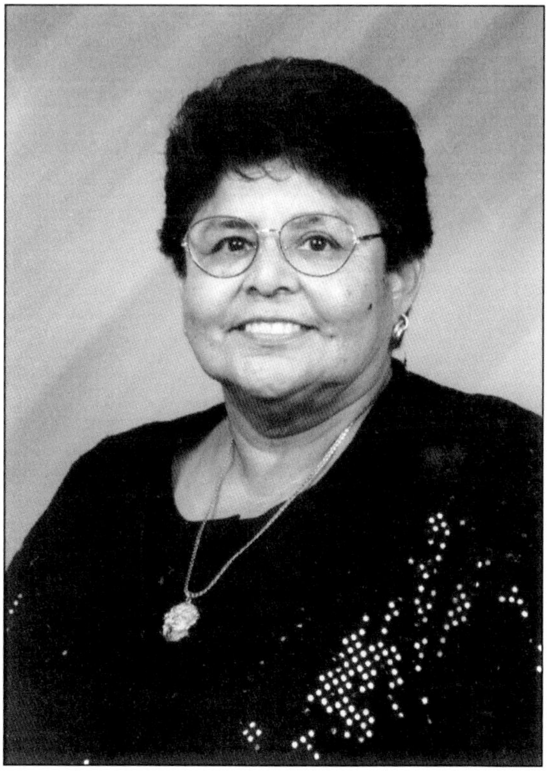

Described as the "Guiding Light for Wilmington's Youth," Connie Calderon has devoted most of her life to mentoring disadvantaged youngsters by creating hundreds of summer jobs, providing a recreational haven for troubled youth, counseling, and connecting families with needed services. The Teen Post provides weight and game rooms, a computer lab, tutoring, and an area for piano lessons in the shadow of nearby refineries. (Connie Calderon.)

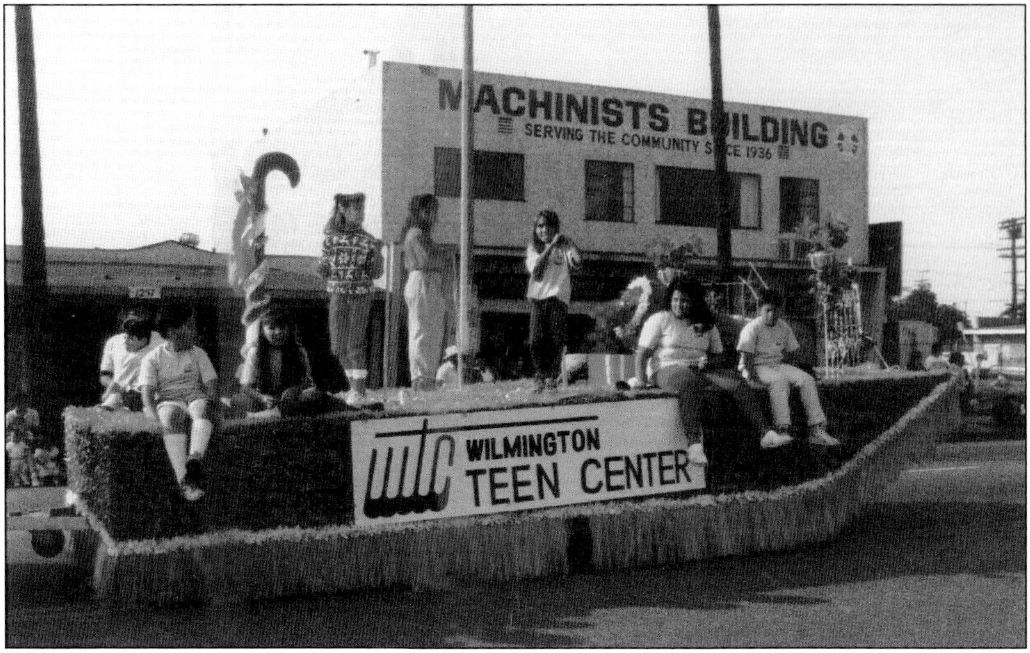

The annual Teen Post Christmas parade is a 40-year tradition in Wilmington, California. Connie Calderon remembers George De La Torre's Juanita's Foods being the float's sponsor. This 1970s photograph showing the Teen Post's float and Christmas spirit was taken in front of the Machinist's Union Hall on Avalon Boulevard. (Connie Calderon.)

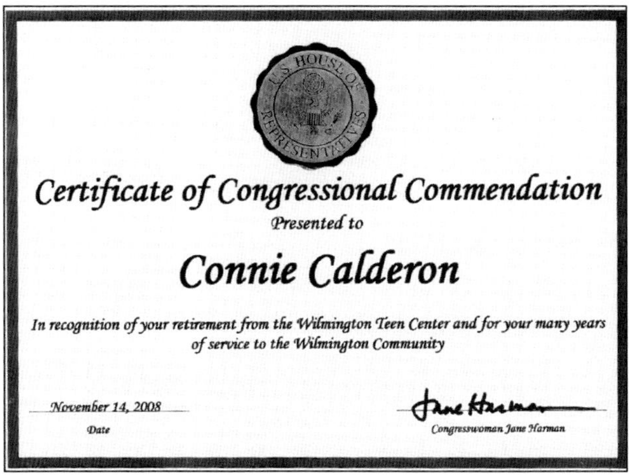

U.S. HOUSE OF REPRESENTATIVES

Certificate of Congressional Commendation

Presented to

Connie Calderon

In recognition of your retirement from the Wilmington Teen Center and for your many years of service to the Wilmington Community

November 14, 2008
Date

Congresswoman Jane Harman

At a retirement dinner in 2008, attended by a multitude of Teen Post "graduates," politicians, and community members, Connie Calderon was honored. In the Washington, D.C., congressional record, she was cited as one of the most active, unselfish, deserving citizens of the Los Angeles Harbor area. This photograph of a congressional commendation awarded to Calderon by congresswoman Jane Harman attests to her community contributions and dedication. (Connie Calderon.)

Abelardo De La Pena emigrated from Chapala, Mexico, 50 years ago. He overcame job discrimination and prejudice to become a hospital administrator, newspaper publisher, author of three books, and honorary mayor of Wilmington, California. He produced the first-ever cancer prevention documentary in Spanish for the American Cancer Society. He has been honored by many civic, religious, and community organizations for his tireless dedication to others. (Abelardo De La Pena.)

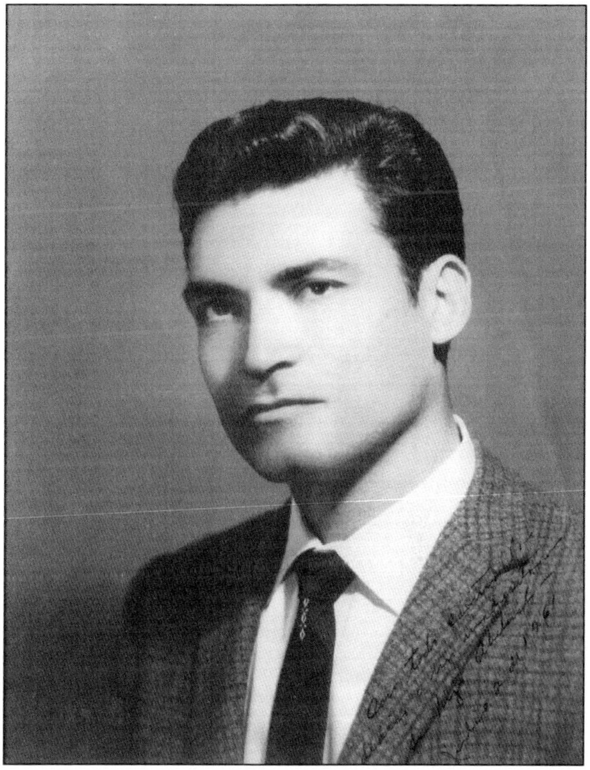

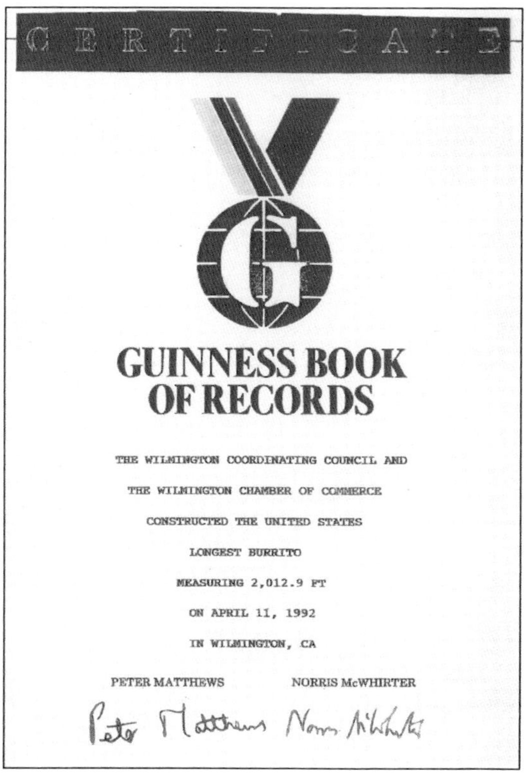

CERTIFICATE

GUINNESS BOOK OF RECORDS

THE WILMINGTON COORDINATING COUNCIL AND
THE WILMINGTON CHAMBER OF COMMERCE
CONSTRUCTED THE UNITED STATES
LONGEST BURRITO
MEASURING 2,012.9 FT
ON APRIL 11, 1992
IN WILMINGTON, CA

PETER MATTHEWS NORRIS McWHIRTER

Peter Matthews Norris McWhirter

The efforts of Abelard De La Pena to build bicultural bridges while inspiring community pride resulted in Wilmington, California, being recognized as the home of the world's largest burrito, stretching over one quarter mile on Avalon Boulevard. This record remains unbroken. He leads a bicultural team planning the traditional celebration of "El Grito," celebrating Mexico's independence. He is currently writing his fourth book. (Abelardo De La Pena.)

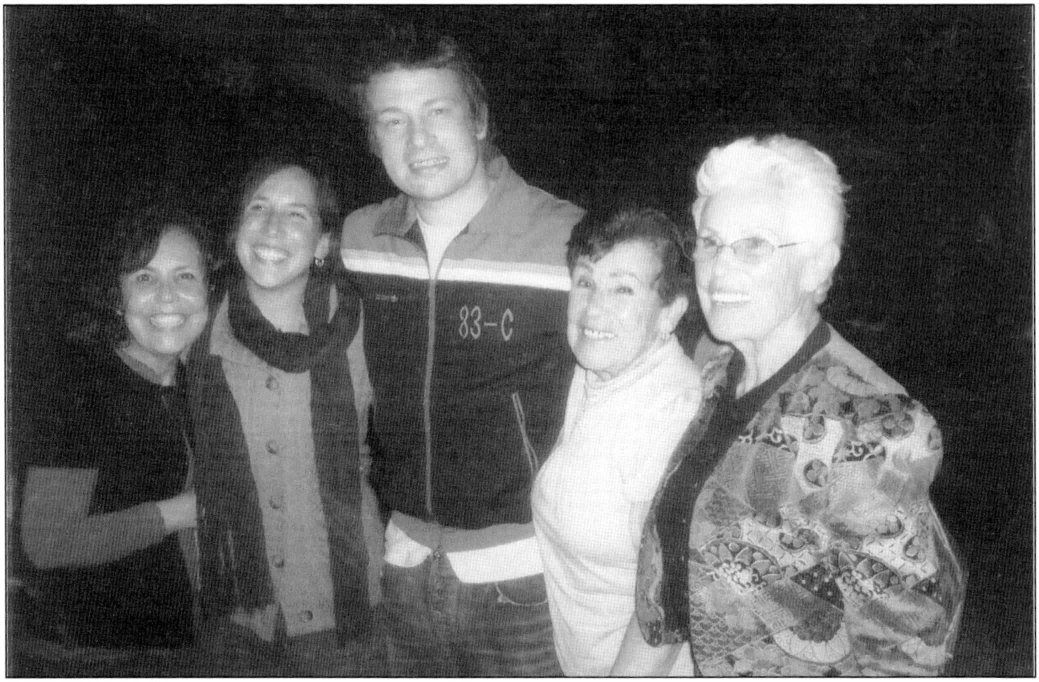

In 2009, British host Jamie Oliver filmed a Mexican cooking documentary at the home of Abelardo and "Cuca" De La Pena for his popular London food show, Naked Chef. Celebrating are, from left to right, Elsa Herrera, Vanessa Herrera, Oliver, Cuca, and Dolores Martinez. Chef Cuca delighted London viewers with her magnificent and authentic Mexican recipes. Abelardo and Cuca have been married for 58 years. (Abelardo De La Pena.)

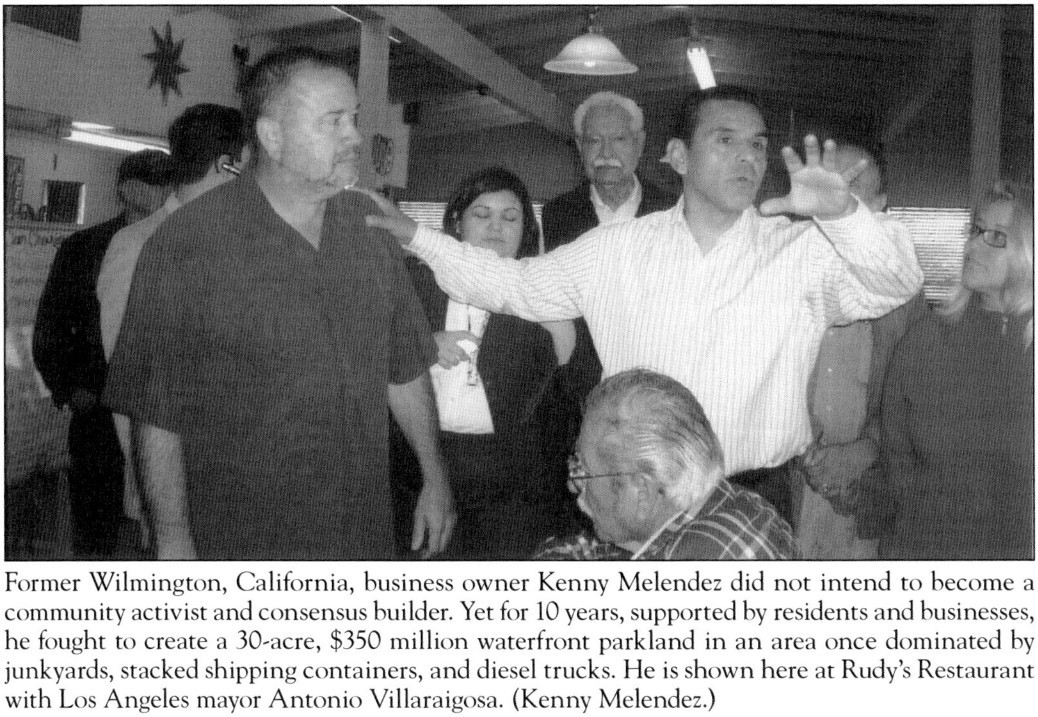

Former Wilmington, California, business owner Kenny Melendez did not intend to become a community activist and consensus builder. Yet for 10 years, supported by residents and businesses, he fought to create a 30-acre, $350 million waterfront parkland in an area once dominated by junkyards, stacked shipping containers, and diesel trucks. He is shown here at Rudy's Restaurant with Los Angeles mayor Antonio Villaraigosa. (Kenny Melendez.)

Kenny Melendez's perseverance and commitment to improving the environmental quality of life for the people of Wilmington is cited in this Certificate of Congressional Commendation signed by Congresswoman Jane Harman, and also in a Wilmington Chamber of Commerce Community Service Award. The development of the Harry Bridges parkland is the first time in history a subcommittee has been responsible for creating a waterfront parkland. (Kenny Melendez.)

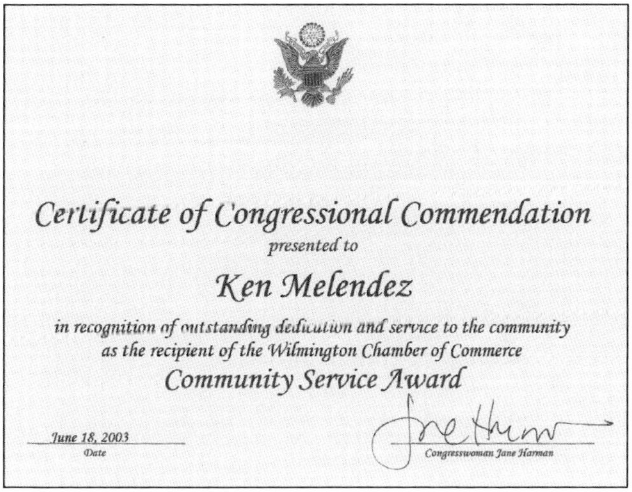

Certificate of Congressional Commendation

presented to

Ken Melendez

in recognition of outstanding dedication and service to the community as the recipient of the Wilmington Chamber of Commerce

Community Service Award

June 18, 2003
Date

Congresswoman Jane Harman

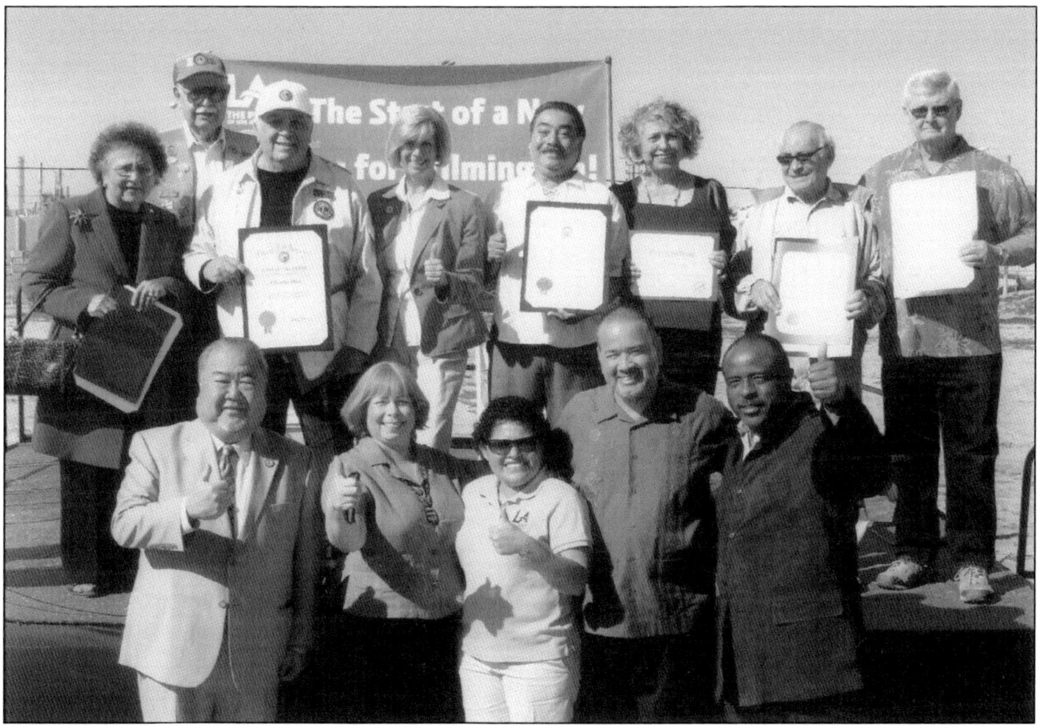

This 2009 photograph shows supporters of Kenny Melendez and his Wilmington Waterfront Development Subcommittee that successfully challenged major shipping firms to create the Harry Bridges waterfront parkland. From left to right are (first row) state assemblyman Warren Furutani, state senator Jenny Oropeza, Cecilia Moreno, Kenny Melendez, and state senator Roderick Wright; (second row) Eleanor Montano, Frank Herrera, Charlie Rico, councilwoman Janice Hahn, Jesse Marquez, Olivia Cueva Fernandez, Abelardo De La Pena, and Gary Kern. (Kenny Melendez.)

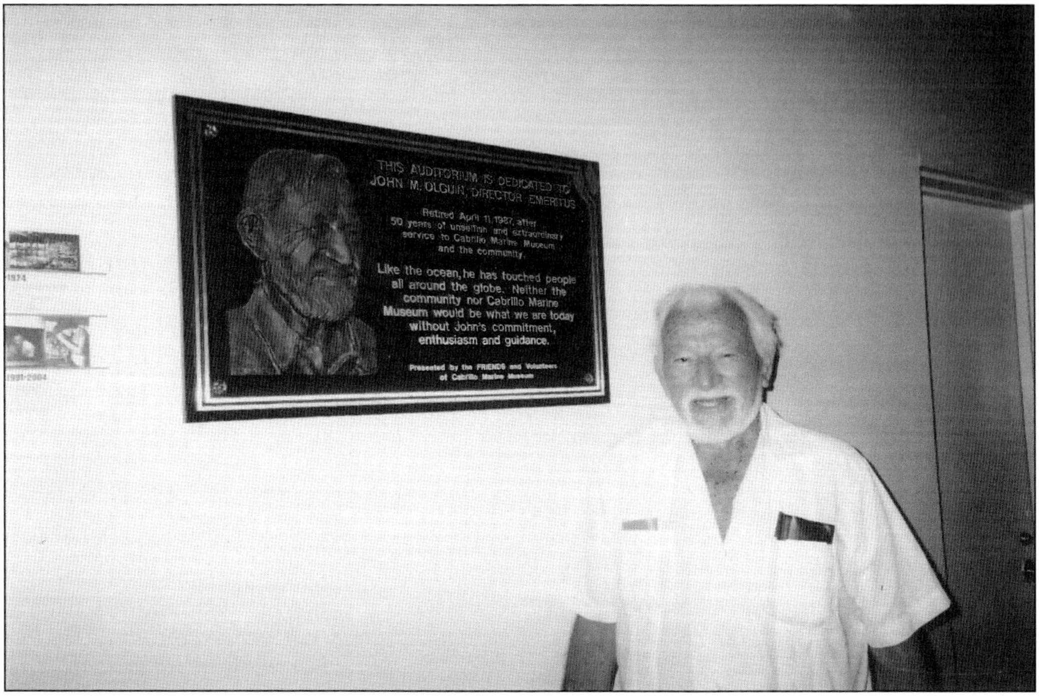

John Olguin, a native of San Pedro, California, started working as a lifeguard at the age of 15, swimming to work from his home near Cabrillo Beach. In 1949, as captain of the Cabrillo Beach lifeguards, he was appointed director of the Cabrillo Museum, later to be named the Cabrillo Marine Aquarium. Upon his retirement in 1987, he was honored by the museum with a commemorative plaque placed in the museum's auditorium. (Author.)

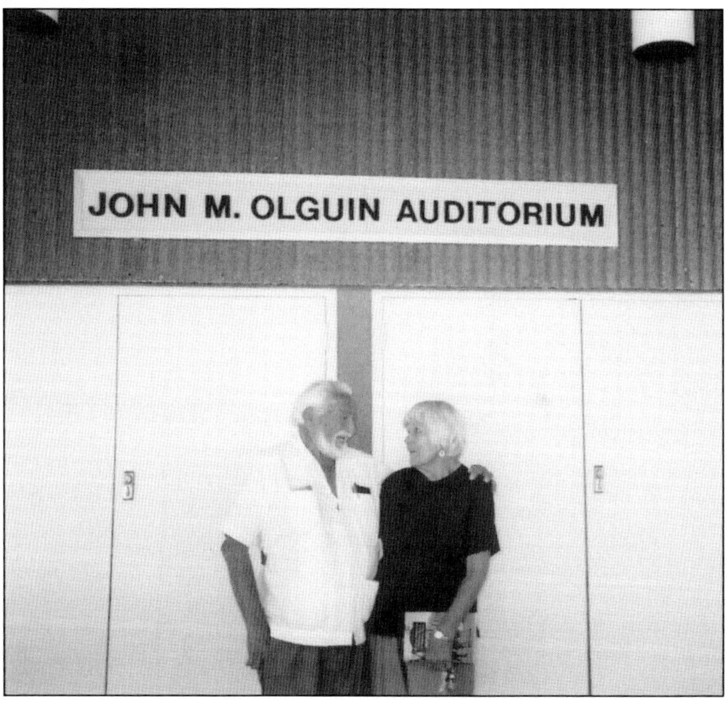

The Cabrillo Marine Aquarium in San Pedro, California, started out in the 1930s when lifeguard John M. Olguin began collecting shells and pieces of marine life brought from Venice Beach to San Pedro. This photograph shows John and his wife, Muriel, in front of the aquarium's auditorium, which is named in his honor. He was proclaimed San Pedro's "Citizen of the Century," after 70 years of service. (Author.)

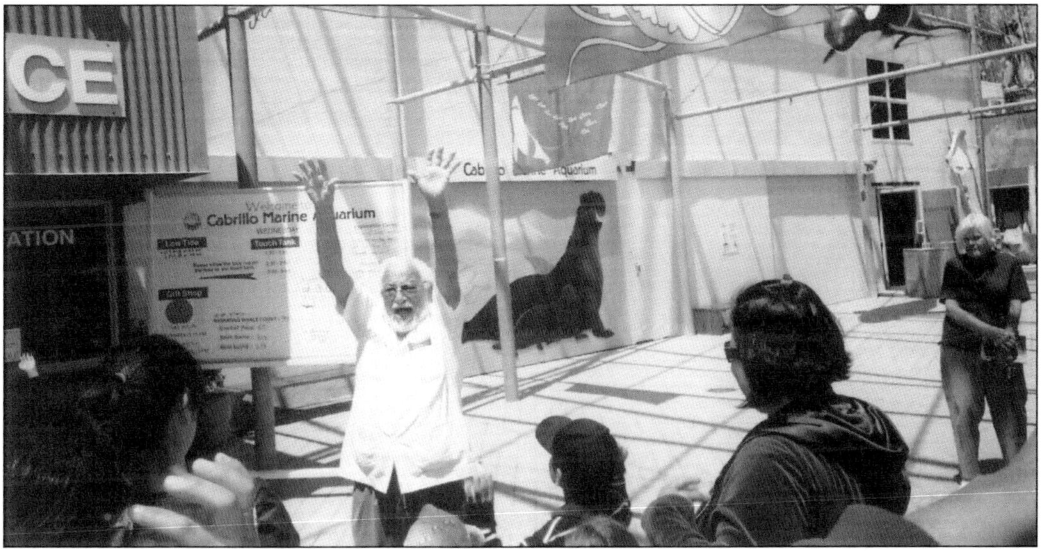

As he has done for several decades, John Olguin captivates youngsters in this photograph with his bilingual tales of the ocean waves and grunion hunting, while teaching them stewardship of the sea. Since 1972, when he initiated a whale-watching program, more than 1 million children and adults have enjoyed the excursions. In its May 1969 issue, *National Geographic* magazine recognized Olguin's night grunion-hunting program. (Author.)

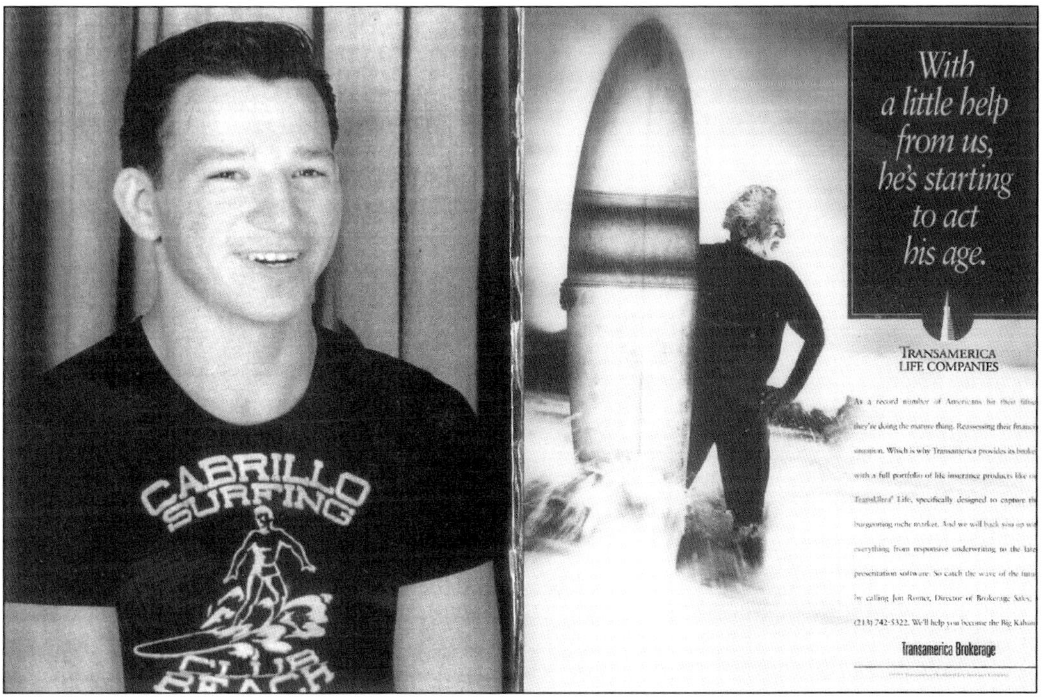

John Olguin's entire life and career have been connected to the sea. From lifeguard to aquarium director, swimming instructor to rower, innovator of marine programs to museum director emeritus, he has done it all. This photograph shows his early and senior years connecting him to the ocean he loves. A number of years ago, he and his wife, Muriel, tried rowing a small boat from Alaska to Northern California. (Transamerica Brokerage.)

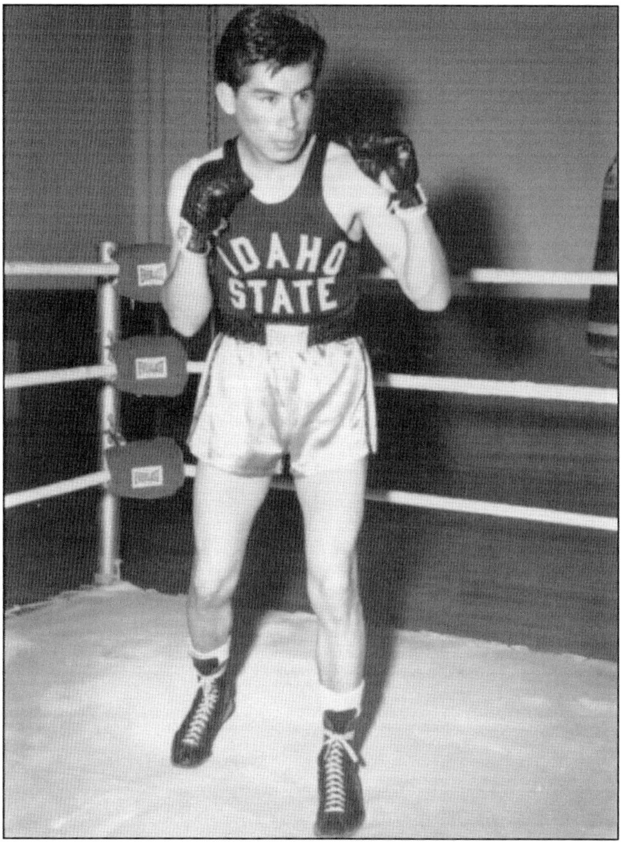

Ray and Ernie Martinez, both San Pedro natives, dedicated their lives to youth and athletics. Ray earned a sports scholarship to Idaho State University in 1947, and later became the program director of the San Pedro Boys Club. From 1978 to 1994, he served as executive director, affecting the lives of hundreds of youths. This photograph shows Ray on the boxing team at Idaho State. He died in 1996. (Ernie Martinez.)

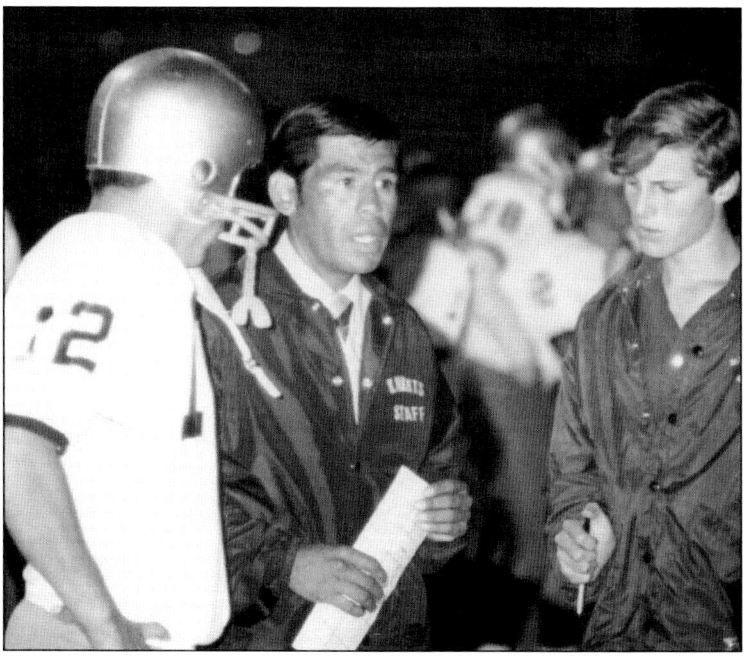

Ernie Martinez was influenced by his brother Ray. He coached for 11 years at San Pedro's Fermin Lasuen Catholic High School and 15 years at Bishop Montgomery in Torrance, California. His coaching philosophy was, "To coach, to win, make gentlemen out of athletes, and teach them good values." Former students include San Pedro judge Peter Mirich, Los Angeles city attorney Carmen Trutanich, and former NFL football star Haven Moses. (Ernie Martinez.)

Coach Ernie Martinez's honors include being named "1970 Assistant South Bay All-Star Football Coach" and 1975 Coach of the Year by *the South Bay Daily Breeze* newspaper. He also won four football league championships for 1973, 1975, 1983, and 1984. He had 21 college scholarships awarded to his players, with seven players drafted to professional sports teams. After retiring in 1985, he became a marine clerk. (Ernie Martinez.)

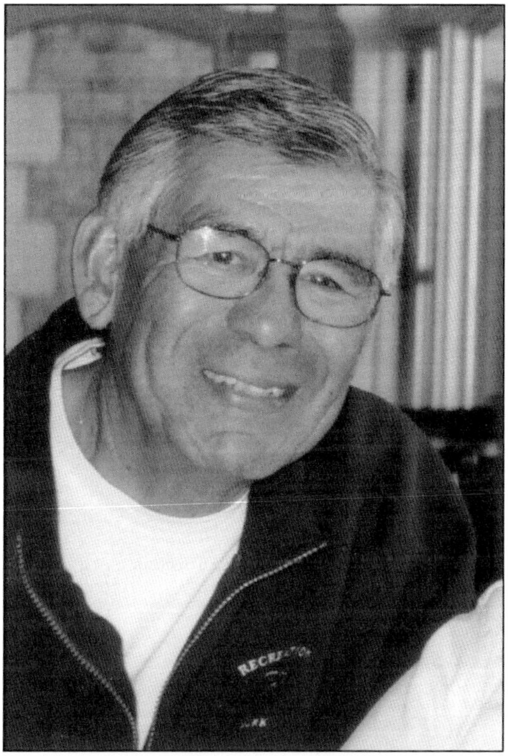

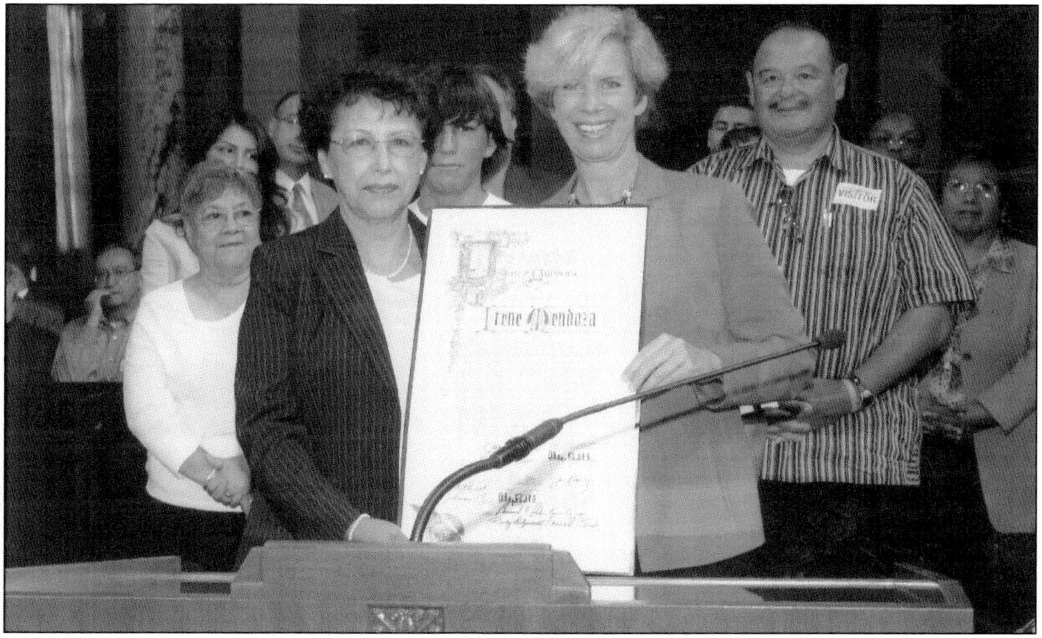

Irene Mendoza, a community advocate in San Pedro, California, is considered the go-to person who helps residents and businesses navigate the Los Angeles city bureaucracy. She served as director of constituent services for Los Angeles city councilwoman Janice Hahn from 2001 to 2005. This photograph shows Mendoza flanked by friend Angie Martinez and husband, Ephraim, receiving an honorary resolution from councilwoman Hahn at her retirement. (Irene Mendoza.)

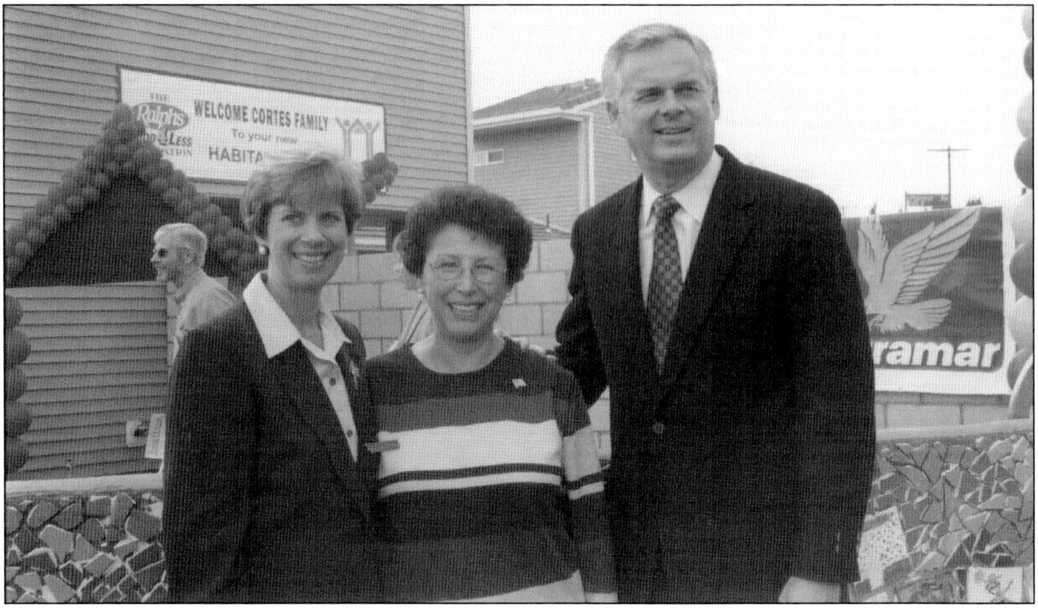

"Sincere and caring promise keeper," is how citizens describe Irene Mendoza. She served as deputy councilwoman for former Los Angeles Harbor councilman Rudy Svorinich. She served on countless boards and committees and is widely known in the harbor district. This photograph shows her with Los Angeles councilwoman Janice Hahn and former Los Angeles mayor James Hahn, dedicating the Habitat for Humanity project in Wilmington, California. (Irene Mendoza.)

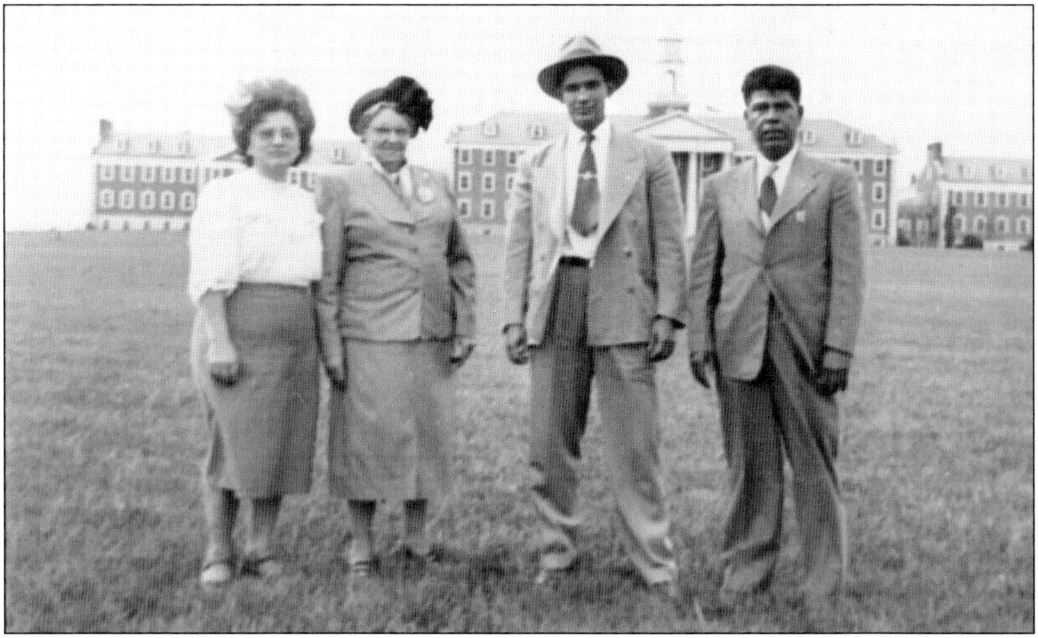

With a fourth grade education, Andrea Gomez came to the United States from Mexico in 1910. By 1924, she was working in the San Pedro fish canneries. By 1933, she was president of the Cannery Workers Union and served as the first female AFL/CIO vice president of the Seafarers International Union. This 1949 photograph shows her at far left at a convention in Washington, D.C. (Evelyn Hamel and Carole Kirkwood.)

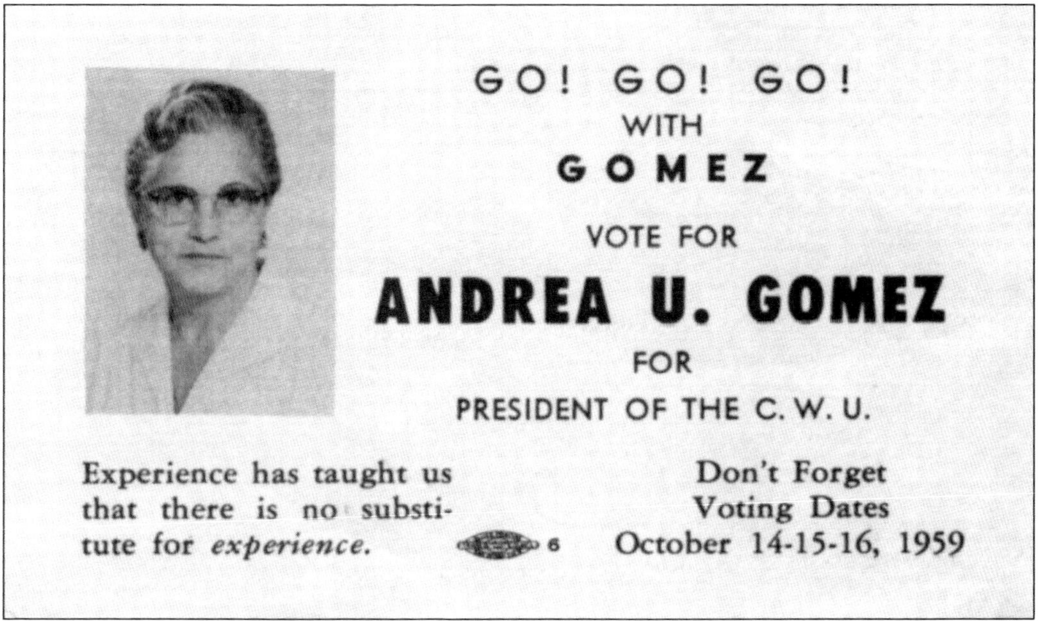

Andrea Gomez's 1949 campaign business card captures her unrelenting spirit to fight for humane working conditions and fair pay. Gomez earned the respect of both labor and management. Often she would stop cannery owner Frank Van Camp to ask that safety and pay problems be corrected. By morning, problems were often solved. She was affectionately called "the sweetheart of the labor movement." (Evelyn Hamel and Carole Kirkwood.)

Though small in stature, Andrea Gomez had a commanding physical presence. In this 1950s photograph, she is addressing the Seafarer's International Union convention in Montreal, Canada. At her left is Paul Hall, president. Andrea was instrumental in organizing workers in Puerto Rico and American Samoa. At her retirement, management and coworkers presented her with a diamond ring and a 1965 Mustang automobile. (Evelyn Hamel and Carole Kirkwood.)

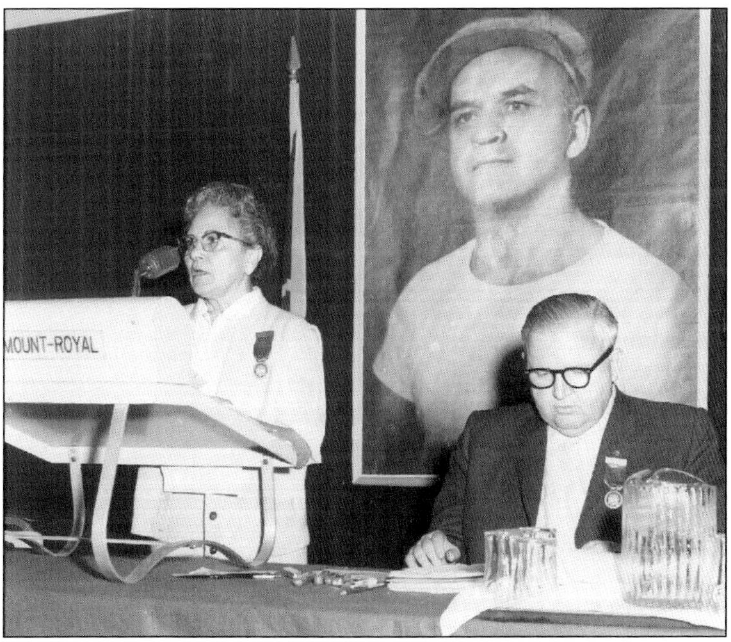

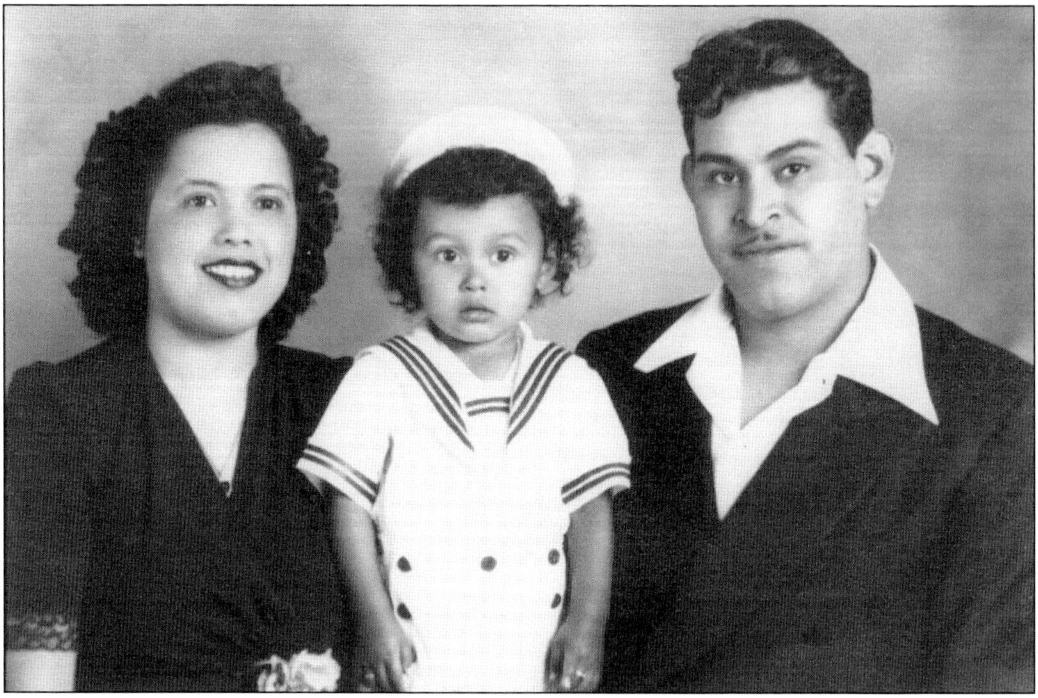

Alice Gonzalez Morales came to San Pedro, California, with her parents in 1920. They lived with about 75 other families in a neighborhood of cold-water cottages and woodstoves called "Mexican Hollywood." A high school graduate, she collected tenants' rents of $9 monthly for the Pacific Steamship Company. Alice and her husband, "Chayo" Morales, are shown in 1944 with their son "Panchito." (Pancho Morales and Rosemarie Cristino.)

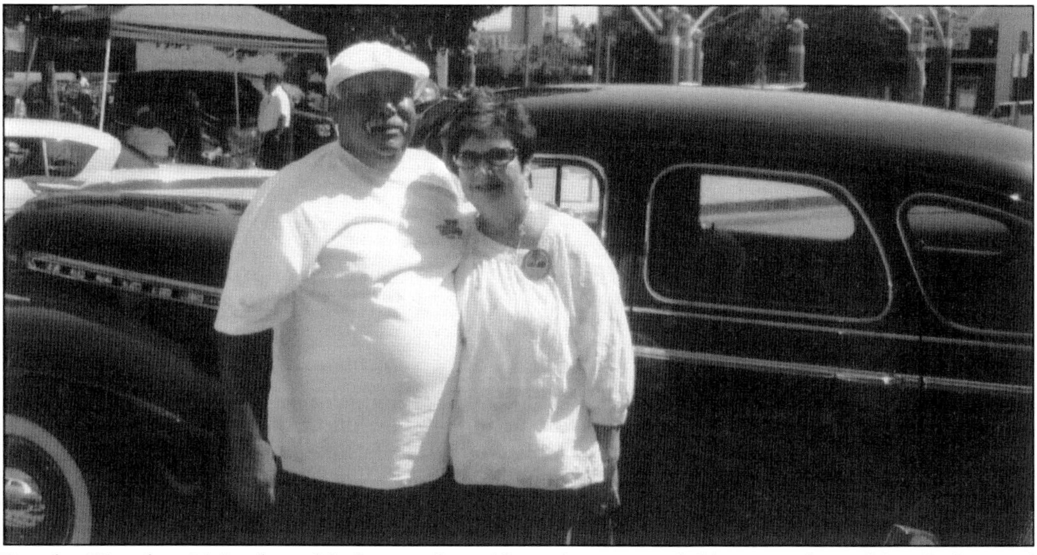

Pancho "Panchito" Morales—like his mother, Alice, above—is a lifelong resident of San Pedro, and like many San Pedro residents, he is a proud retired member of the ILWU Local No. 13. Pancho is shown in this recent photograph with his wife, Yolie, exhibiting his classic 1941 Chevrolet sedan at a San Pedro classic car show, coincidentally near Berth 93, the former site of "Mexican Hollywood." (Pancho and Yolie Morales.)

Starting by making confetti eggs for school fund-raisers 50 years ago, Lucy Delgado continues volunteering in her community of Boyle Heights in East Los Angeles. She has fought prisons, dangerous pipelines, toxic incinerators, and helped save a Jewish synagogue. In 2005, she was honored by her community with this special plaque. Her motto is, "First my faith, then my love for Boyle Heights." (Lucy Delgado.)

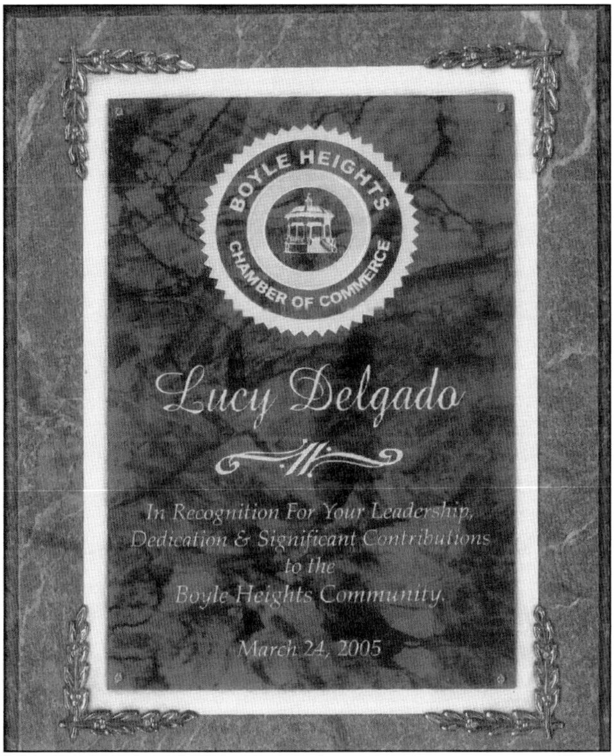

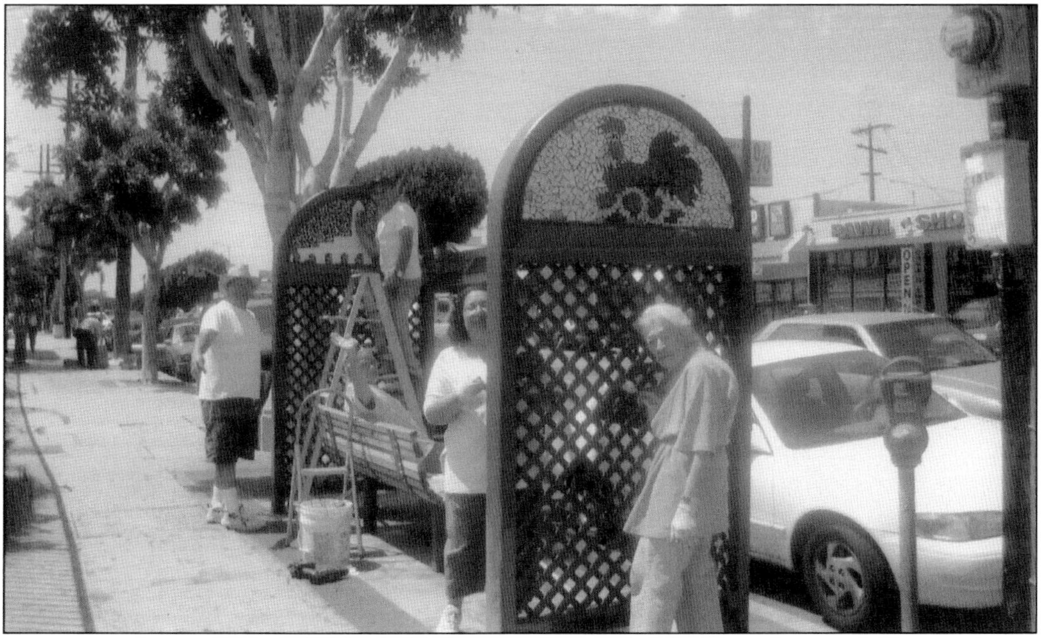

Tree planting, painting, litter removal, and bus station beautification are some of Lucy Delgado's daily activities. The arch in the foreground shows the ceramic tile skills acquired in her youth. She is a founding member of the Boyle Heights Neighborhood Organization, which spearheads continuous community improvement programs. She also finds time to participate in the Japanese community's Nisei parade honoring Japanese World War II veterans. (Lucy Delgado.)

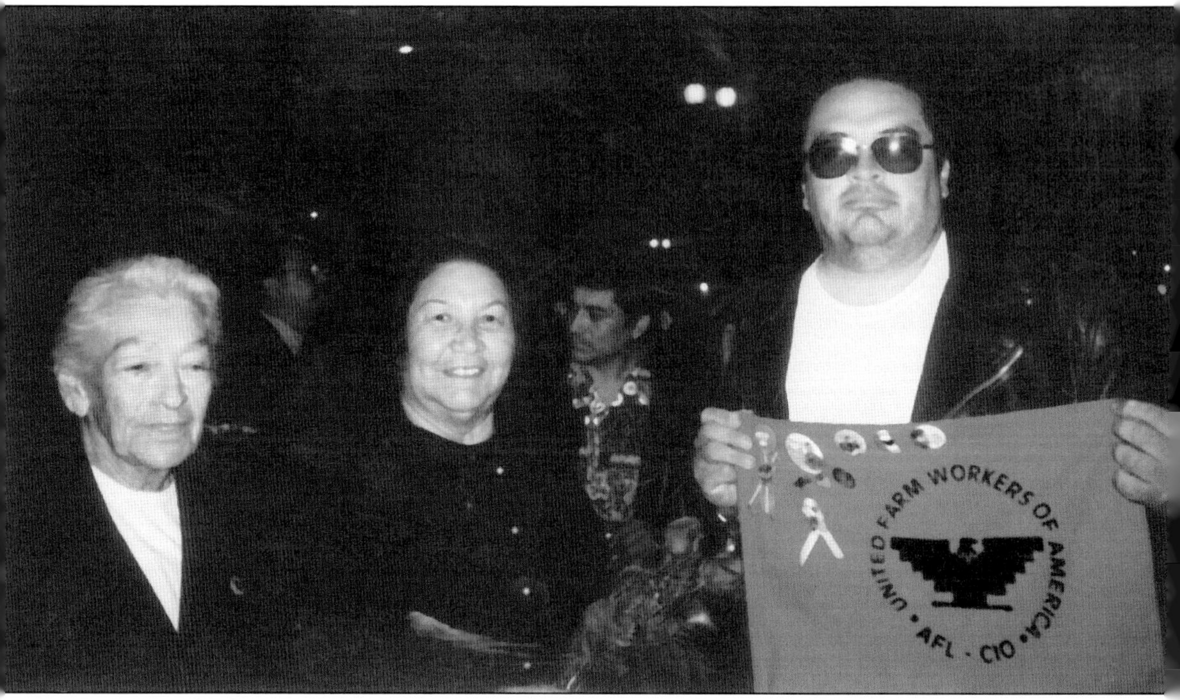

Lucy Delgado is a community activist who has supported the campaigns of past California governors Edmund "Pat" Brown and Jerry Brown, and activist David Sanchez. She campaigned for the late Robert F. Kennedy and advocated for labor leader Cesar Chavez, by joining Kennedy at Chavez's hunger fasts. Shown at a 2002 commemorative march for Cesar Chavez are, from left to right, Lucy, Helen Chavez—Cesar's widow, and Victor Delgado—Lucy's son. (Lucy Delgado.)

Three

Political Figures

The historic election of Edward R. Roybal to the Los Angeles City Council in 1949 was a political watershed event for the Mexican American population of the city. Roybal became the first Mexican American to serve on the council since 1881. For 65 years, the Los Angeles Latino community had remained voiceless and without viable political representation, despite the fact that the city was, and continues to be, home to the largest Latino population outside of Mexico City. Since Roybal's election, the city's Mexican American population has grown exponentially. With that growth, there has come a rapid awareness that the community's future political, social, economic, and cultural needs would only be fulfilled by a dramatically increased participation in the political process.

Early awareness of the importance of participation in political life began with the return of large numbers of Mexican American soldiers from World War II, who for the first time began attending college under the G.I. Bill. Education and the purchase of homes in middle class neighborhoods outside of the barrios (neighborhoods) increased the feelings of mainstreaming and social acceptance. This in turn led to a sense of empowerment that they were now stakeholders and participants in American life. This was not a reality before World War II. In the 1960s and 1970s, the period of social and political activism, which became known as the "Chicano—or Mexican American—Movement," provided a second and stronger source of political awareness and motivation. This movement ignited the community's repressed dream of achieving political power. Equipped with larger numbers of college-educated Mexican Americans, the community quickly recognized that achieving their dream of political strength rested in their ability to identify and support large numbers of male and female candidates who could be successfully elected to public office. The political figures of Mexican American heritage mentioned in this chapter are only a few of the many who continue adding to the growing political presence of Latinos in the city of Los Angeles and the state of California.

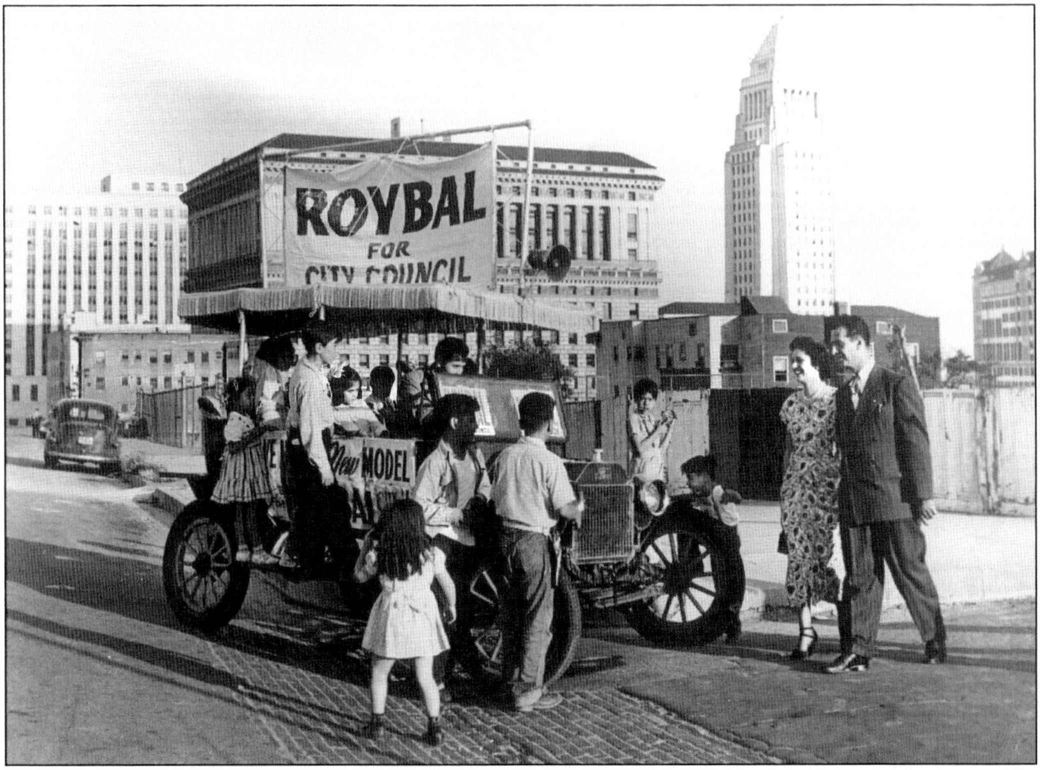

In 1949, Edward R. Roybal was the first Mexican American elected to the Los Angeles City Council since 1881. He later became a congressman. He graduated from Roosevelt High School and married his wife, Lucille Beserra, in 1940. This 1949 photograph shows him and his wife during his campaign, with a sign on an old car stating, "We need a new model, vote for Ed Roybal." He unlocked doors for many people. (UCLA archives and the Roybal family.)

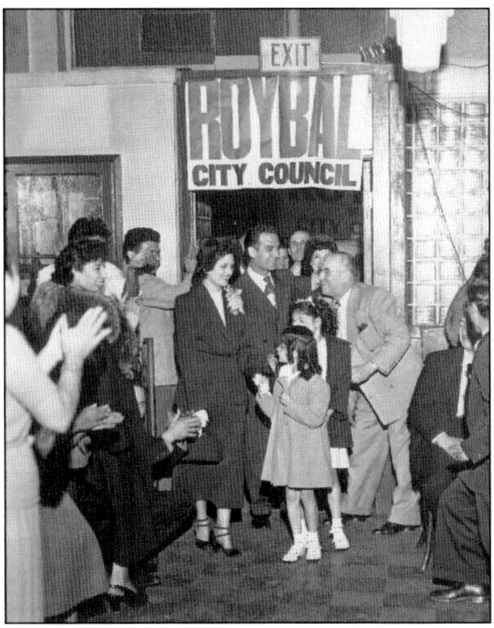

Edward Roybal's campaign for Los Angeles City Council was welcomed with enthusiastic support from many of his constituents. This 1949 image taken during the campaign shows the level of support he received during his campaign stops. Four Roybal family members are pictured in this photograph. From left to right are wife, Lucille Roybal, and daughters Lucille and Lillian. (UCLA archives and the Roybal family.)

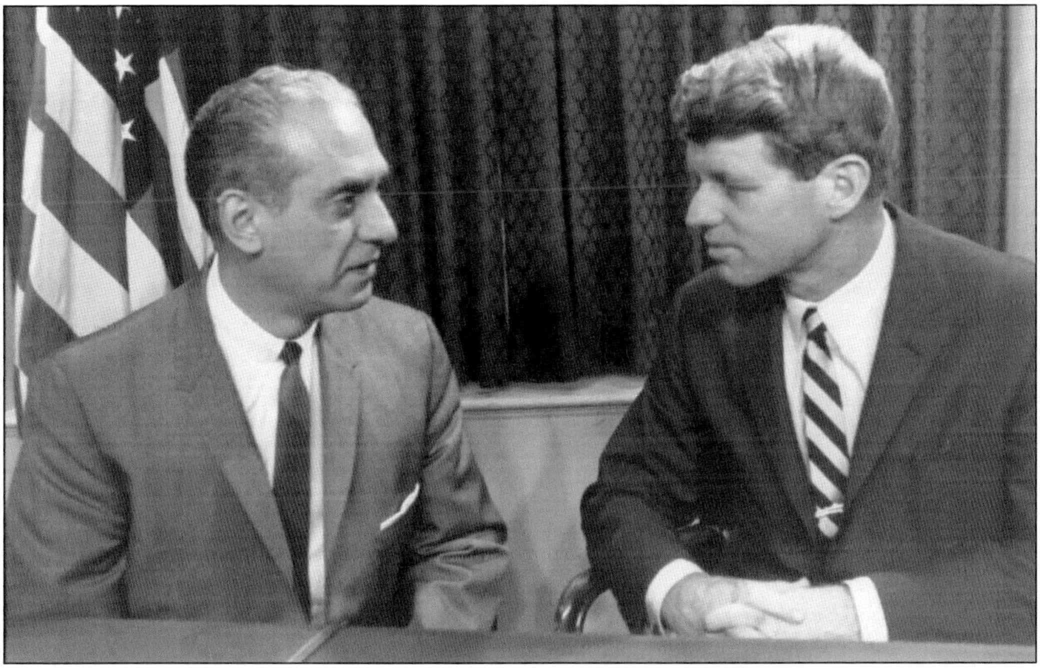

After serving as a Los Angeles city councilman from 1949 to 1962, Edward Roybal was elected to Congress in 1963 and was the first Hispanic congressman from California to sit in Congress since Romauldo Pacheco in 1879. He was a powerful advocate for civil rights, health, and education programs. In this photograph, he is seen conferring with Democratic senator Robert F. Kennedy. (UCLA archives and the Roybal family.)

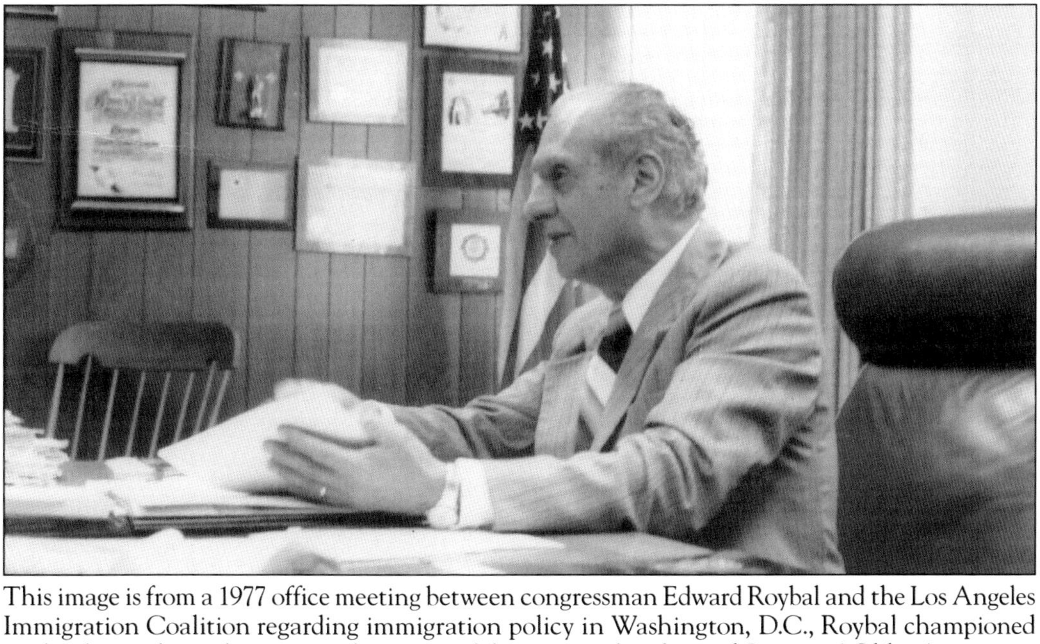

This image is from a 1977 office meeting between congressman Edward Roybal and the Los Angeles Immigration Coalition regarding immigration policy in Washington, D.C., Roybal championed civil rights and social justice, and was one of the principal authors of Congress' Older Americans Act. In 2001, Pres. Bill Clinton awarded him the Presidential Citizens Medal for over 50 years of service to the nation. He died in 2005. (Rosalio Munoz.)

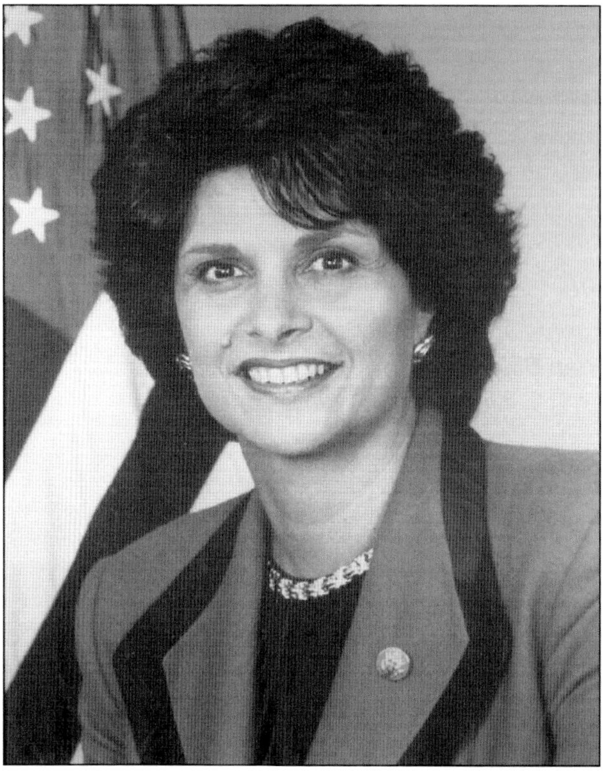

In 1992, Lucille Roybal Allard was the first woman of Mexican American heritage to be elected to the U.S. Congress. From 1987 to 1992, she served as a California state assemblywoman chairing the ways and means subcommittee on health. When senior congressman Edward Roybal left Congress in 1992, she continued his legacy of effective representation and local empowerment. (UCLA Archives and the Roybal family.)

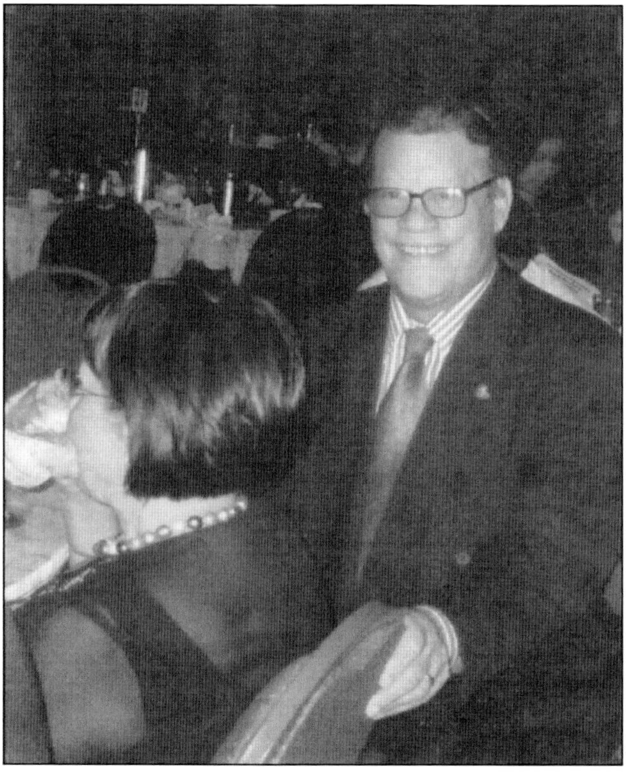

Congressman Esteban Torres was one of the first Mexican Americans elected to Congress and served for 16 years, retiring in 1998. During his career, he fought for workers' rights and community activism. He was among the founding members of the East Los Angeles Community Union (TELACU). Despite his retirement, he continues to be active in the community. An East Los Angeles High School bears his name. (Rosalio Munoz.)

County supervisor Gloria Molina was the first Mexican American woman elected to the California legislature, the Los Angeles City Council, and the Los Angeles County Board of Supervisors. Early in her career, she helped the Mothers of East Los Angeles (MELA) successfully oppose the building of a prison in East Los Angeles. This photograph shows her being sworn in as supervisor by Congressman Edward Roybal. (Alycia Enciso.)

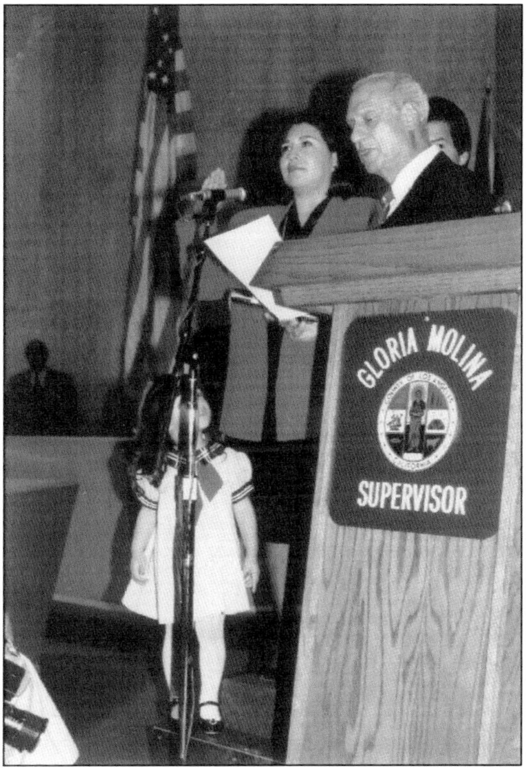

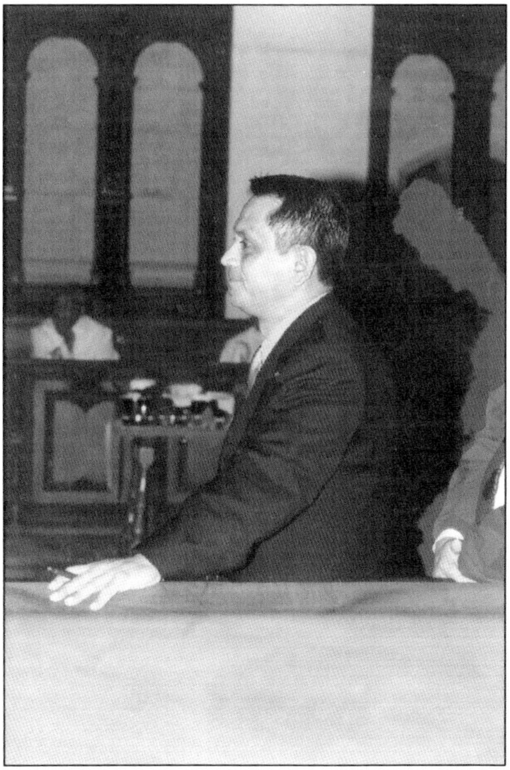

Gil Cedillo, raised in the East Los Angeles neighborhood of Boyle Heights, served three terms in the California State Assembly. In 2002, he was elected to the state senate. He was re-elected in 2006 by a landslide. He supports access to healthcare and employees' right to unionize Los Angeles hotels, while promoting economic development in the downtown area. He was a close friend of labor activist Bert Corona. (Rosalio Munoz.)

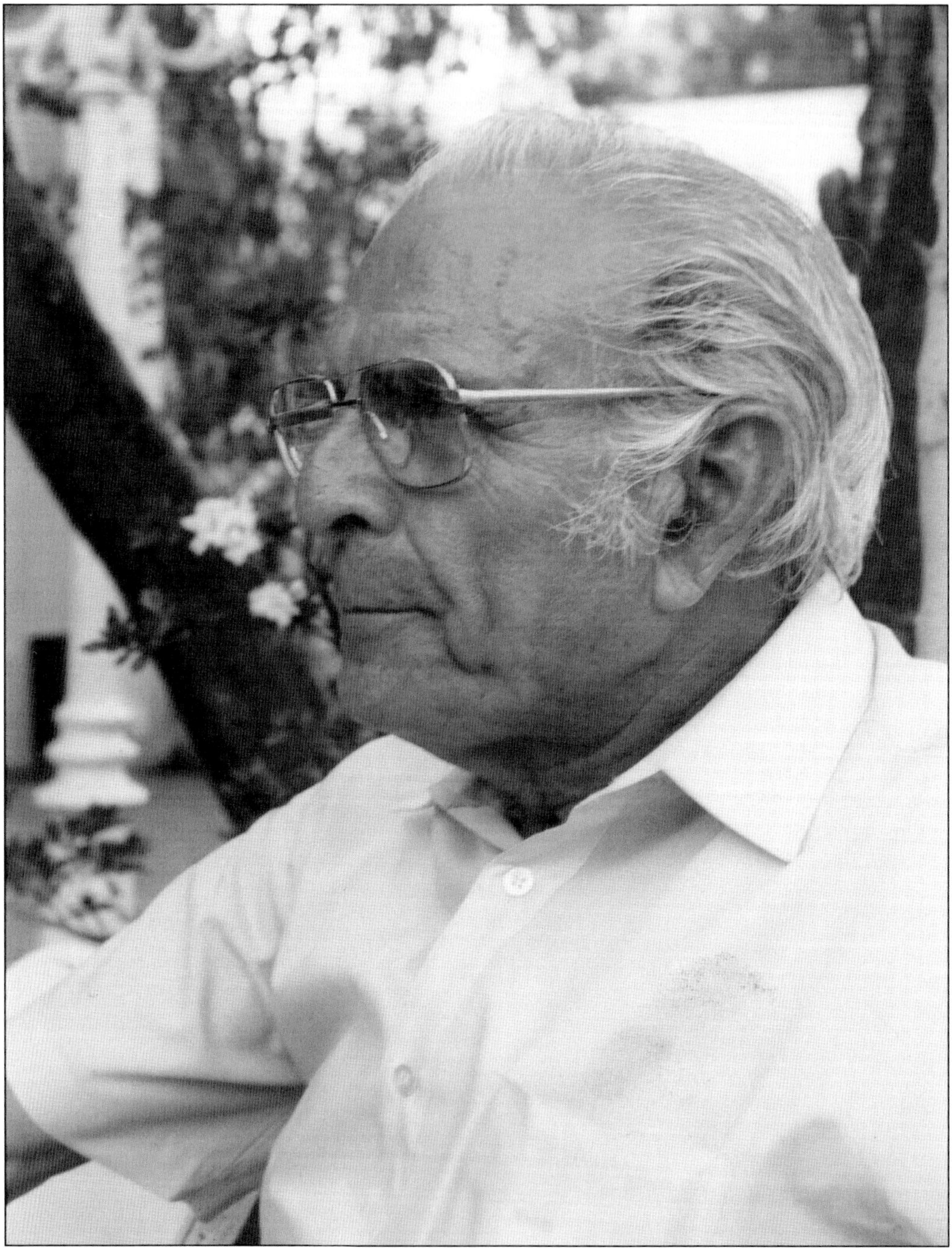

Bert Corona was an organizer of undocumented workers, agricultural workers, and factory workers. He was a World War II military veteran, a union official, and a college professor. He was instrumental in starting the Community Service Organization, which played an important part in electing Edward R. Roybal to public office in the late 1940s. With Roybal, he founded the Mexican American Political Association (MAPA). Since the 1940s, he dedicated his life to fighting for social and economic justice for the average worker regardless of ethnicity. He spearheaded the Latino civil rights movement of the 1960s and 1970s. He died in 2001. (Rosalio Munoz.)

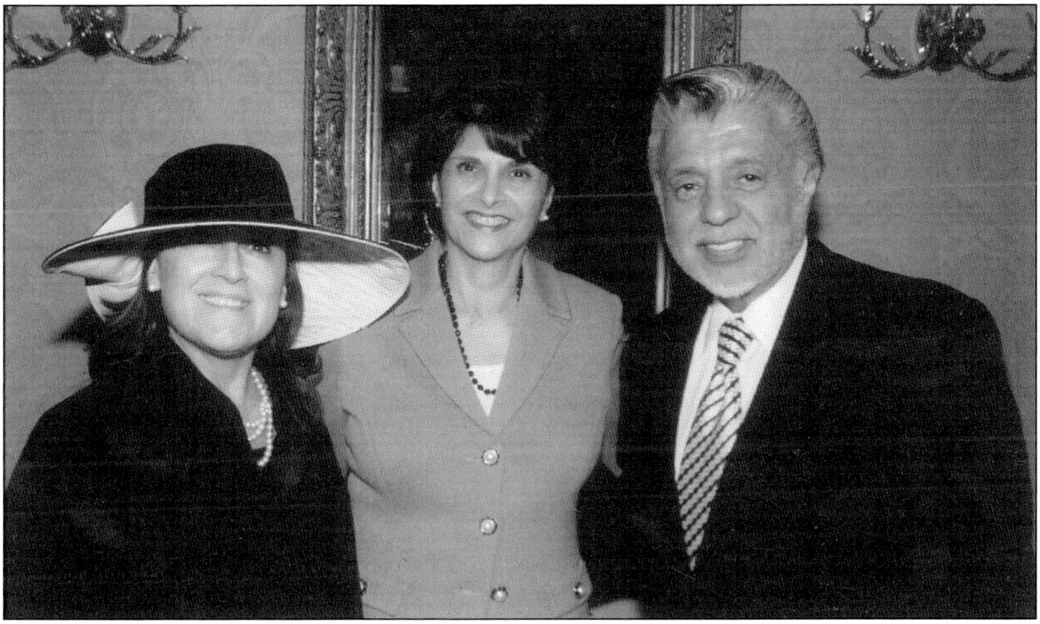

David C. Lizarraga, right, has overseen the growth and expansion of the East Los Angeles Community Union (TELACU) since its founding in 1968. This nonprofit, community building organization manages real estate, construction, financial loans, and an education foundation benefiting families and seniors. Here he attends a community event with Congresswoman Lucille Roybal Allard, center, and Alycia Enciso, left. (Alycia Enciso.)

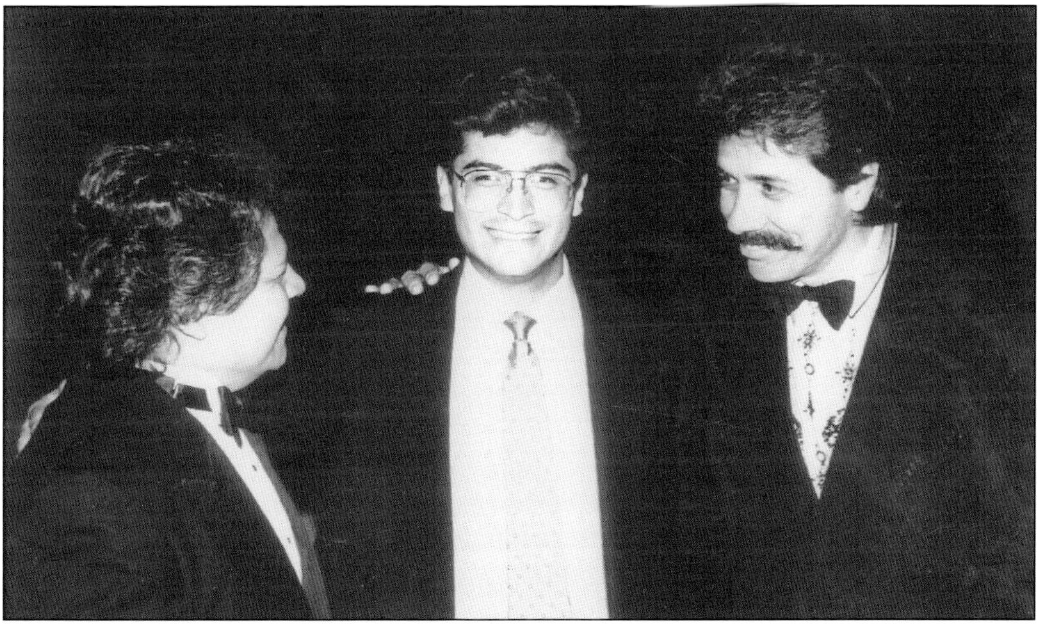

Xavier Becerra, center, a California congressman since 1993, is the first Latino to serve on the House Ways and Means Committee, and is a permanent member of the Hispanic Caucus. He has supported strengthening Medicare and Social Security for women and minorities. He is shown with Frank Villalobos, FAIA, left, and actor Edward James Olmos, right. He is a Stanford University Law School graduate. (Frank Villalobos, FAIA.)

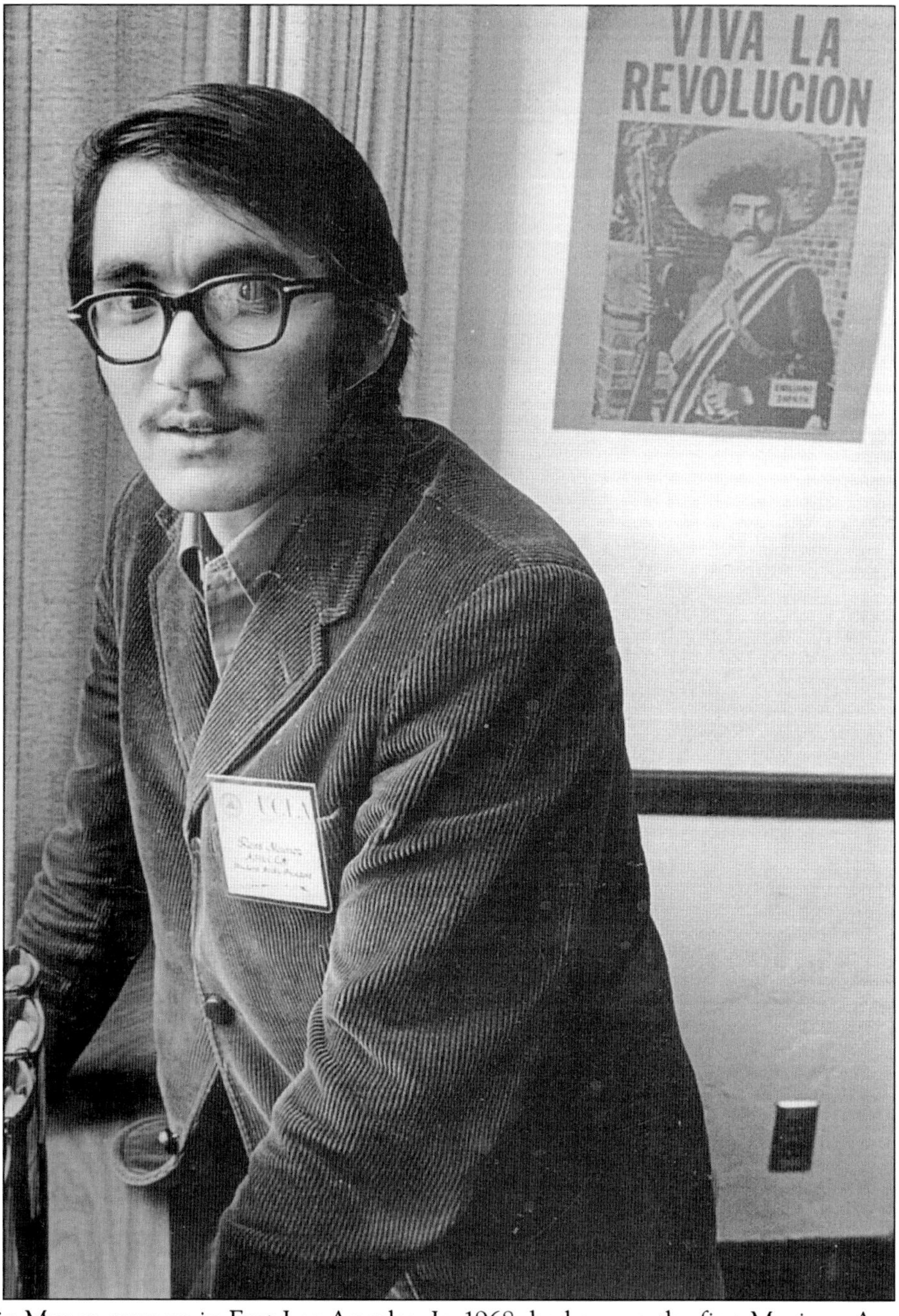

Rosalio Munoz grew up in East Los Angeles. In 1968, he became the first Mexican American student body president at UCLA. He became an anti-war activist, protesting the disproportionate number of Mexican American military casualties that were occurring in the Vietnam War. In 1969, Munoz decided that, if he were drafted, he would refuse to fight. On August 29, 1970, he cochaired the Chicano Moratorium antiwar rally in East Los Angeles. Coincidentally, he received his military draft eligibility notice on September 16, 1970, Mexican Independence Day. Rosalio Munoz is credited with being the match that ignited the Los Angeles Chicano civil rights movement of the 1960s and 1970s. (George Rodriguez.)

The son of a Methodist minister, Rosalio Munoz's strong sense of social justice directed him to continue motivating Mexican American communities to increase their political awareness and strength in order to inspire their political, economic, and social self-determination. Today he remains committed to helping others achieve social justice through labor organizing activities. (Author.)

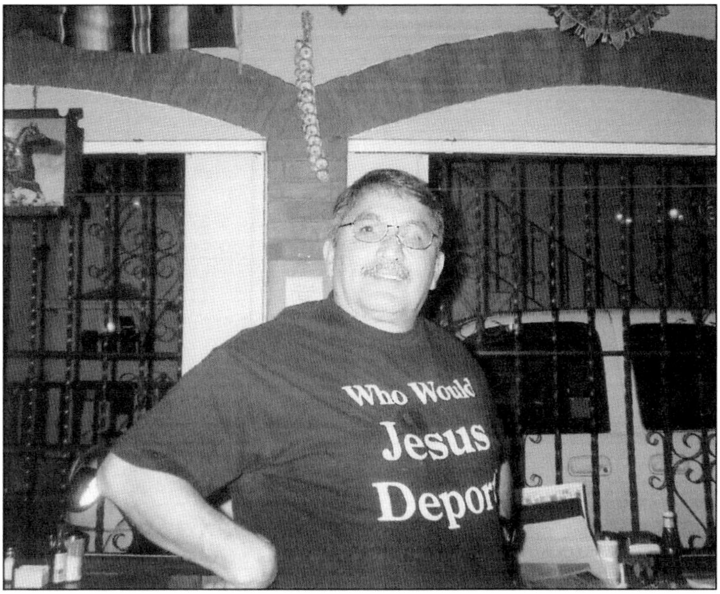

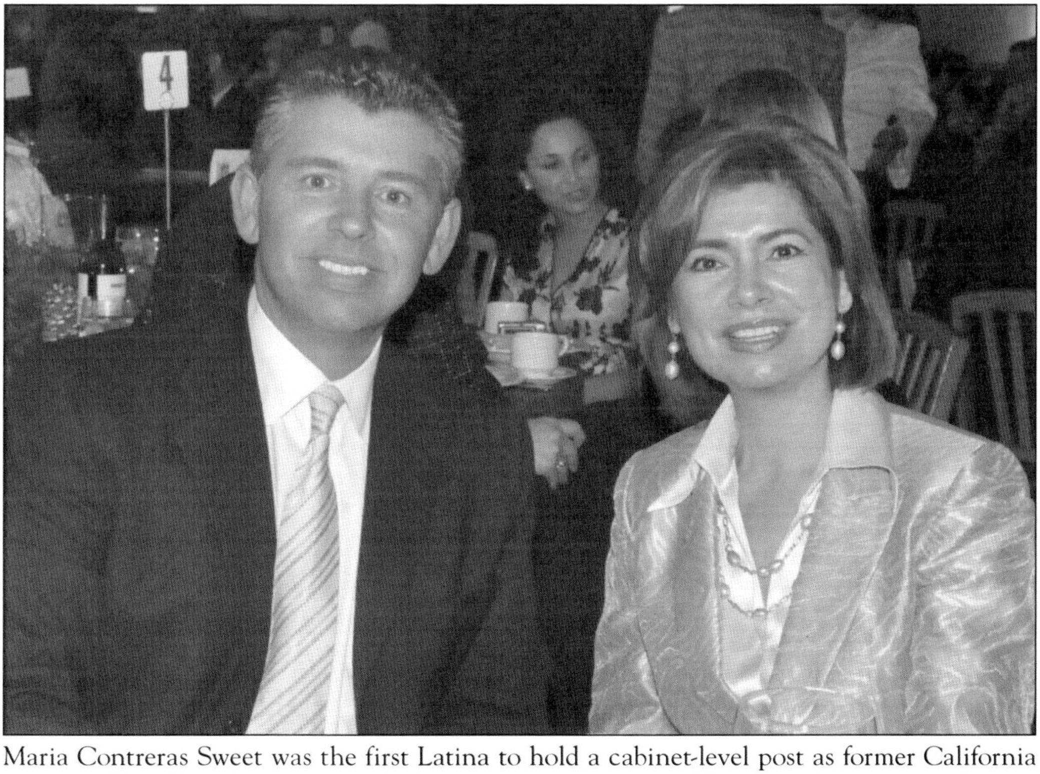

Maria Contreras Sweet was the first Latina to hold a cabinet-level post as former California governor Gray Davis's secretary of business, transportation, and housing. As secretary, she was responsible for a $14 million budget and thousands of state employees. She is the president of Promerica Bank, which serves as a leading bank for Latino entrepreneurs. (MAOF.)

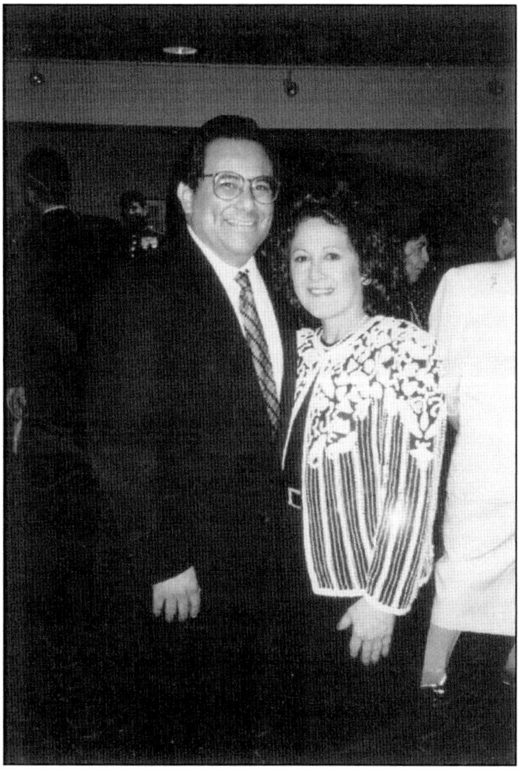

From 1998 until his retirement in 2002, Richard Polanco, left, with friend Alycia Enciso, served as California Senate majority leader and chaired the state's Hispanic caucus. He pioneered the citizen education program, assisting half a million Californians to become naturalized citizens, and tripled the representation of Latino state legislators. His legislation created the state holiday honoring labor leader Cesar Chavez. (Alycia Enciso.)

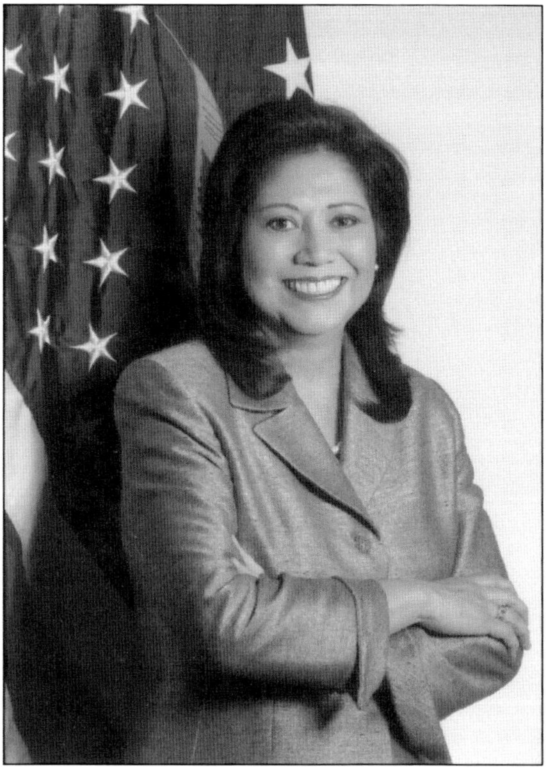

In 2009, Hilda Solis became U.S. Secretary of Labor and the first Latina in the United States to serve nationally in a regular cabinet position. Before becoming secretary, she served in the California State Assembly, and then became the first Latina elected to the California State Senate. From 2001 to 2009, she served in Congress representing East Los Angeles. She is a lifelong supporter of labor causes. (MAOF.)

In 1957, Judge Carlos Teran became the first Mexican American judge of the East Los Angeles municipal court. In 1959, he was promoted to the Superior Court. He possessed a strong sense of civic duty, especially in supporting disadvantaged youth. He attained the rank of colonel in the U.S. Air Force Reserve. Despite his accomplishments, he remained humble throughout his life and loved helping people. He died in 2009. (MAOF.)

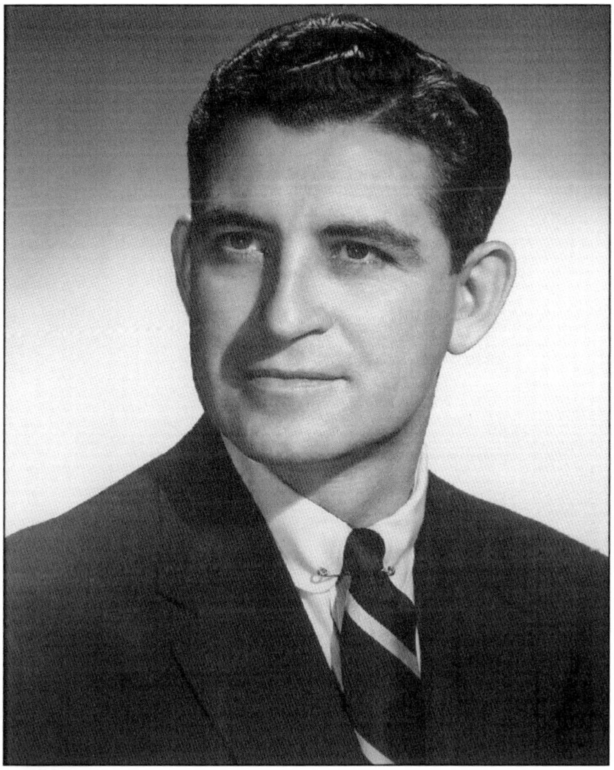

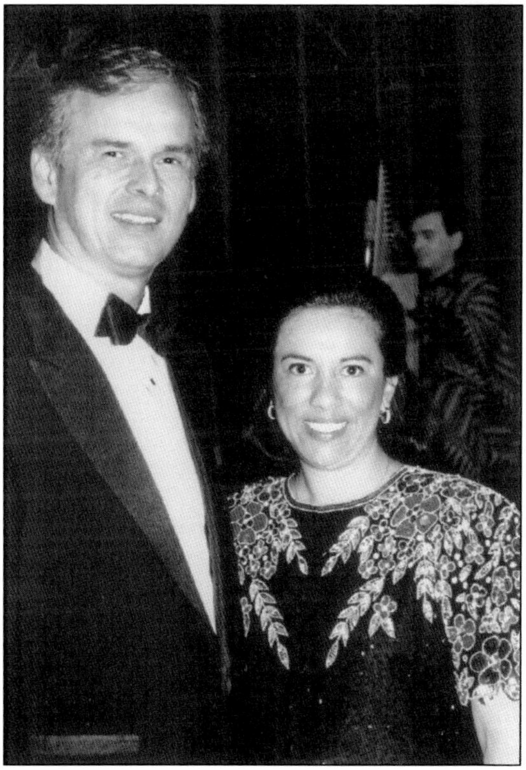

Attorney Antonia Hernandez headed the Los Angeles office of the Mexican American Legal Defense and Education Fund (MALDEF) for more than 23 years, protecting Latino voting rights and helping Latinos take their place in mainstream American society. In 2004, she became president and chief executive officer of the California Community Foundation, to continue serving the Latino community. This 1980s photograph shows her with former Los Angeles mayor James Hahn. (Alycia Enciso.)

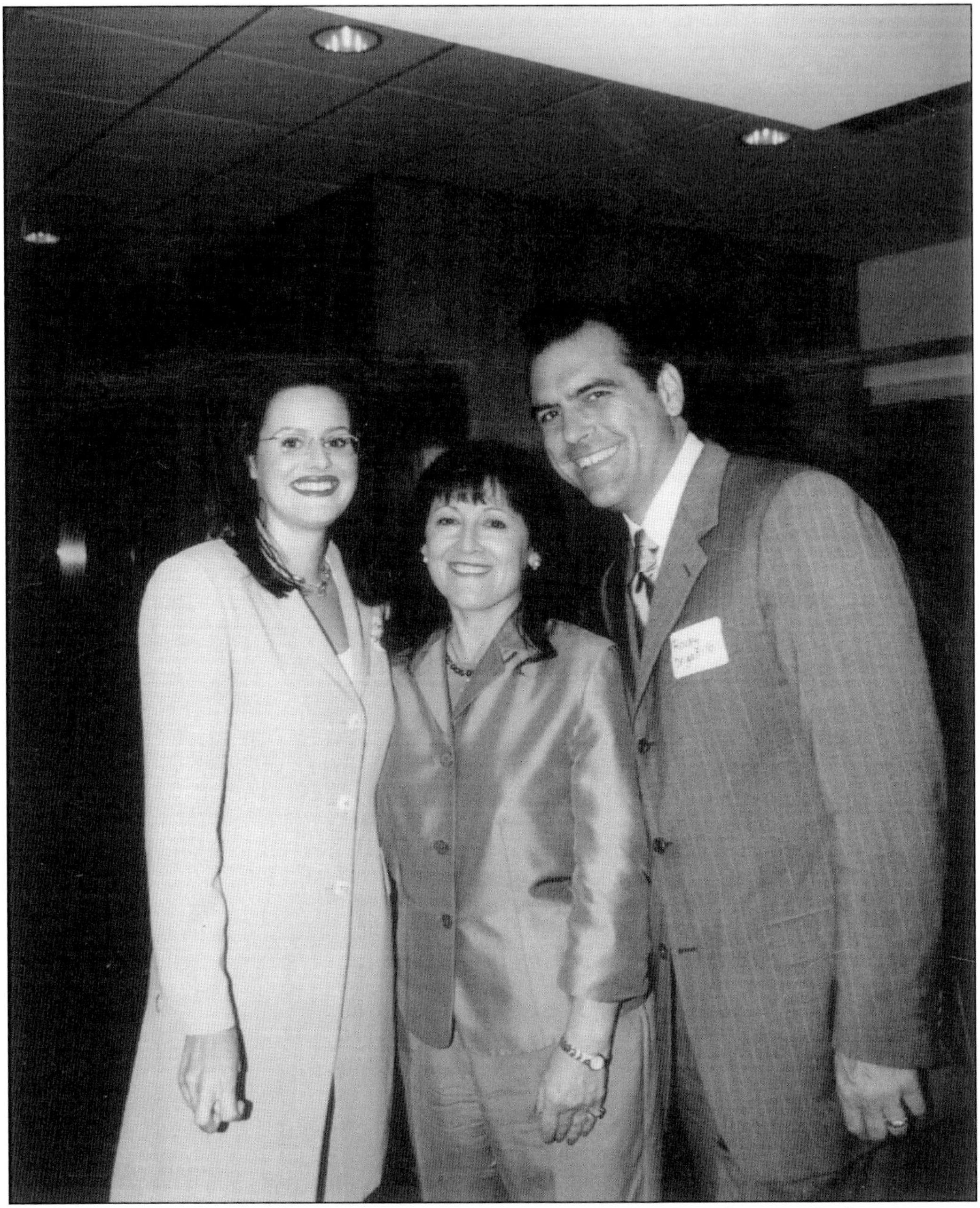

Rocky Delgadillo, a graduate of Columbia University Law School, in 2001 became the first Latino in over 100 years to win the office of Los Angeles City Attorney. He was re-elected in 2005. Delgadillo was deputy mayor under former mayor Richard Riordon after the 1992 Los Angeles riots, later working on tough gang injunctions. Shown here farthest left is his wife, Michelle, and at center is award-winning Latina interior designer Alycia Enciso. Enciso has practiced in Los Angeles for 30 years and has also served as a City of Los Angeles cultural affairs commissioner. She is the founder of the nationally recognized Latinos in Hollywood photographic exhibit, highlighting the participation and achievements of Latinos in the film industry from its inception to the present. Her photographic exhibits have received national acclaim. (Alycia Enciso.)

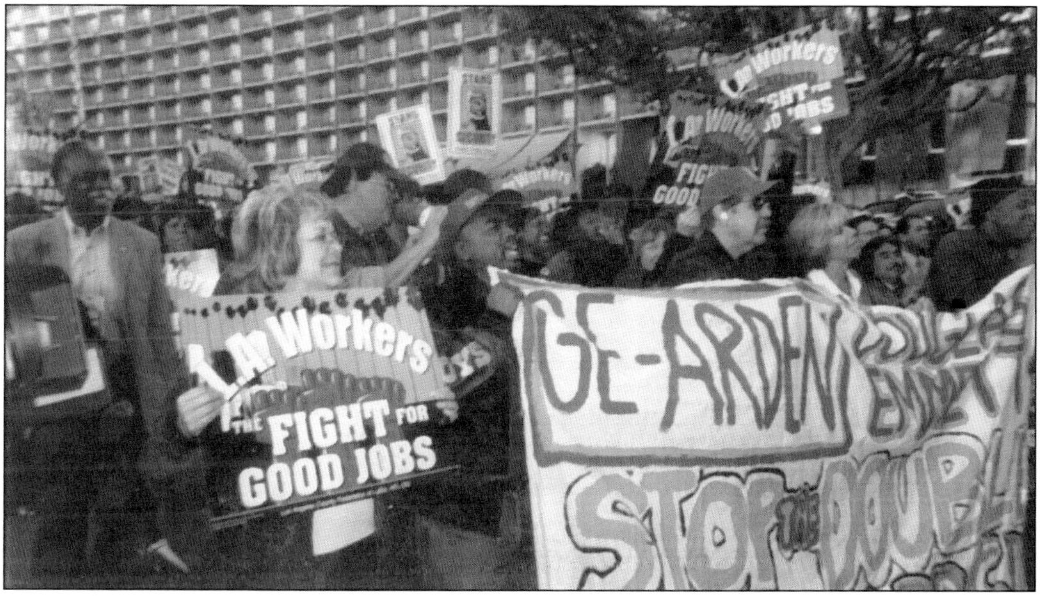

Maria Elena Durazo became executive secretary-treasurer of the Los Angeles Federation of Labor in 2006, representing 800,000 workers in industry. Her late husband, labor leader Miguel Contreras, preceded her in the secretary-treasurer position. She is a law school graduate and an alum of Saint Mary's College in Moraga, California. In this 2007 photograph, at left, she leads a union rally of Los Angeles hotel workers. (Alycia Enciso.)

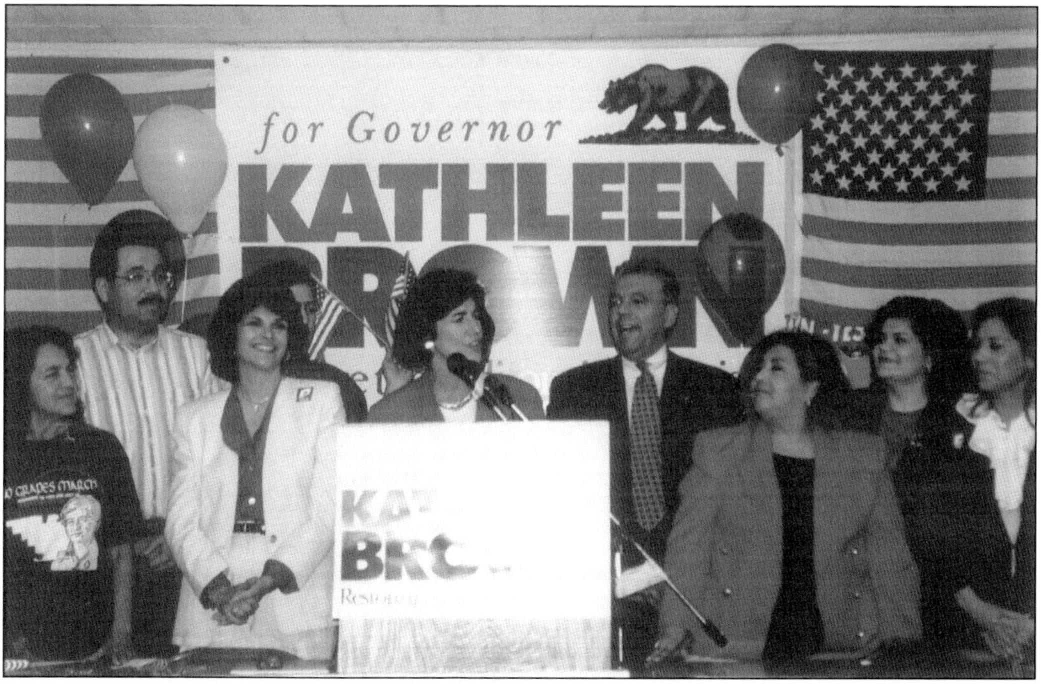

This c. 1993 photograph of Kathleen Brown's gubernatorial campaign rally in Los Angeles shows the growing solicitation of Latino voting strength by major politicians. Beginning with the 1949 election of city councilman Edward R. Roybal, Mexican Americans have been sought after as voters and have seen increasing numbers of candidates successfully run for political office. (Alycia Enciso.)

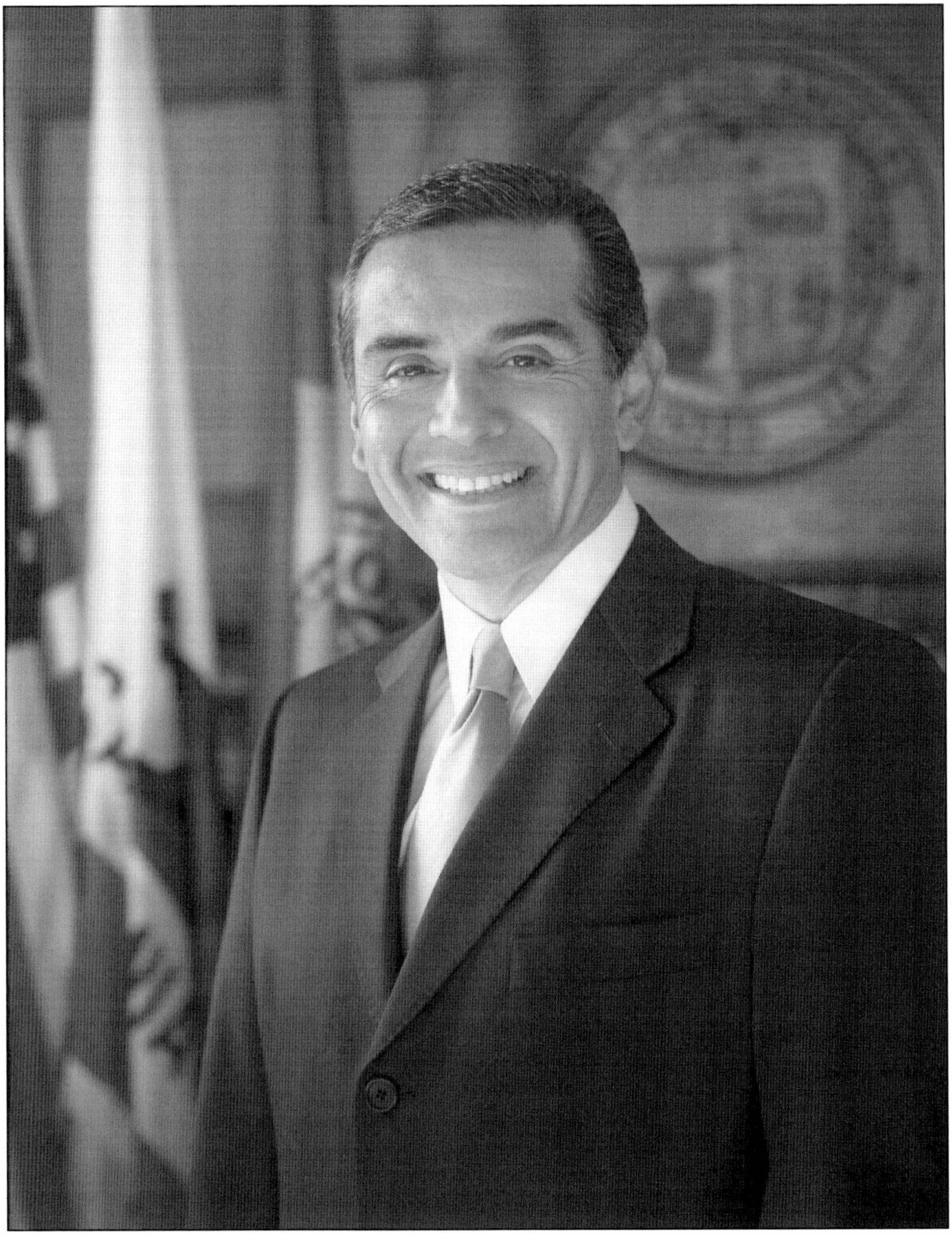

In 2005, Los Angeles mayor Antonio R. Villaraigosa became the first Mexican American mayor of Los Angeles since 1872, a period of 133 years. Beginning as a civil rights activist at age 15, supporting farm workers, he rose to union organizer, member of the Los Angeles County Metropolitan Transit Authority, State of California assemblyman, speaker of the assembly, city councilman, and ultimately mayor. A UCLA graduate, he has championed the causes of education, health care, civil rights, and protection of the underserved throughout his career. His political success has been attributed to his ability to build broad coalitions of supporters, his astuteness, tireless campaigning, optimistic spirit, and being a consummate consensus builder. In 2004, he was chosen by Sen. John Kerry as one of the campaign chairs in his presidential bid. He is seen as a leading Latino politician. (Ricardo Hong.)

Four

EDUCATION

Before World War II, Mexican Americans were present in limited numbers on college campuses in Los Angeles. There existed little encouragement for higher education, mainly due to economic factors faced by Mexican American families. Moreover, before 1945, there was no Mexican American intellectual tradition in higher education, similar to the lack of growth and development of African American colleges and universities until the Civil War. The numbers of Mexican Americans attending college began to climb after World War II as a result of the financial assistance for education provided by the G.I. Bill. In the 1960s and 1970s, African Americans' large push for educational opportunity and civil rights influenced the Mexican American civil rights movement to make the same demands for educational equality.

For the Mexican American community, the Chicano civil rights movement defined the need for political and educational equality with two additional requirements: self-assertion and self-determination. Self-assertion was evidenced in the late 1960s, when East Los Angeles high school students took it upon themselves to walk out of classrooms protesting instruction that was not culturally relevant and offered few college-track opportunities. Self-determination would be achieved by hiring more Latino teachers who shared their values and cultural background and who understood how to lead them to relevant college careers. The students believed that the way to gain self-determination and meaningful education was to become stakeholders in their own education. They were strongly influenced by the increasing numbers of Latino college students who had successfully initiated Chicano studies programs on university campuses. Currently, the increased number of Latinos attending and graduating from college has led to more people of Hispanic background pursuing graduate degrees in various fields. This is one of the lasting benefits of the student activism of the Chicano civil rights movement.

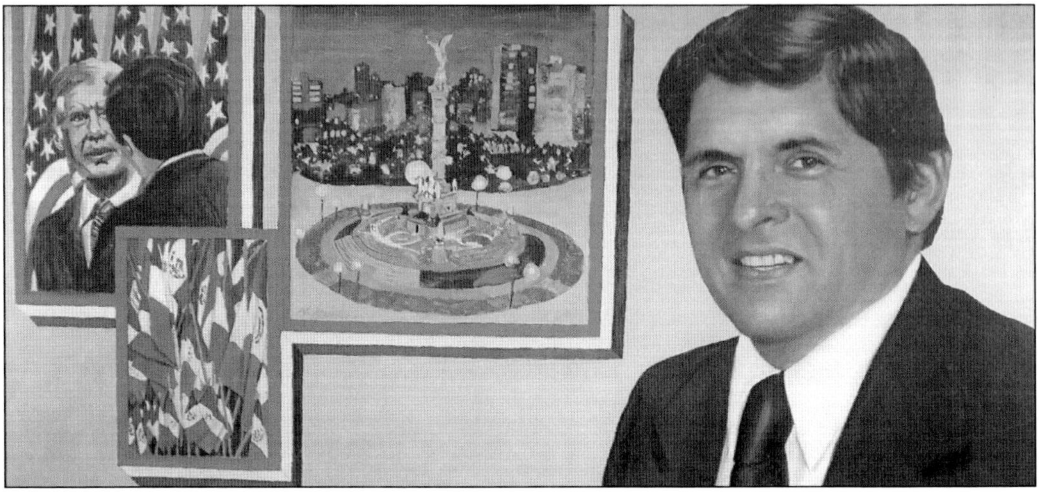

Julian Nava, Ph.D., is a Mexican American educator and diplomat. He earned a doctorate in history at Harvard University. He became the first Latino to serve on the board of education for Los Angeles schools. In 1980, he became the first Mexican American U.S. Ambassador to Mexico. In 1993, he served as a pallbearer at labor leader Cesar Chavez's funeral. (MAOF.)

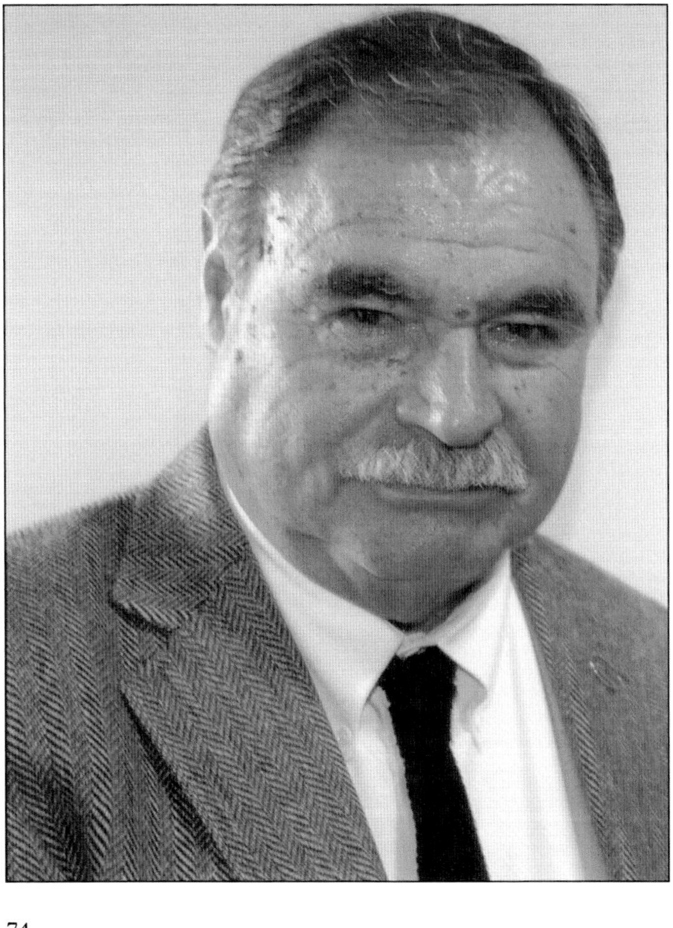

Sal Castro, educator and activist, was born in Los Angeles in 1943. He is known for leading five East Los Angeles high schools in student walkouts, protesting years of inferior and culturally irrelevant education of Mexican American students. He is a pioneer of the Chicano movement who continues contributing to students through his Chicano youth leadership conferences. In 2009, a middle school was named in his honor. (Rosalio Munoz.)

This photograph of an unidentified East Los Angeles high school student reflects the sentiments of many students in the 1968 high school walkouts. Students at Roosevelt, Wilson, Lincoln, Garfield and Belmont High Schools left their classrooms to protest the poor quality of education and lack of college opportunities. The walkouts were led by high school teacher Sal Castro. (Harry Gamboa Jr.)

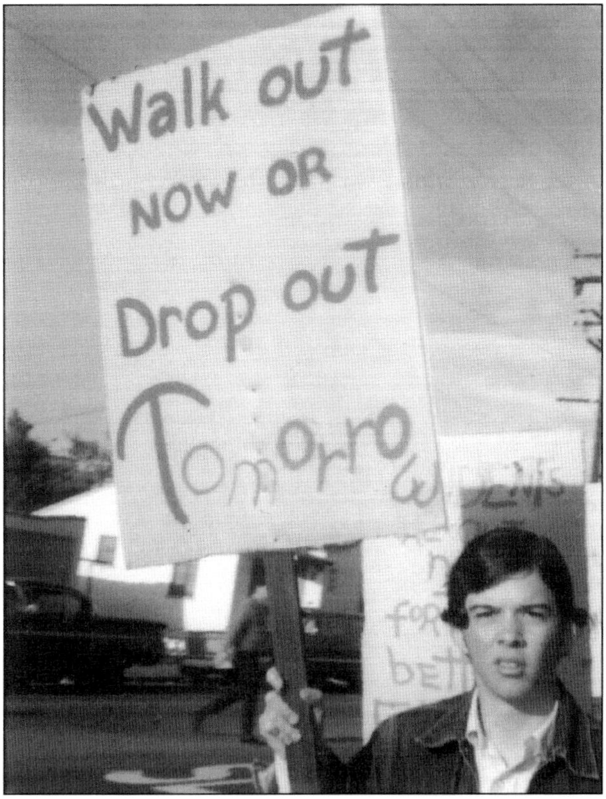

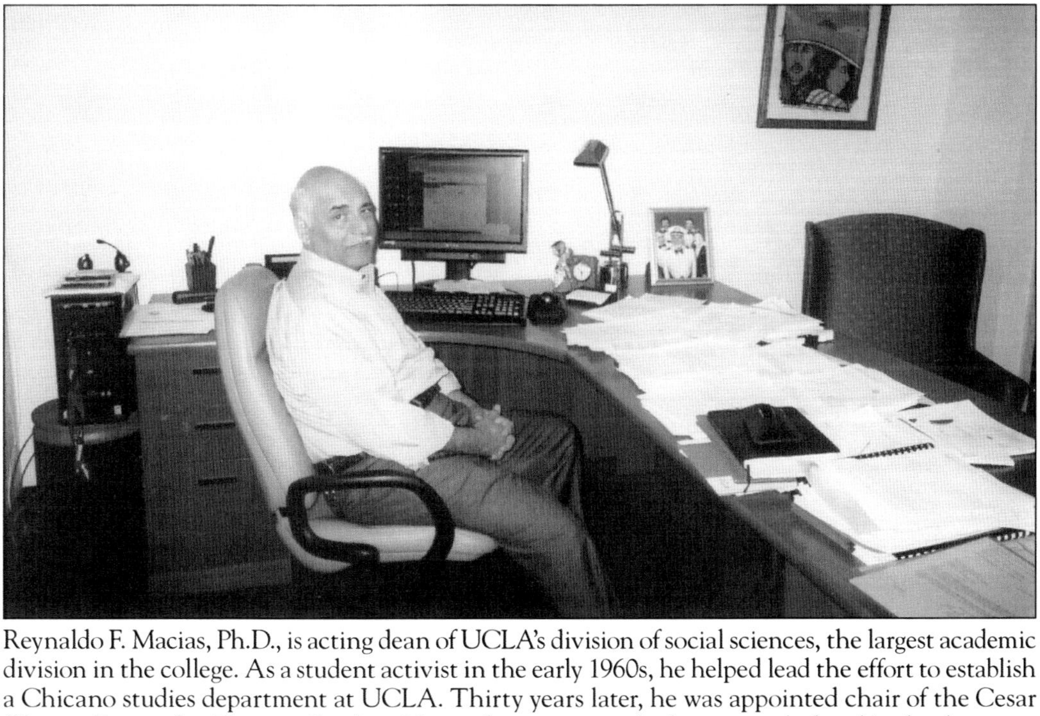

Reynaldo F. Macias, Ph.D., is acting dean of UCLA's division of social sciences, the largest academic division in the college. As a student activist in the early 1960s, he helped lead the effort to establish a Chicano studies department at UCLA. Thirty years later, he was appointed chair of the Cesar Chavez Center for Chicano Studies. He is a linguistics and education scholar. (Author.)

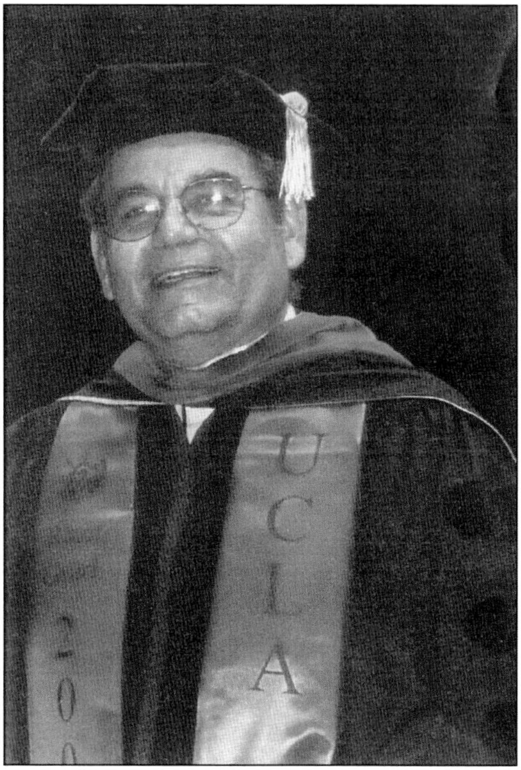

Carlos Manuel Haro, Ph.D., has been assistant director of the UCLA Chicano Studies Research Center overseeing research activities. He was a student at UCLA in the mid-1960s, experiencing the early stages of the Chicano student movement. As a retired professor, he directs research projects and scholarly conferences dealing with germane subjects, such as school desegregation cases. (Reynaldo Macias, Ph.D.)

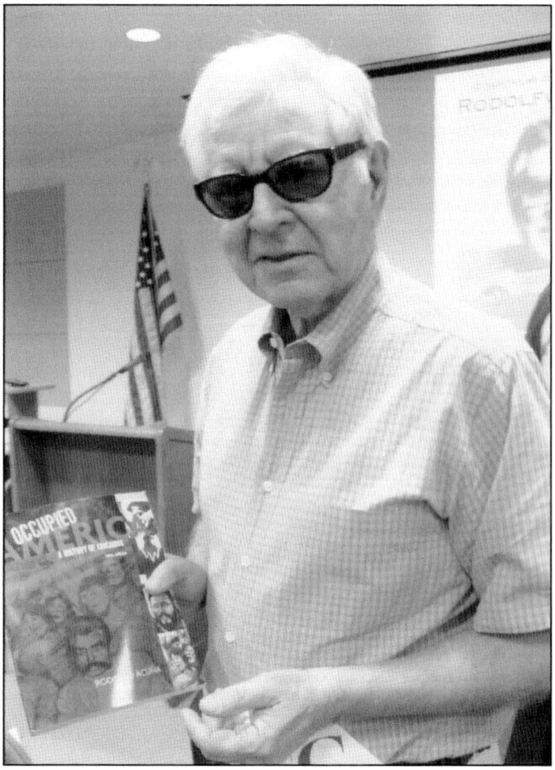

Rodolfo Acuna, Ph.D., from Boyle Heights, is a professor, activist, and historian and is considered the father of Chicano/a studies. His pioneering efforts and scholarly research led to the legitimization of Chicano/a Studies as an academic major at universities. He founded the CSU Northridge Chicano/a studies department. Acuna authored the seminal work, *Occupied America, A History of Chicanos*. Acuna was motivated to pursue a doctorate in history when a counselor said, "Mexicans don't have a history." (Rosalio Munoz.)

Juan Gomez-Quinones, Ph. D, is a history professor at UCLA. For many years, he has been active in civic affairs and recognized as an effective community organizer. His activities have included civil rights, electoral politics, and legal defense. He is coeditor of the *Plan de Santa Barbara*, a manifesto for the implementation of Chicano Studies nationwide. He is also a published poet. (Juan Gomez Quinones.)

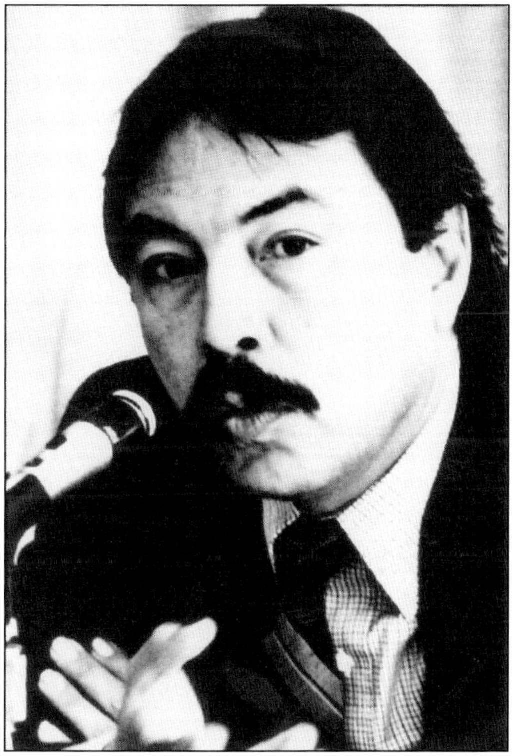

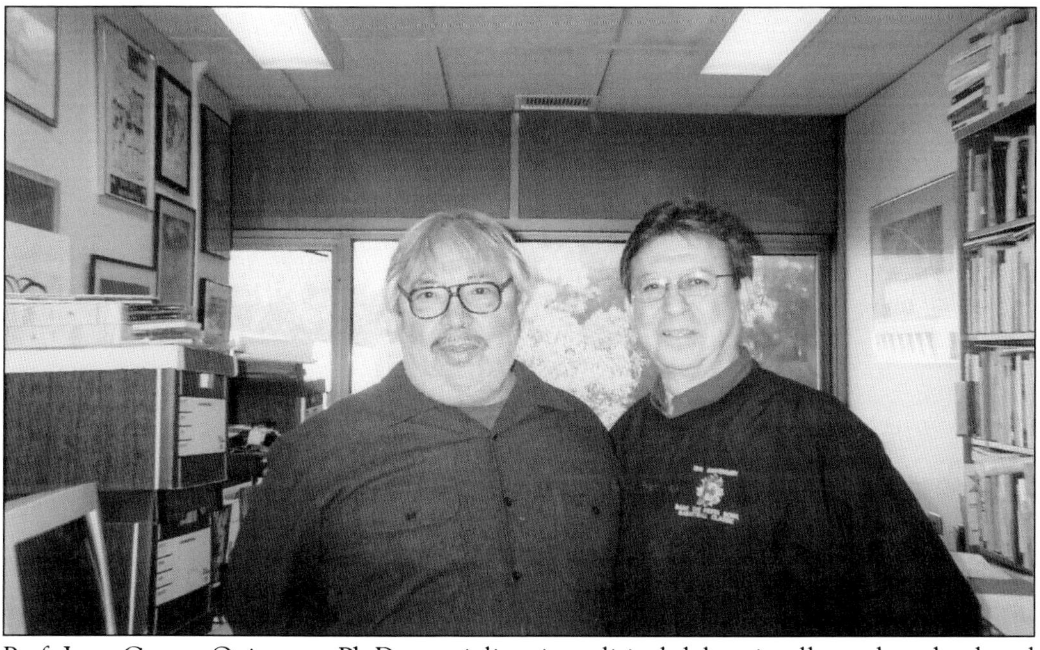

Prof. Juan Gomez-Quinones, Ph.D., specializes in political, labor, intellectual, and cultural history. His career at UCLA has included delivering research papers before historical societies in the United States and Mexico, and he has published more than 40 scholarly works such as *Mexican American Labor, 1790–1990*. He is shown (left) with the author, in his office at UCLA in 2009. (Author.)

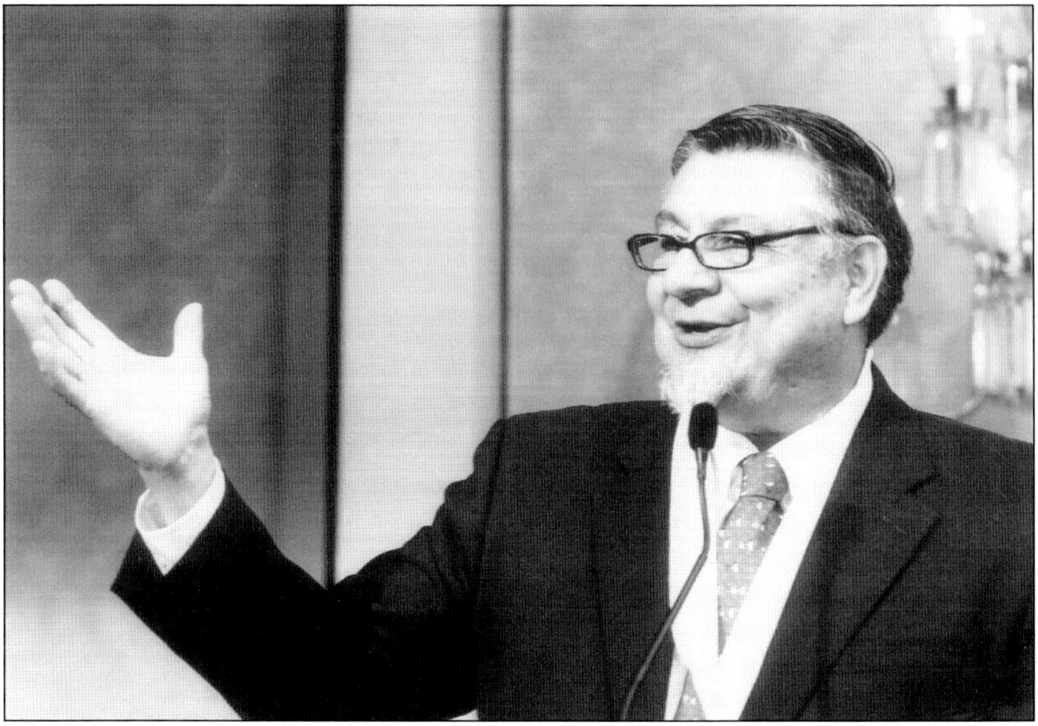

Dr. David Hayes-Bautista, a professor of medicine at UCLA, is the director of the Center for the Study of Latino Health and Culture. He is internationally recognized for his use of quantitative data and qualitative observations. He is the author of *La Nueva California: Latinos in the Golden State*. In his research, he discovered that a 1880s Mexican American California legislator named Reginaldo Del Valle was instrumental in the founding of UCLA. (David Hayes-Bautista.)

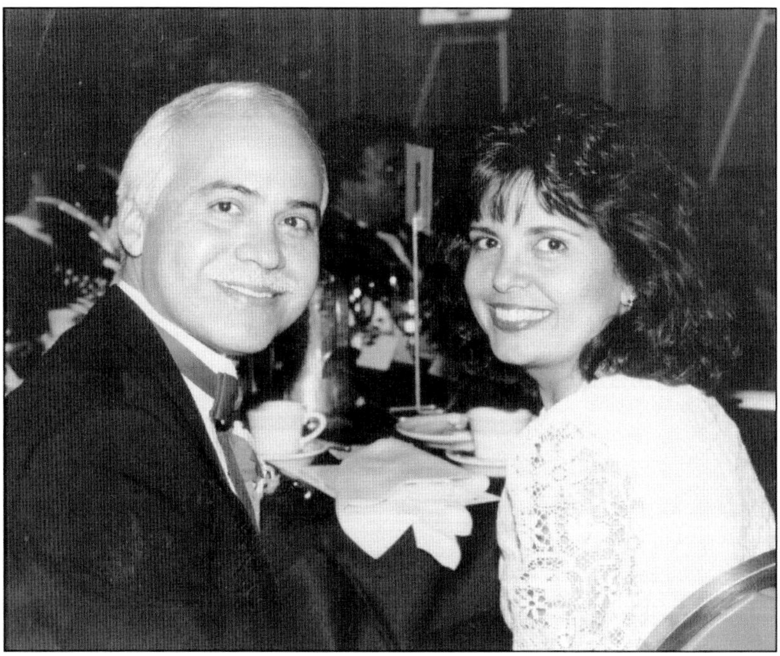

Leo Estrada, Ph.D., is a professor of urban planning and a demographer at UCLA's School of Public Policy and Social Research, and an authority on racial demographic trends. He is an expert in political redistricting, and he was a key figure in the election of Los Angeles' first Latina county supervisor. He is shown in this c. 1991 photograph with his wife, Ivelisse. (Alycia Enciso.)

Five

Sports

In the past three decades, Mexican Americans have increasingly joined the ranks of professional sports. This trend reverses some old public perceptions that Hispanics are unwilling to compete or lack the drive to succeed. Early role models operate as motivators for those aspiring to be successful in the sports world. Parents and siblings often act as role models, creating first impressions and someone to emulate. Role models also develop through exposure to neighborhood peers and relationships with teachers and coaches in high school and college. If individuals do not have strong role models to emulate while growing up, the likelihood of them becoming professional athletes is significantly reduced.

In the decades before the 1950s, economics played a significant role in whether Mexican Americans participated in sports. Because families tended to be large, the first priority was financial well-being. Participation in sports was largely dependent on how much work revenue would be sacrificed if a family member's time was dedicated to this extracurricular. The cost of personal transportation and equipment needed for after-school sports also had an impact. These financial pressures were not dissimilar to the experience of Anglo children growing up on small, rural farms in the past.

The number of Mexican Americans in professional sports is growing. In Los Angeles baseball during the 1980s, Dodgers' pitcher Fernando Valenzuela created the phenomenon of "Fernandomania," with pitching that rattled even seasoned baseball veterans. He was later joined by Nomar Garciaparra. In professional football, Mark Sanchez, the outstanding quarterback at the University of Southern California, recently joined the professional National Football League as a quarterback for the New York Jets. Although the number of Mexican American professional sports figures could be greater, professional baseball is currently leading a national trend in hiring more Latino athletes.

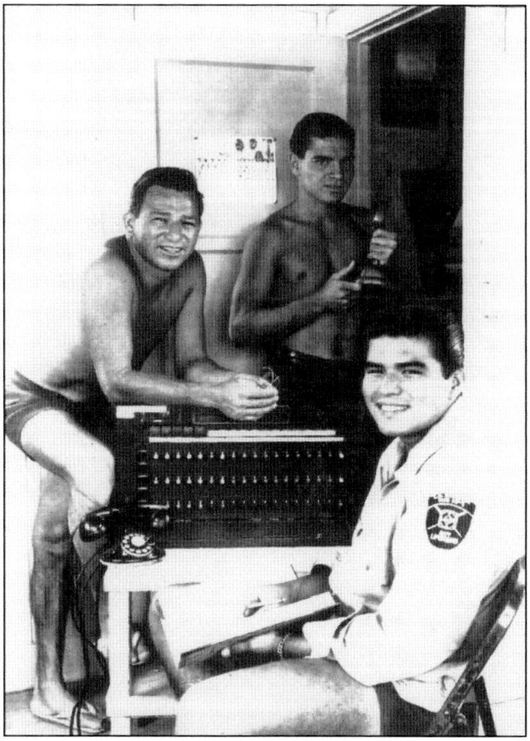

This 1960 image shows John Olguin, left, Gilbert Sales, right, and Robert Tonjes, top, as the first Mexican American lifeguards to work for the County of Los Angeles. Olguin, a World War II soldier and Silver Star recipient, became the first Mexican American lifeguard captain. He later founded and directed the Cabrillo Marine Museum in San Pedro, California. Gilbert Sales became a NASA physician. (Arthur Verge, Ph.D.)

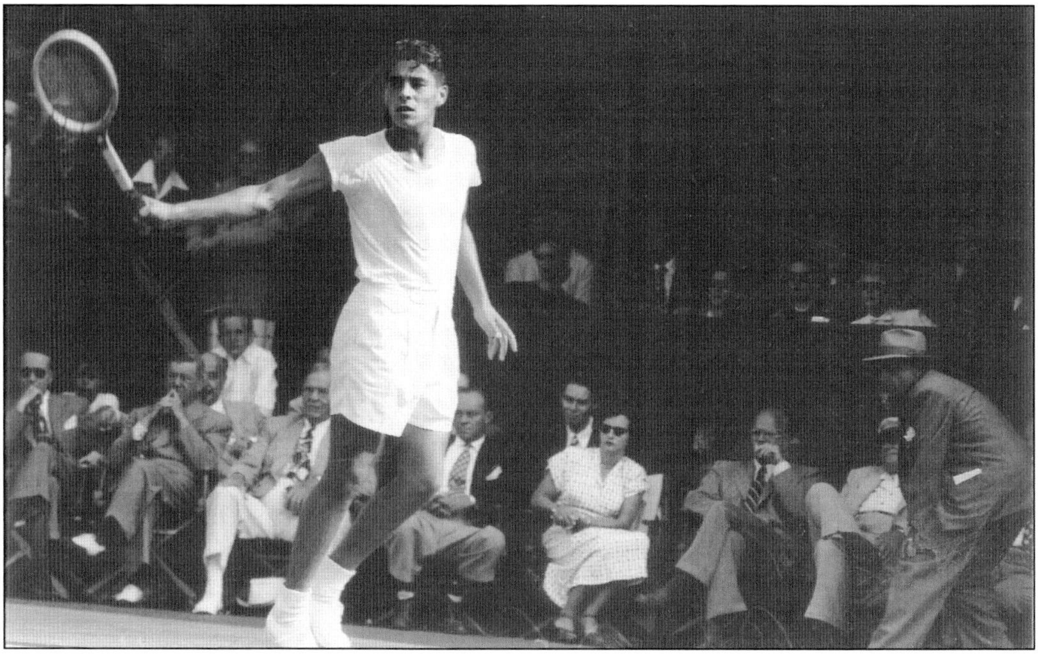

Richard Alonzo "Pancho" Gonzalez, a Los Angeles native and tennis player, broke the color line in tennis in 1945. Despite his racial isolation and being entirely self-taught, within three years, he defeated three top competitors to become the top-ranked California player. Between 1953 and 1962, he won several world championships. He was described as the most powerful player of the century. (UCLA archives.)

This c. 1953 photograph of Art Aragon, known as the original "Golden Boy," was probably taken at the Los Angeles Grand Olympic Auditorium's office. Aragon entered the ring wearing gold trunks and robes. He was known for his powerful left hook and drew standing-room-only crowds. He was born in Belen, New Mexico, and grew up in East Los Angeles. (UCLA archives.)

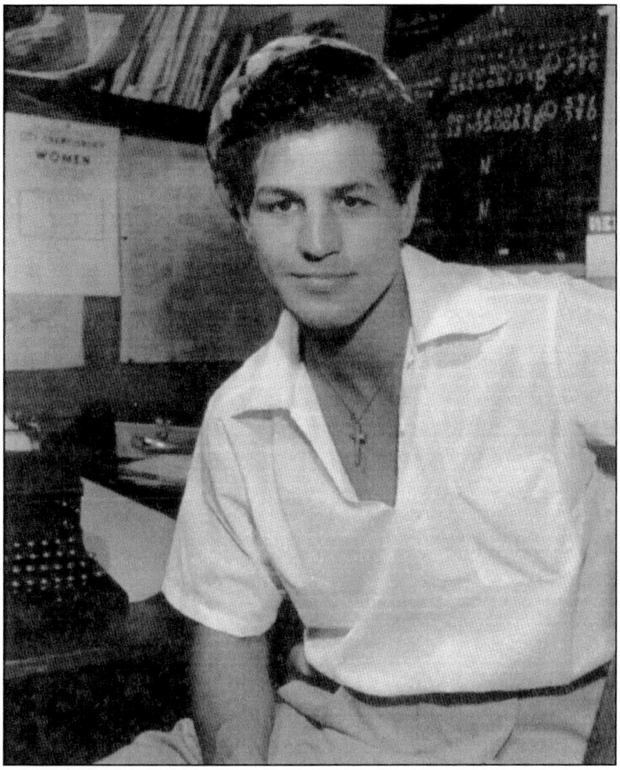

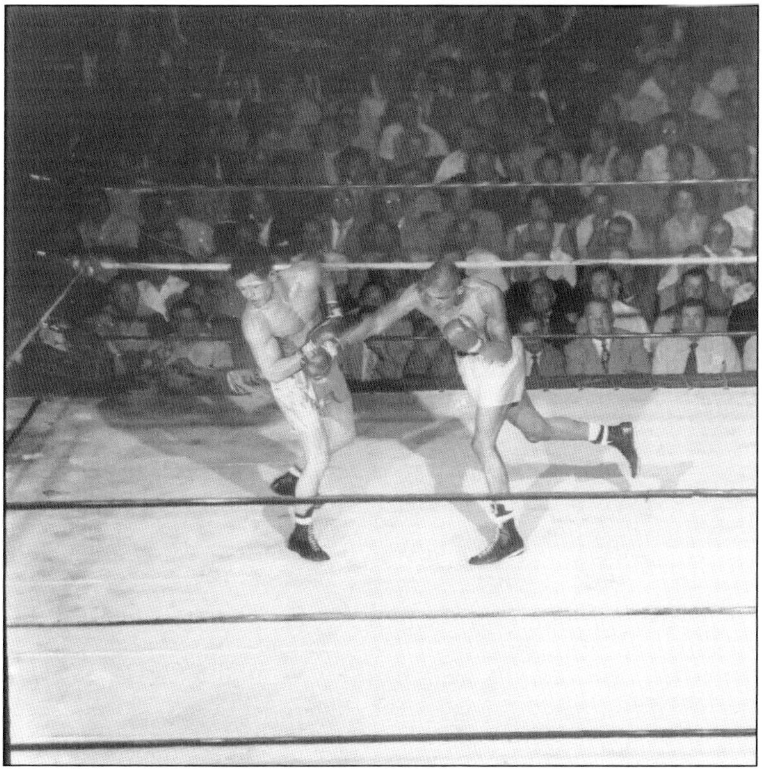

Lightweight fighter Art Aragon, left, in this image, is fighting Don Jordan at the Grand Olympic Auditorium in Los Angeles in 1955. Aragon attended Roosevelt High School in East Los Angeles and entered the ring at age 16. He did not always train hard for fights, but consistently won. He was a proud convert to Judaism and is buried at Mount Sinai Cemetery in Los Angeles. (UCLA archives.)

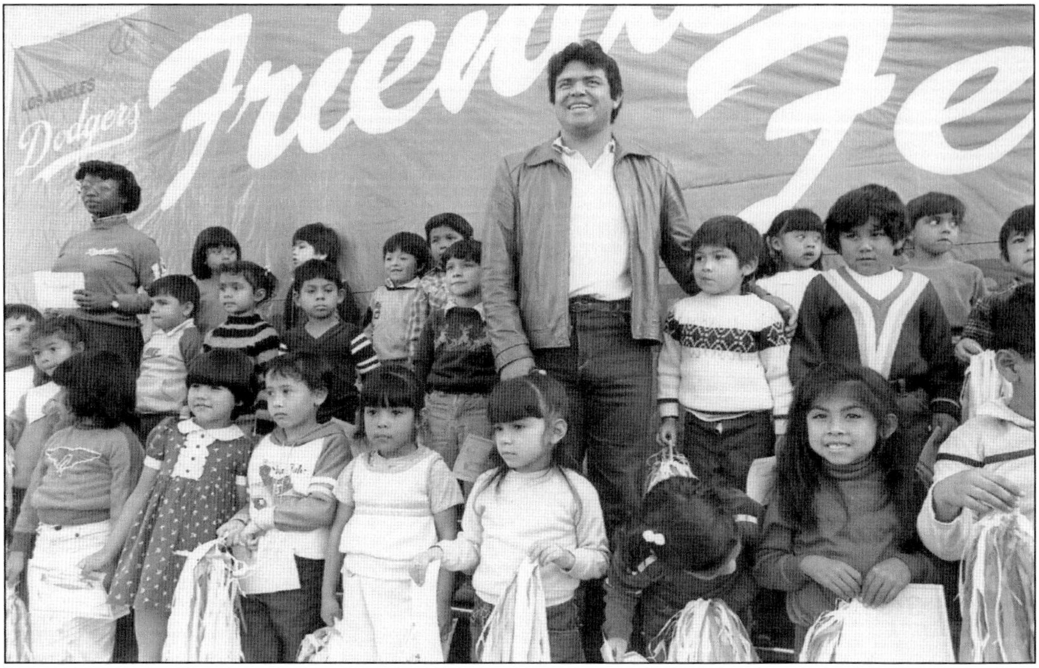

Los Angeles Dodgers left hand pitcher Fernando "El Toro" (the bull) Valenzuela was given this nickname by his fans for his tenacity. In the 1980s, he touched off a craze called "Fernandomania." He was the only player in major league history to win both Rookie of the Year and the Cy Young Award in the same 1981 season. He learned baseball in Mexico from his brother Rafael. (UCLA archives.)

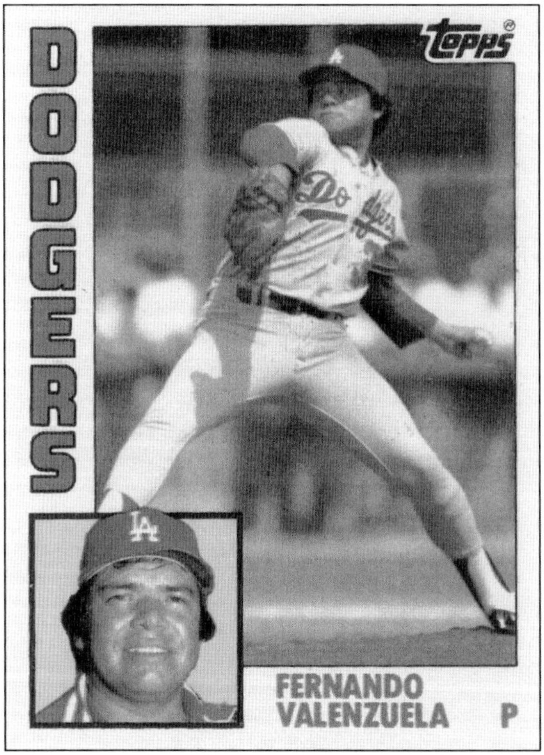

Los Angeles Dodgers pitcher Fernando Valenzuela's 1981 season was called, "the best ever season for a rookie pitcher." The left-hander pitched five shutouts in his first seven major league baseball starts. In 1981, he was named the "First Rookie Strikeout Champion." Today he is co-anchor of Spanish language broadcasts for Dodger games. (Tops Cards.)

Los Angeles Dodgers pitcher Fernando Valenzuela was born in Etchohuaquila, Sonora, Mexico (population 150) in November 1960. He played for the Dodgers from 1980 to 1990. His fame came from his devastating screwball, which baffled opposing players. In 2003, he was inducted into the Hispanic Heritage Baseball Hall of Fame. (Tops Cards.)

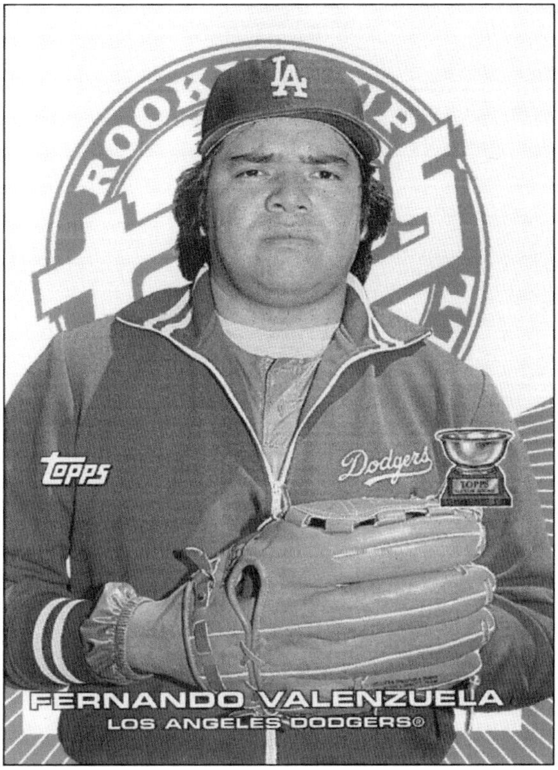

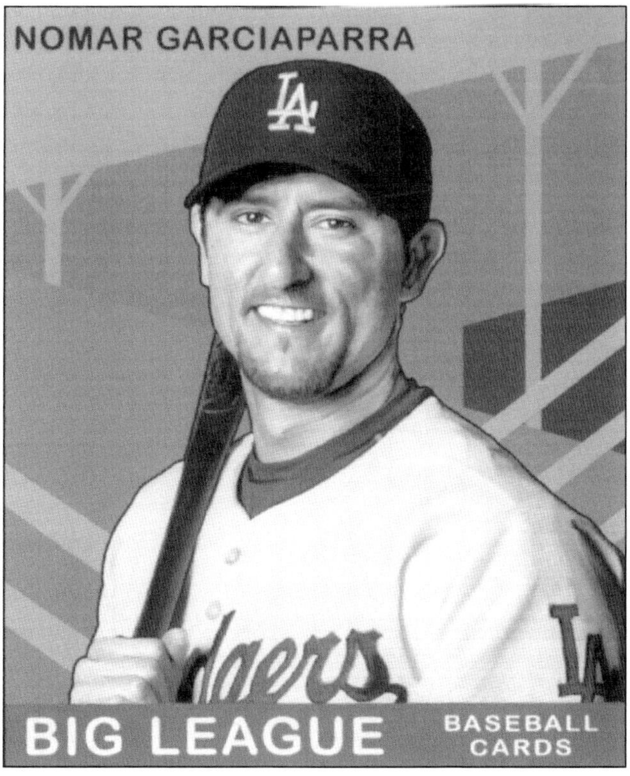

Nomar Garciaparra, born in Whittier, California, in 1973, was valedictorian at St. John Bosco High School, and played shortstop for the Los Angeles Dodgers. He is one of 13 players in major league history to hit two grand slams during a single game. He was a six-time all star from 1997 to 2006. In five post-season series, he batted .323 with a slugging percentage of .625. (Tops Cards.)

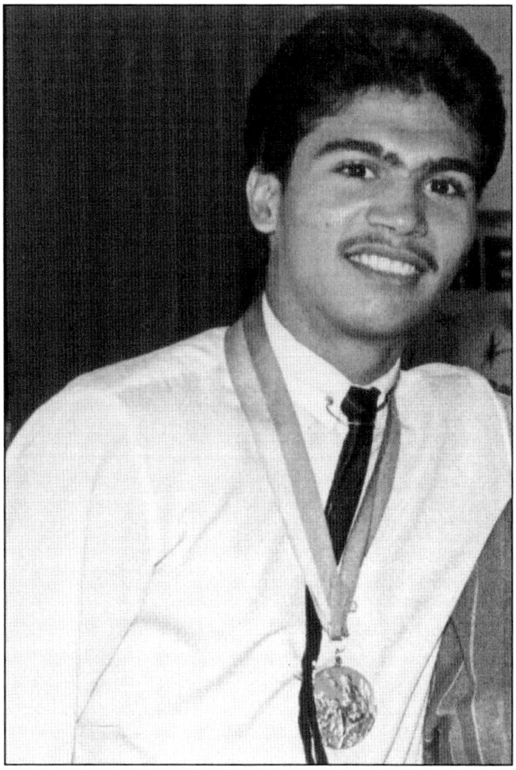

Paul Gonzalez, the 1984 Olympic gold medal boxing champion, was born April 18, 1964, in East Los Angeles' Aliso Village. He won gold as a light flyweight at the summer games in Los Angeles. He was the first Mexican American to win an Olympic gold medal in boxing and was inducted into the World Boxing Hall of Fame in Los Angeles. In 1994, he announced his retirement. (Connie Calderon.)

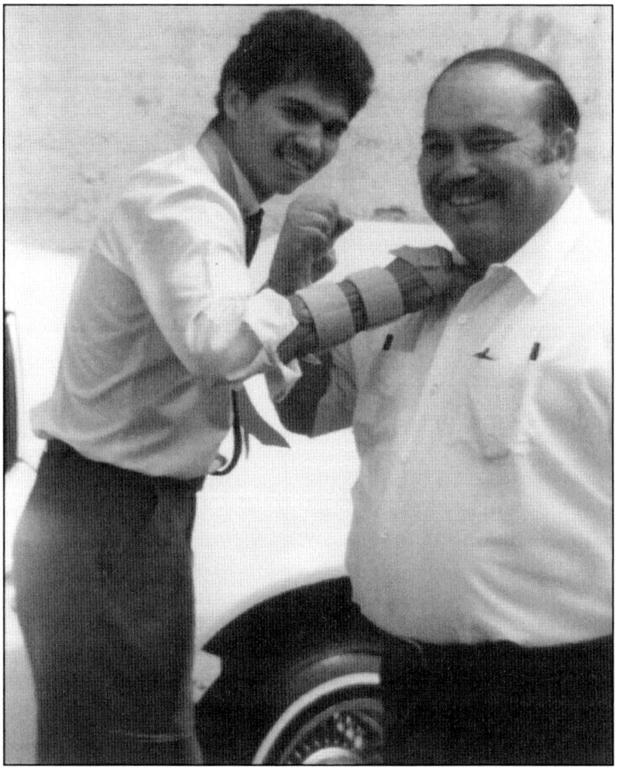

In this 1980s photograph, Olympic gold medal boxing champion Paul Gonzalez of East Los Angeles is seen playfully sparring with Wilmington, California's, Teen Post director Johnny Mendez. Gonzalez frequently supported youth activities such as teen centers. (Connie Calderon.)

Oscar De La Hoya was born in East Los Angeles, and he began boxing at the age of six. His father and brother were both boxers. He won 10 world titles in six different weight classes, earning the title "Golden Boy." In 1992, he won an Olympic gold medal in Barcelona, Spain. Before retiring in 2009, he generated more money than any other boxer in history. (MAOF.)

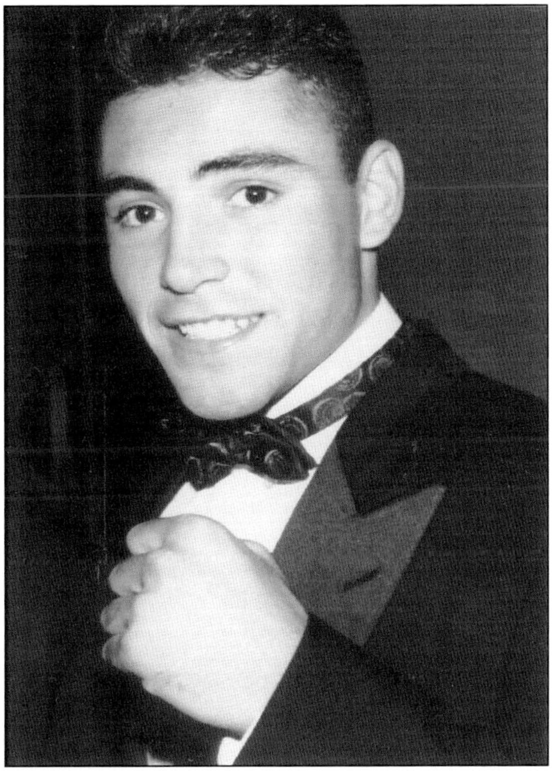

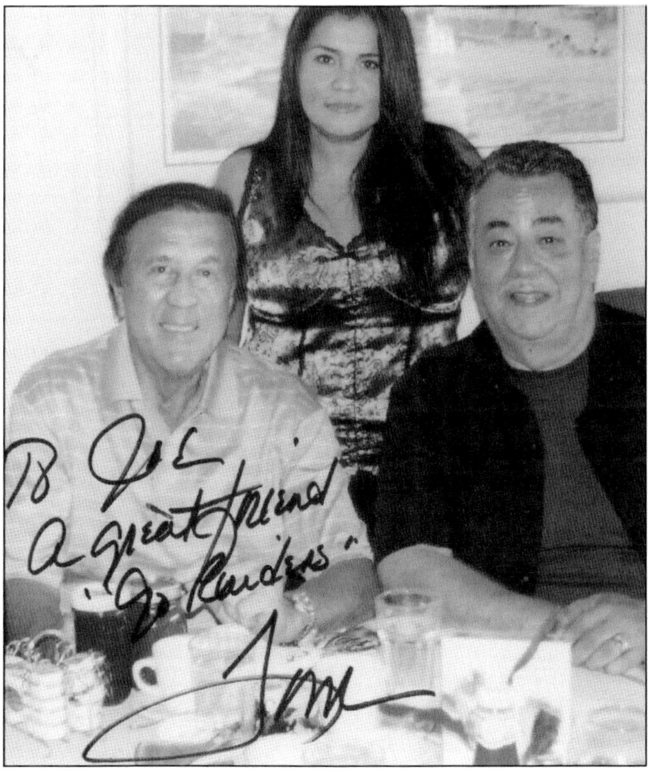

Raiders football coach Tom Flores, left, is shown with Los Angeles publicist Joe Ortiz, right, and Liz Campos in this c. 2006 photograph. In 1979, Flores became the first Hispanic head coach in the National Football League. In the 1980s, he led the Los Angeles Raiders to their first Super Bowl victory. Flores is also the author of the book, *Fire in the Iceman*. (Joe Ortiz.)

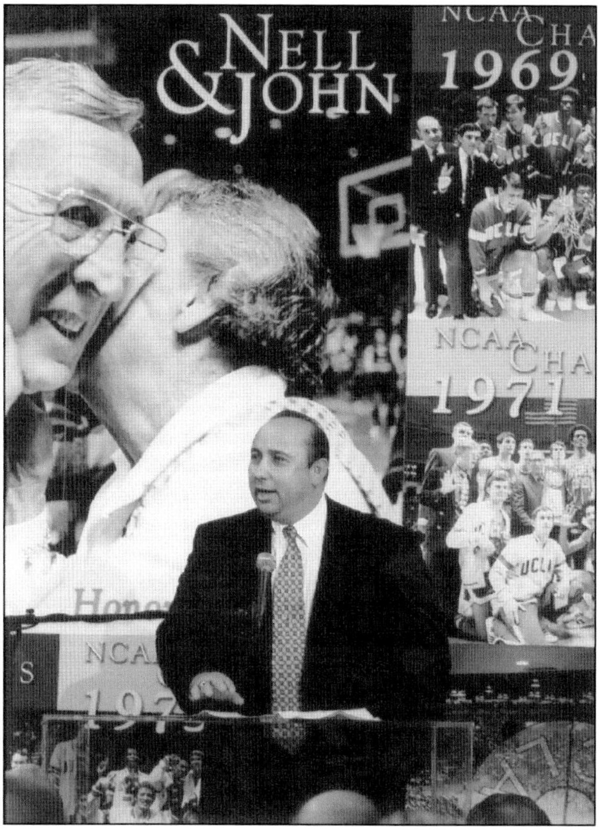

Dan Guerrero is the current director of athletics at UCLA. He is a former student athlete who is now making the calls at his alma mater. This December 2003 photograph shows Guerrero addressing a pregame UCLA luncheon for the naming of the Bruins' basketball court for Nell and John Wooden. Guerrero was named West Region Athletic Director of the Year. (UCLA Athletic Department.)

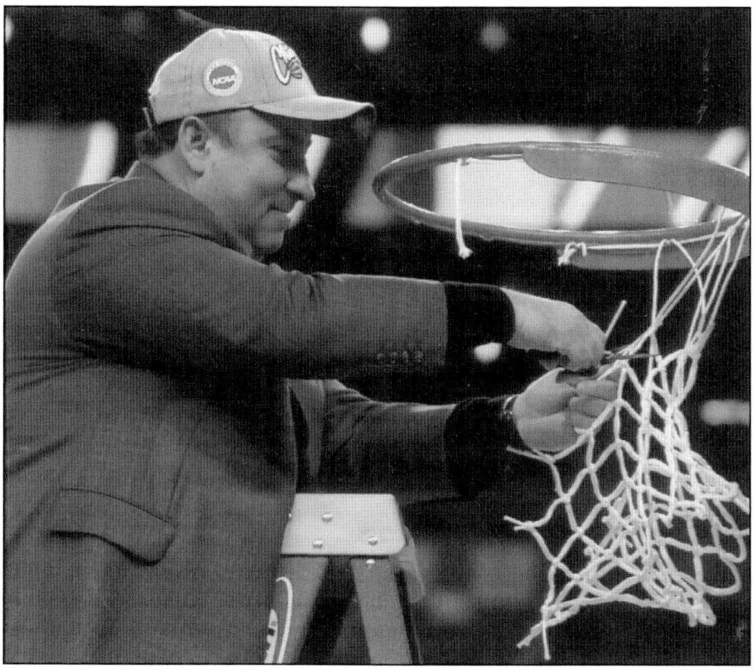

This image shows UCLA's athletic director Dan Guerrero cutting a piece of the net after defeating the Memphis Tigers to claim a spot at the Final Four basketball tournament in Indianapolis, Indiana, the team's first trip to the tournament under Guerrero. Guerrero grew up in Wilmington, California, and is listed as number 38 among the most influential minorities in sports by *Sports Illustrated* magazine. (UCLA Athletic Department.)

Six

Journalists, Writers, and Artists

The profession of a journalist is rarely rivaled in terms of public importance. With the power of the press, journalists are responsible for informing many American citizens about public life. What journalists communicate makes them key participants in the democratic process, making their profession a necessary arm of civilization and an important part of the public trust. Among their chief missions are the responsibilities of synthesizing and communicating complex information objectively, while seeking the truth. In seeking truth, they are not necessarily serving the interests of persons in power or of the state. They are the public watchdogs of government. In Los Angeles' history, two deceased *Los Angeles Times* journalists of Mexican American heritage, Ruben Salazar and Frank del Olmo, served as beacons of truth. Salazar, who wrote critiques about police brutality, was killed by a sheriff's deputy while covering the 1970 Chicano Moratorium rally in East Los Angeles. The deputy was later exonerated. Del Olmo succeeded Salazar to become the conscience of the Latino community at the *Los Angeles Times*, winning a Pulitzer Prize for reporting on issues facing the Mexican American community. He died of a heart attack at his desk in 2004. Both reporters were outstanding role models. The community suffered a deep loss with their passing.

Mexican American artists are important vehicles of visual communication. Their artistic language conveys complex ideas through visual symbols that are as important as the written word. Moreover, their visual language is one that all people speak, cutting across racial, cultural, social, and economic levels. Their artistic work integrates the mind, body, and spirit of the Mexican American community in Los Angeles. During the period of political activism of the 1960s and 1970s, Mexican American artists created graphic murals and art that appeared on public buildings, schools, and parks that reflected the urgent social and political struggles of the time and often had more communication value than the written word.

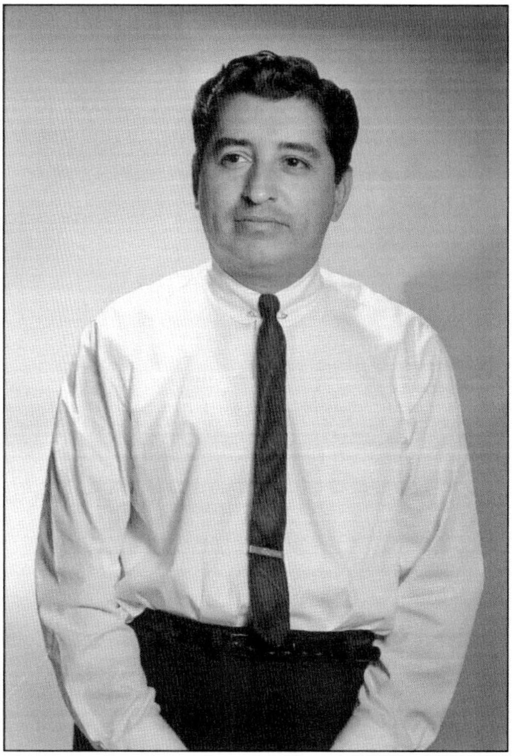

Ruben Salazar, a Mexican American journalist for the *Los Angeles Times*, was killed by a sheriff's deputy at the Silver Dollar Café on August 29, 1970, in East Los Angeles, while covering the Chicano Moratorium anti–Vietnam War rally. Salazar criticized the unjust treatment of Mexican Americans by law enforcement and is considered the first martyr of the Chicano movement. He described the complexity of the Mexican American experience in Los Angeles. In 2008, the U.S. Postal Service issued a postage stamp commemorating his life. (UCLA archives.)

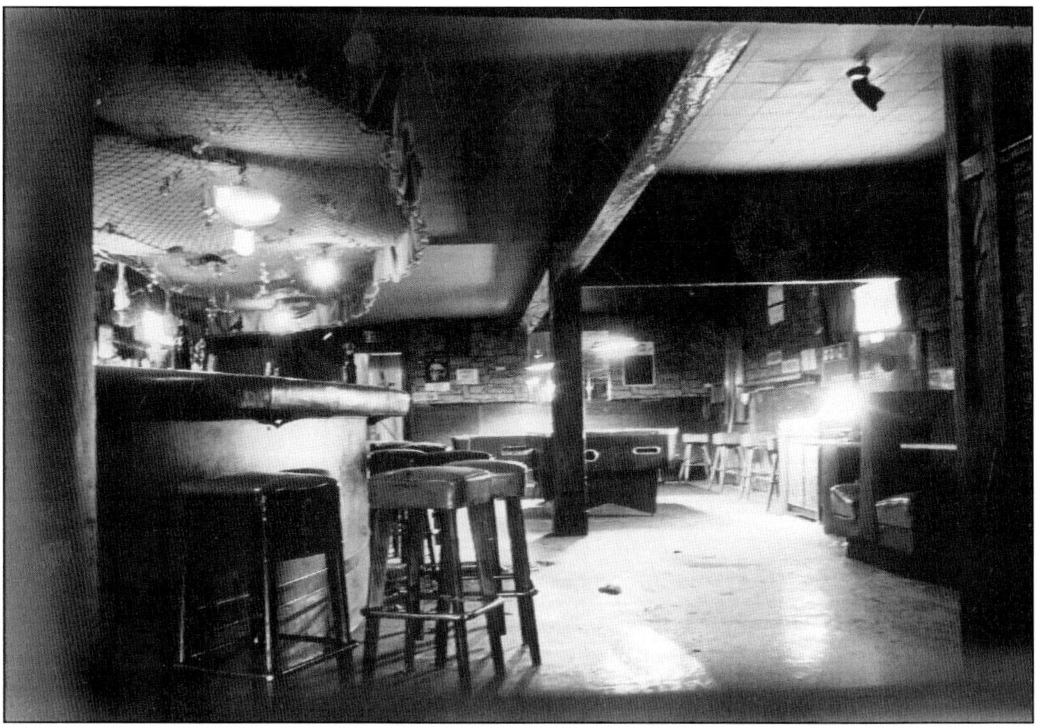

This image shows the interior of the Silver Dollar Café where journalist Ruben Salazar was killed. It was taken on August 30, 1970, the day after he died. (UCLA archives.)

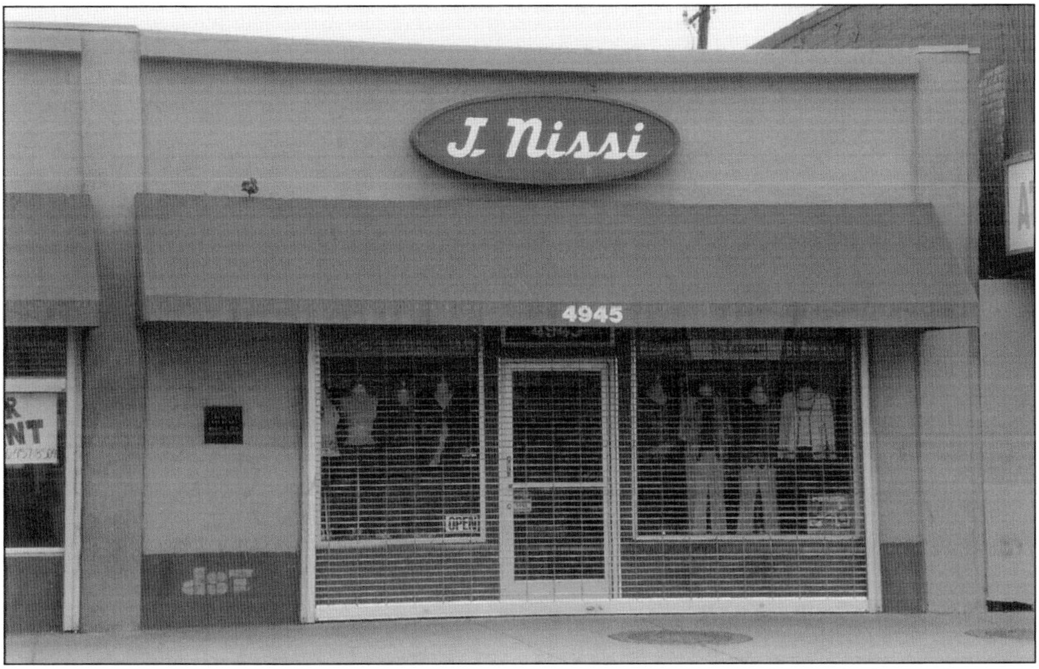

This 2009 image shows the exterior of what was once the Silver Dollar Café, located at 4945 Whittier Boulevard in East Los Angeles, where Ruben Salazar died. Since 1970, the building has been a fabric and notions store, and it is now a dress shop. A commemorative plaque is seen as the small square at left, between the column and the window. (Author.)

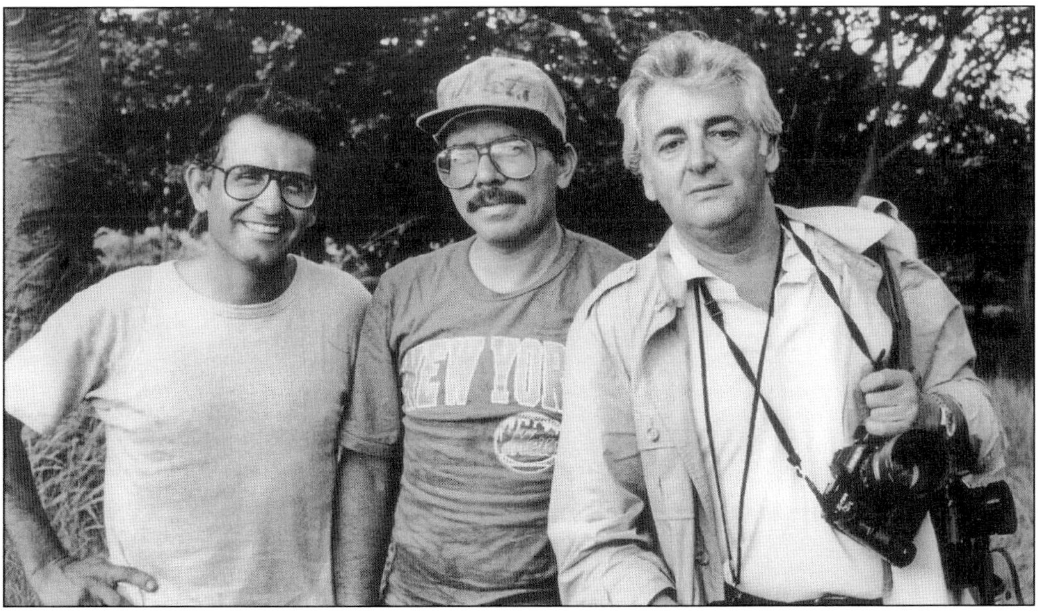

Journalist and writer Ron Arias, left, is shown on assignment with Nicaraguan president Daniel Ortega, center, and photographer Harry Benson, near Managua in the 1980s. Arias has written for the Copley newspapers and *People* magazine, with articles appearing in the *New York Times* and the *Christian Science Monitor*. The author of several books including *The Road to Tamanzunchale* and *Moving Target*, he is a National Book Award nominee. (Ron Arias.)

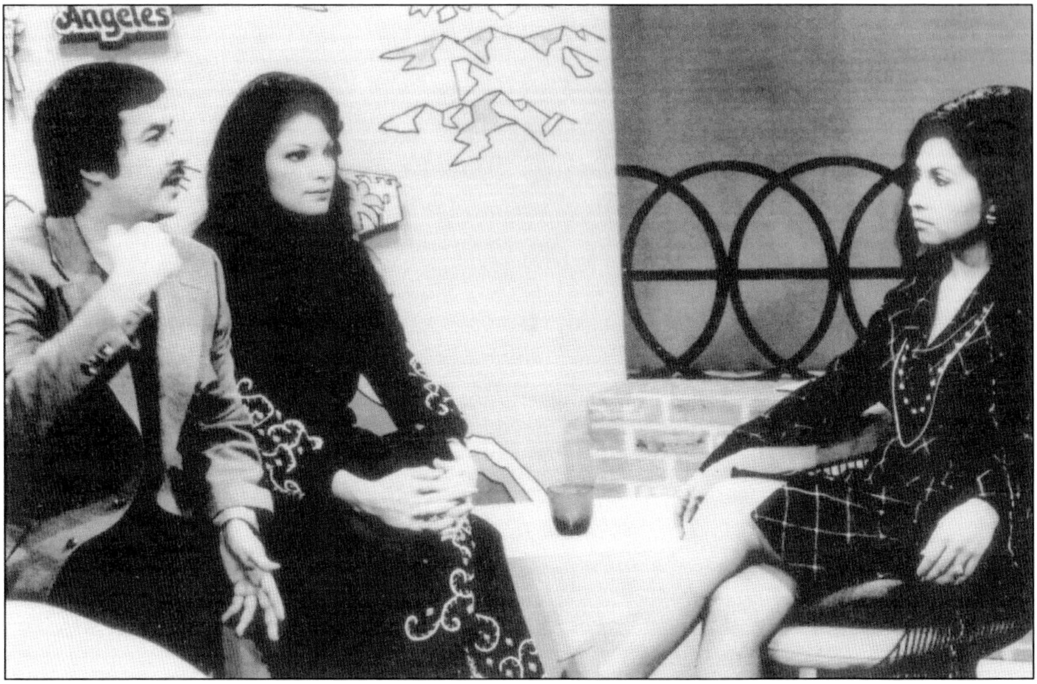

Writer and radio and television talk show host, Joe Ortiz, far left, and cohost Diana Munatones, center, are shown in this 1972 image from their television show, *Bienvenidos* (Welcome). At right is Gloria Molina, now Los Angeles County supervisor. The show's topic was women's issues. Ortiz founded Joe Ortiz and Associates after retiring from broadcasting. Among Ortiz's clients are actress Rita Moreno and coach Tom Flores. (Joe Ortiz.)

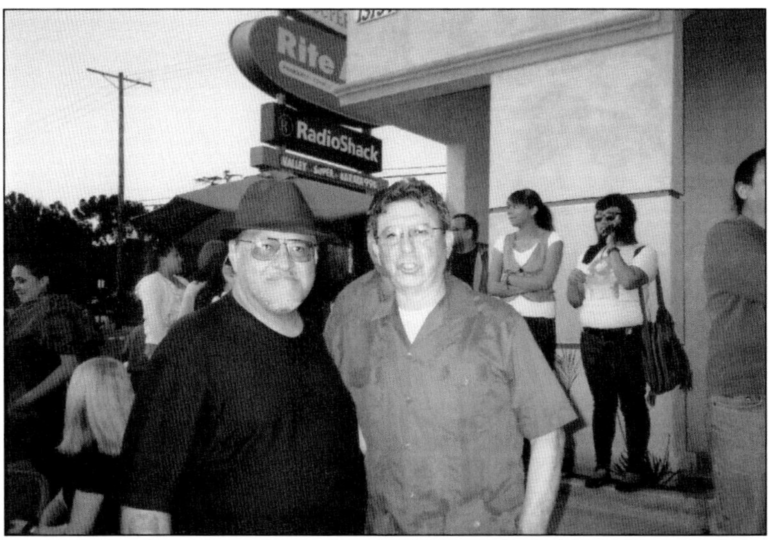

Luis Rodriguez, a Mexican American author and poet, is shown on the left in this 2009 photograph with the author, taken at his Tia Cucha's Cultural Center in Sylmar, California. He is the author of the powerful book, *Always Running: La Vida Loca, Gang Days in L.A.* (Linda Areyan.)

Rose Soto was a longtime columnist for Eastern Group Publications, covering the vast East Los Angeles region. Her column, *East L.A. and Beyond,* highlighted the accomplishments of often-overlooked Latinos in the community. Periodically she wrote under the byline of Irma La Bomba. Her publisher Dolores Sanchez writes that Soto quipped that her tombstone would read, "That's all she wrote." She died September 4, 2009. (Joe Ortiz.)

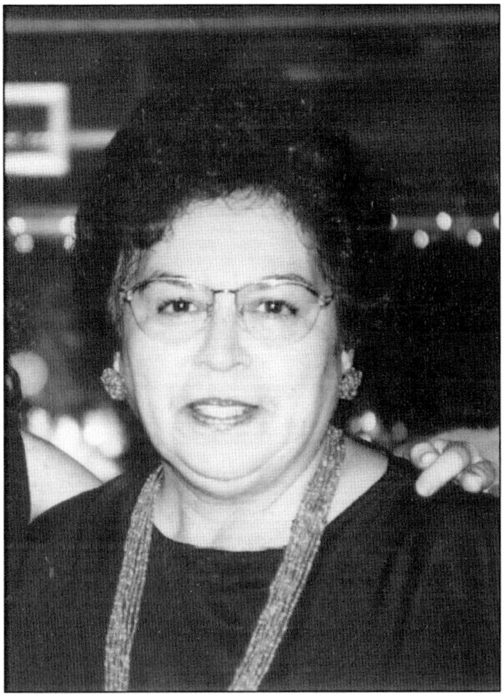

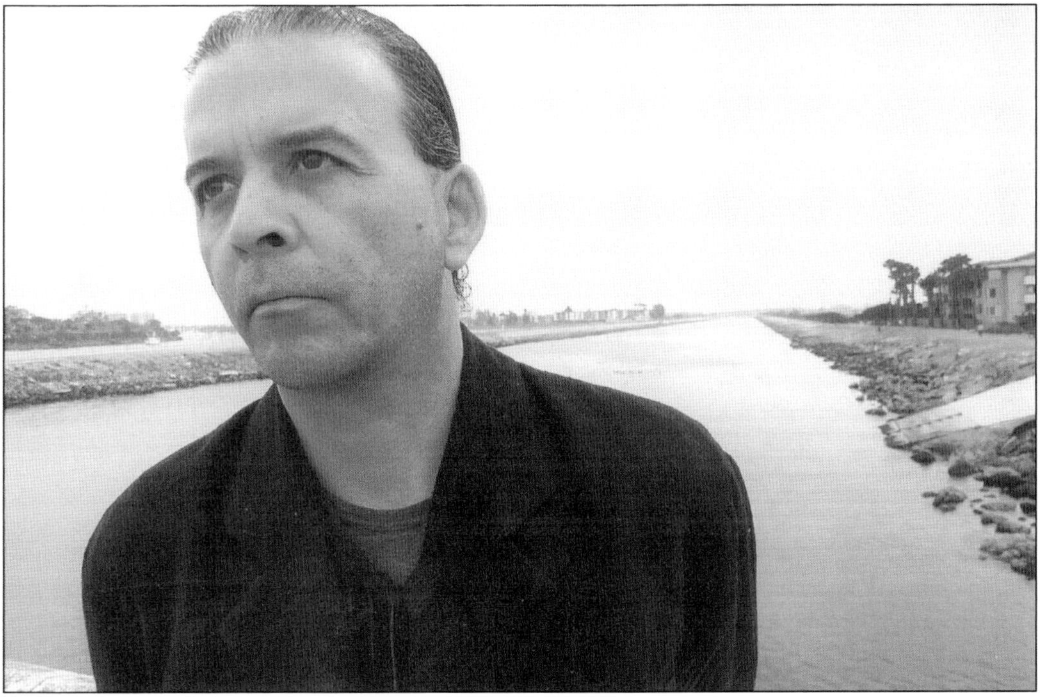

Harry Gamboa Jr. is a photographer, essayist, and performance artist who brings together media to find the correct vehicle to transport his artistic vision. He is one of the founders of the art collective, Asco (Spanish for nausea), which was active between 1971 and 1985. Gamboa's artwork deals with the forces subjugating people in urban environments. The background of this photograph is Ballona Creek. (Harry Gamboa Jr.)

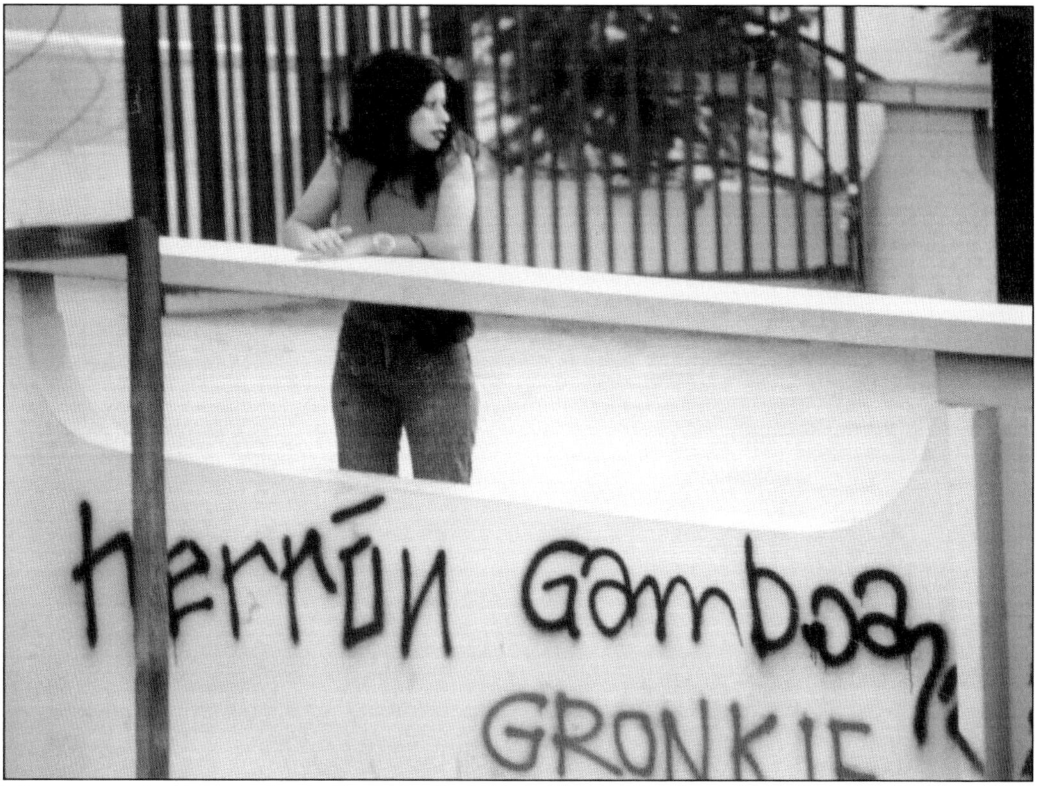

This iconic photograph shows the names of three early Chicano artists who spray-painted their names outside the Los Angeles County Museum of Art in 1972. Pictured is artist Patssi Valdez, who would later join their protest. Artist Harry Gamboa Jr. inspired Willie Herron and Gronkie to spray their names to protest a museum official's comment that, "Mexicans aren't into art; they're into gangs." (Henry Gamboa Jr.)

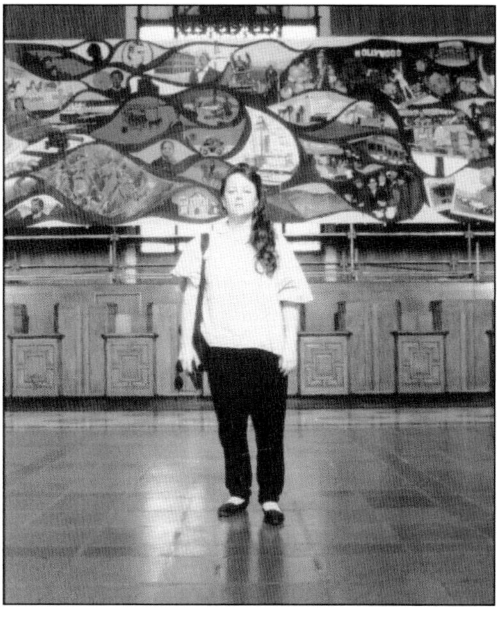

Barbara Carrasco, a Chicana artist and muralist, is pictured in this 1992 photograph with her mural, *L.A. History: A Mexican Perspective*, at Union Train Station in Los Angeles. Her artwork explores race, gender, class, and strong women who have changed the world. Dolores Huerta, cofounder of the United Farm Workers is one of her role models. She has also painted murals in Russia and Armenia. (Henry Gamboa Jr.)

Gilbert "Magu" Lujan, an influential Chicano sculptor, muralist, and painter, grew up in East Los Angeles. With a master's degree in art, he joined the early socio-political art movement of the 1960s and founded the Chicano art collective known as Los Four (the four), who established Chicano art as a valid form of artistic expression. His anthropomorphic animals and low-rider cars are well known. (Harry Gamboa Jr.)

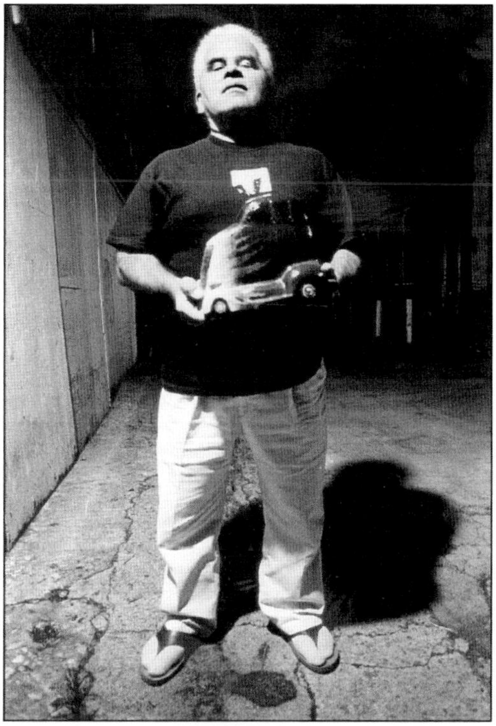

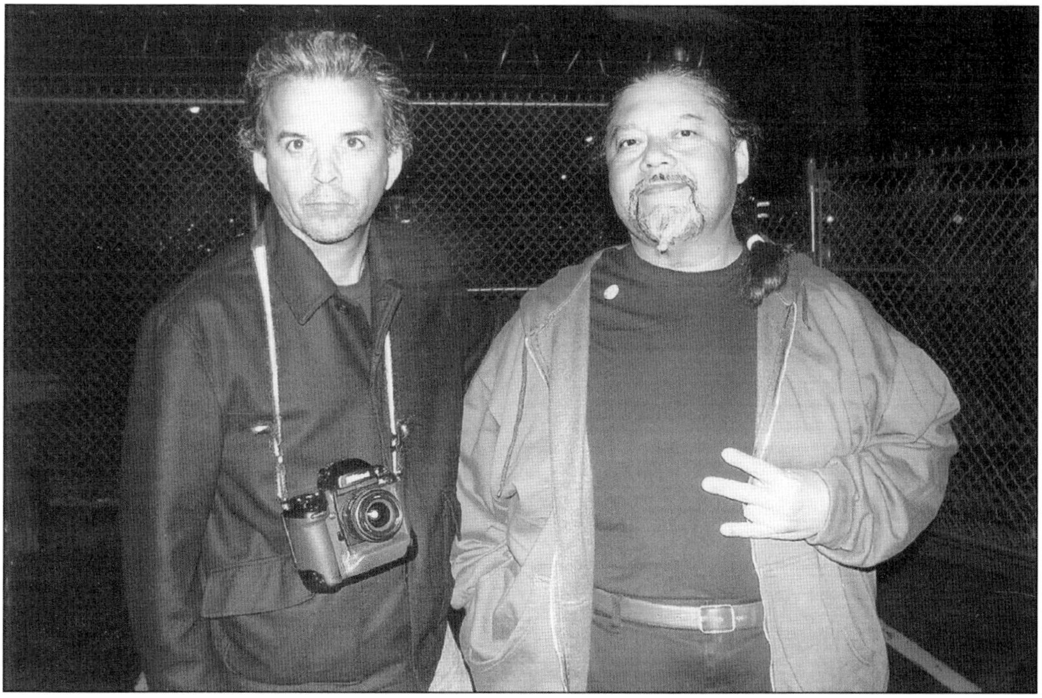

Artist Leo Limon, right, with photographer Harry Gamboa Jr., left, was born and still resides in East Los Angeles. He is described as an art ambassador for the Eastside. He is known for painting cheerful cats on the Los Angeles river walls. Limon focuses his effort on reviving the river area as a tourist attraction. This photograph is from a Gamboa night photo shoot. (Harry Gamboa Jr.)

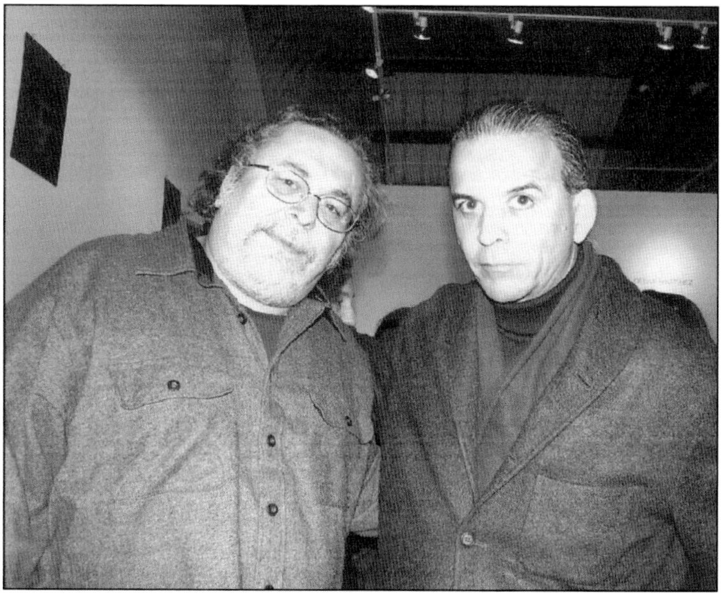

Artist John Valadez, left, with Harry Gamboa Jr., right, is an East Los Angeles artist who is internationally recognized for his realistic photograph-like murals. His 1981–1982 mural, at 242 Broadway Avenue in downtown Los Angeles, is considered one of the most extraordinary achievements of the Los Angeles mural movement. His work is in the permanent collection of the Smithsonian Institute in Washington, D.C. (Barbara Carrasco.)

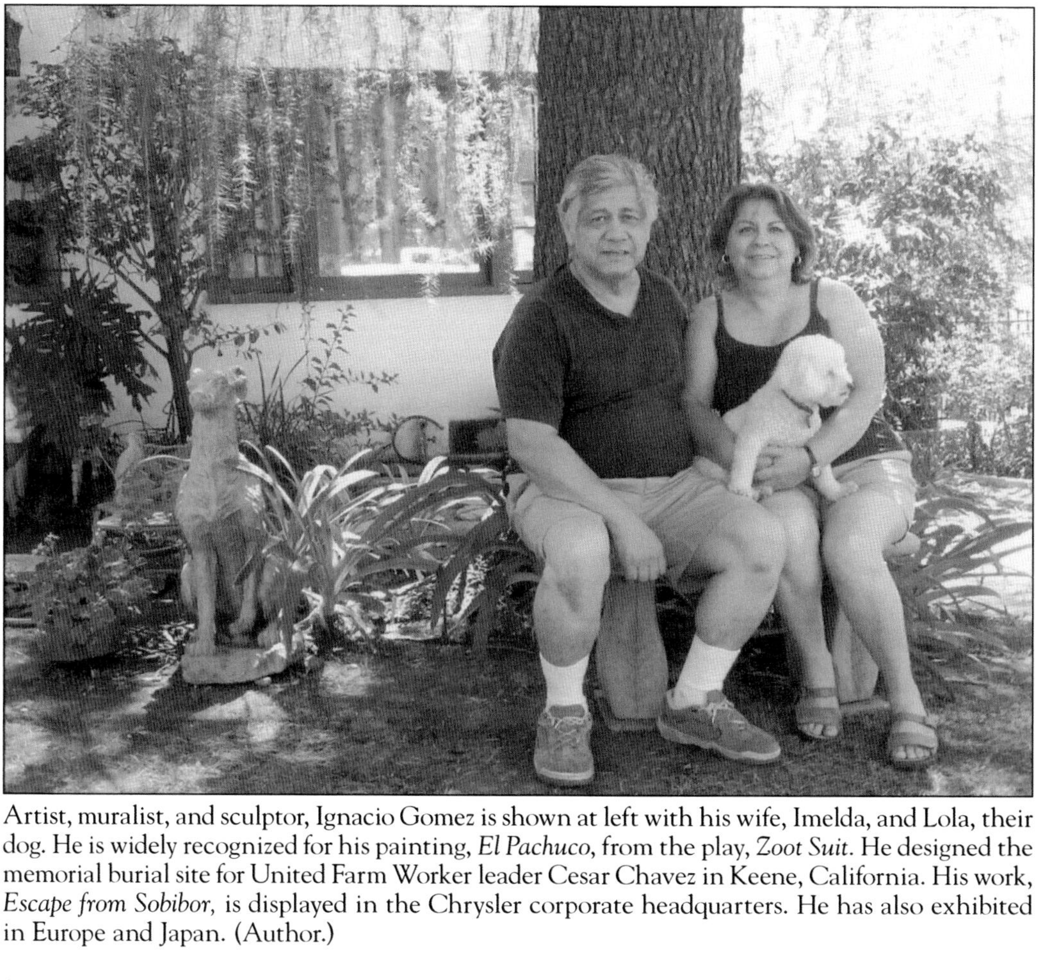

Artist, muralist, and sculptor, Ignacio Gomez is shown at left with his wife, Imelda, and Lola, their dog. He is widely recognized for his painting, *El Pachuco,* from the play, *Zoot Suit*. He designed the memorial burial site for United Farm Worker leader Cesar Chavez in Keene, California. His work, *Escape from Sobibor,* is displayed in the Chrysler corporate headquarters. He has also exhibited in Europe and Japan. (Author.)

Seven

Military Veterans

Many Mexican Americans who fought in World War II collected money from family and friends to pay for transportation to the nearest city to enlist, since recruiting stations did not exist where they lived. While they fought overseas, often their families had the oldest daughters working in aircraft defense plants as "Rosie the Riveters." At home, parents had stars posted on their windows proudly displaying the number of men and women from their households who were serving in the armed forces. It is widely unknown that Mexico, the original country of many soldiers' parents, joined the United States in 1942 in a blockade of the Axis powers' sea-lanes. Mexico also provided a squadron of 300 volunteers and 38 fighter pilots, known as the "Escuadron 201," in support of the U.S. war effort. Unfortunately, these facts have been absent from historical accounts of World War II.

When the thousands of World War II–era Mexican American veterans returned home from theaters of war and years of combat, they came with an understanding of what it was like to be treated as equals in the military. Prior to the war, they were largely relegated to second-class status in American society. However, returning veterans felt that they had gone to fight racial and political tyranny overseas only to return to face the similar tyranny at home. Their experiences in World War II gave the Mexican American veterans a new sense of political assertiveness and leadership. They had demonstrated their patriotism and courage during the war; Latinos were awarded 13 Congressional Medals of Honor for service in World War II. After the war, in order to protect their civil rights and to ensure their path toward full inclusion into American life, veterans formed the League of Latin American Citizens (LULAC) and the American G.I. Forum.

In the Korean War, Latino veterans earned eight medals of honor; in Vietnam, they were awarded 17. The total number of Congressional Medals of Honor awarded to Latinos in the three wars was 38, the largest percentage of medals awarded to any ethnic minority in the history of the United States. This tradition of outstanding military service by the Mexican American community continues today.

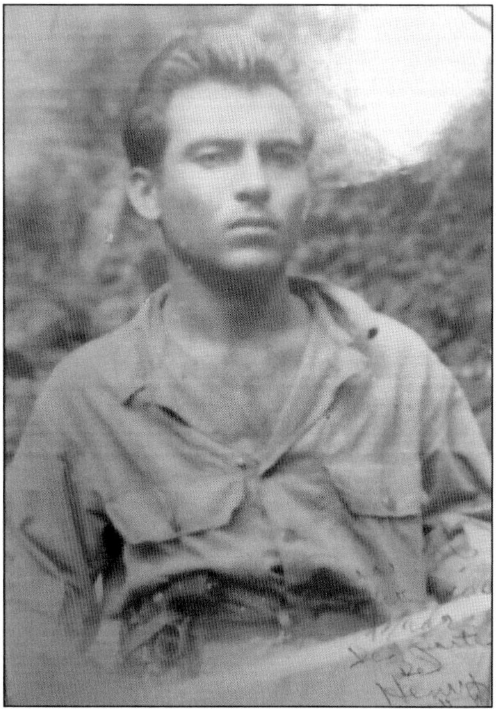

From East Los Angeles to the jungles of the Philippines in World War II, Henry Garduno lived with determination and courage, earning two Purple Hearts and a Bronze Star. As an advance scout, he ensured that soldiers would be safe in advancing to their next position. He was also an amateur boxer with a record of 18 wins and 1 loss. Between battles, he entertained troops as a fighter. (Ron Garduno.)

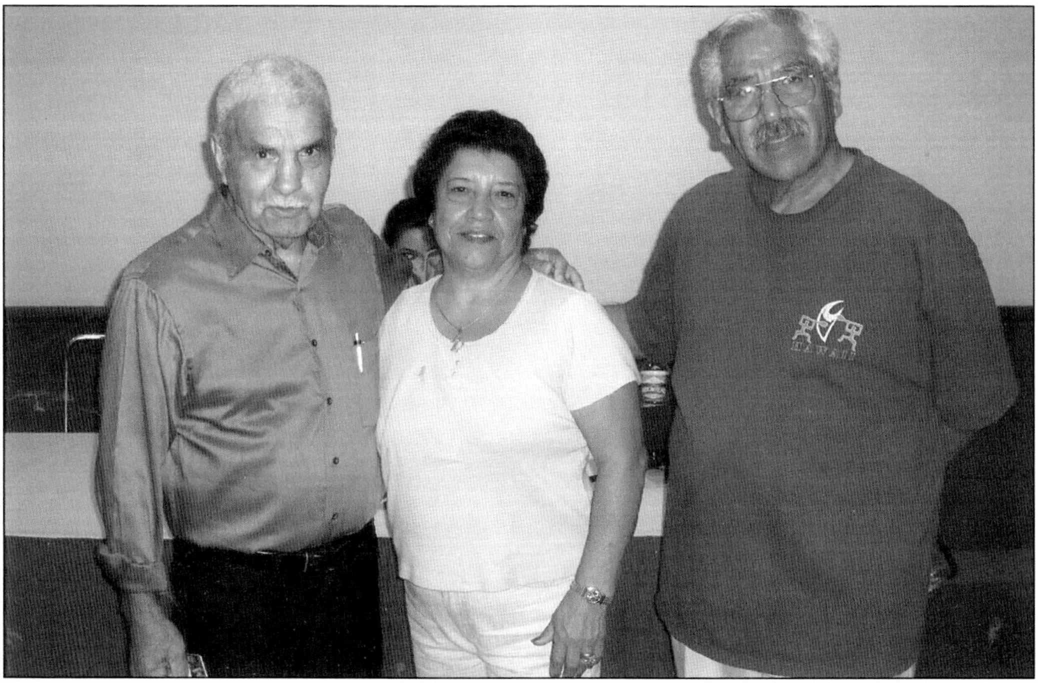

Born in East Los Angeles and raised by a Japanese family, marine Guy Gabaldon (left) single-handedly captured more than 1,000 Japanese soldiers on Saipan Island using the Japanese language he learned at home. In 1957, his story was told on the television program, *This Is Your Life*. He was called the "Pied Piper of Saipan," but despite his heroism, he never received the Congressional Medal of Honor. (*Saipan Tribune*.)

San Pedro, California, native Sgt. John Olguin served with the First Cavalry Division in the Philippine Islands during World War II. While patrolling a beach defense perimeter, despite enemy fire and casualties among his men, he was able to save another soldier's life. In this *c.* 1945 photograph, he is not wearing the Silver Star he was awarded for gallantry. (John Olguin.)

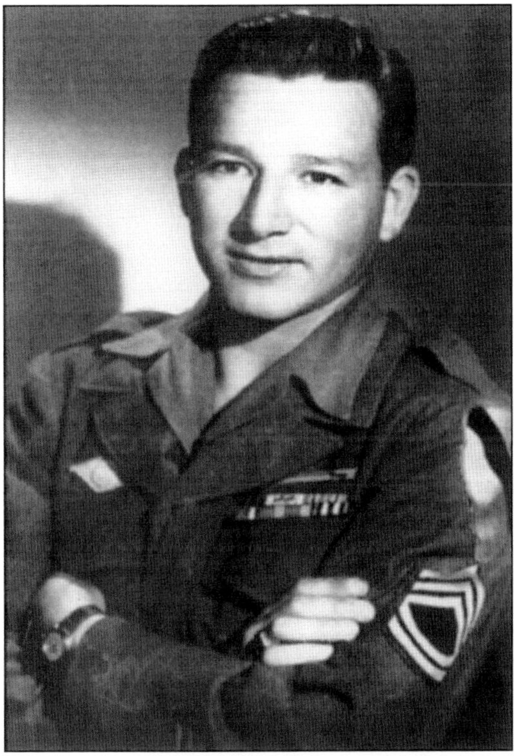

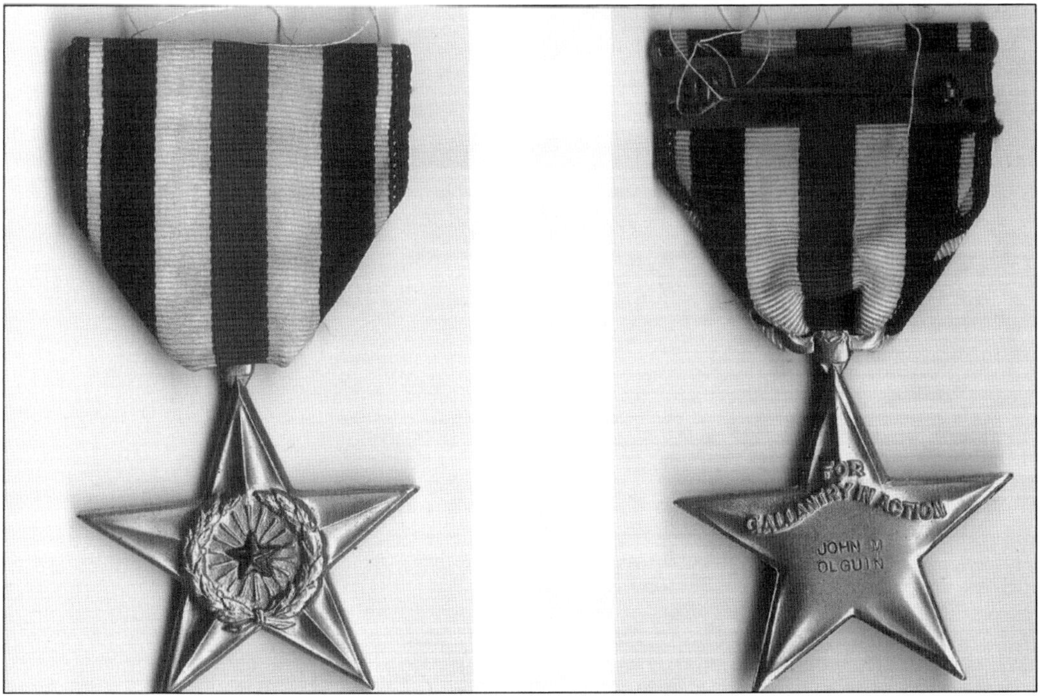

This is a rare image of the front and reverse sides of the army's Silver Star medal, which was awarded for gallantry to Sgt. John Olguin of San Pedro, California, during World War II, after he saved the life of a fellow soldier. (John Olguin.)

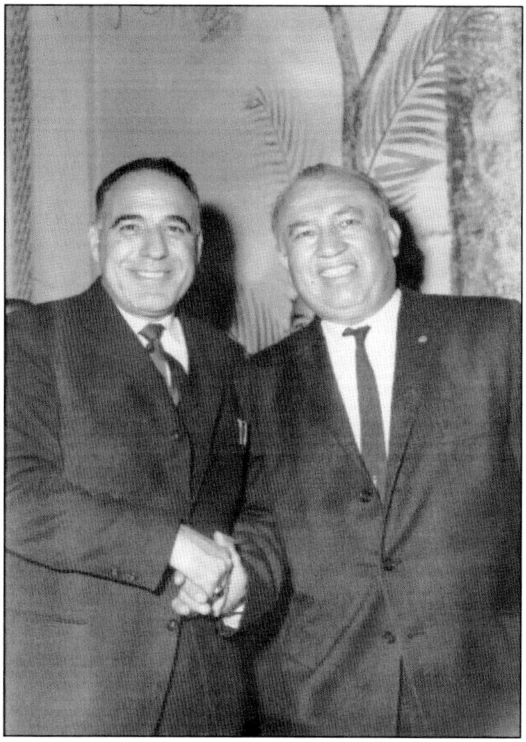

Raul Morin, a Los Angeles resident, was a World War II Purple Heart veteran and an author who wrote, *Among the Valiant*, a book documenting the heroic actions of Mexican American soldiers in World War II and Korea. He is shown, right, in this 1965 photograph with congressman Henry Gonzales of Texas, where Morin was born. (Eddie Morin.)

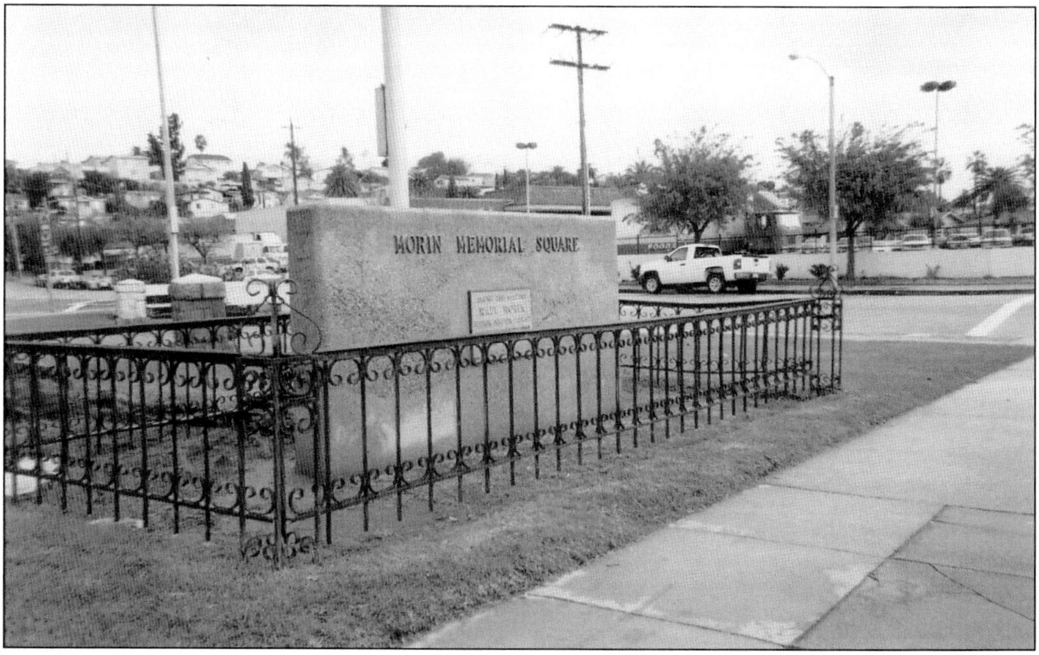

The Raul Morin Memorial Square in East Los Angeles, erected in 1967, is dedicated to Morin for his efforts in documenting the heroism of Mexican American World War II and Korean War heroes. Mexican Americans received the highest percentage of Congressional Medals of Honor of any minority in the United States during these times. Eddie Morin, a Vietnam veteran and Raul's son, has authored, *Valor and Discord*, a book about Vietnam veterans. (Author.)

California congressman Edward Roybal, left, presents a copy of Raul Morin's book, *Among the Valiant*, to Pres. Lyndon B. Johnson in this mid-1960s photograph. Congressman Roybal was a World War II veteran and an admirer of the book. President Johnson, also a supporter of Morin's work, wrote the introduction to the book. (UCLA archives.)

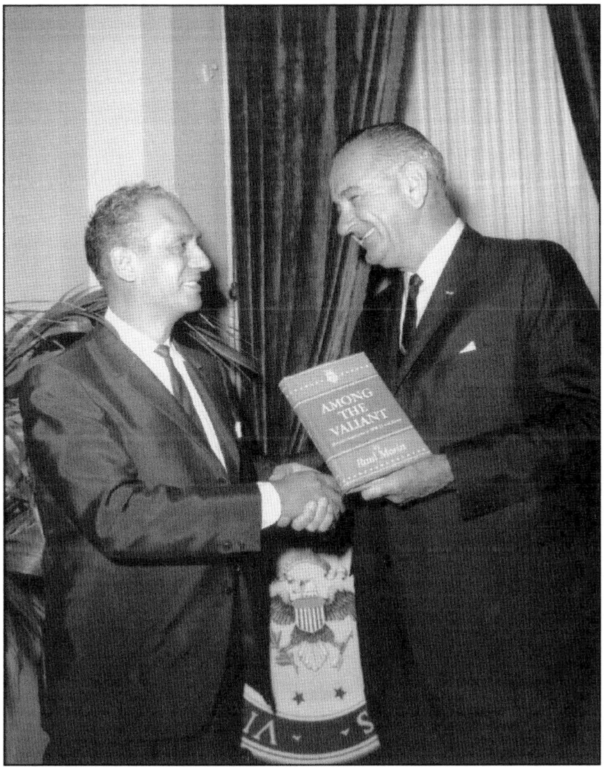

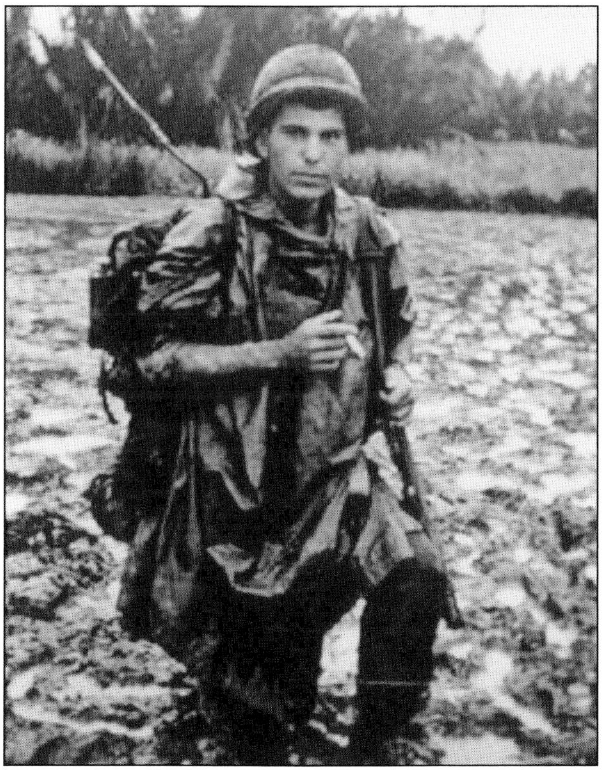

Army specialist Louis Dominguez of San Pedro, California, is seen in this 1968 image in the Mekong Delta of Vietnam, knee-deep in mud during monsoon season. After this photograph was taken, he was wounded on a search-and-destroy mission while acting as a forward infantry observer for his group. After Vietnam, he returned from active duty to earn a college degree. (Louis Dominguez.)

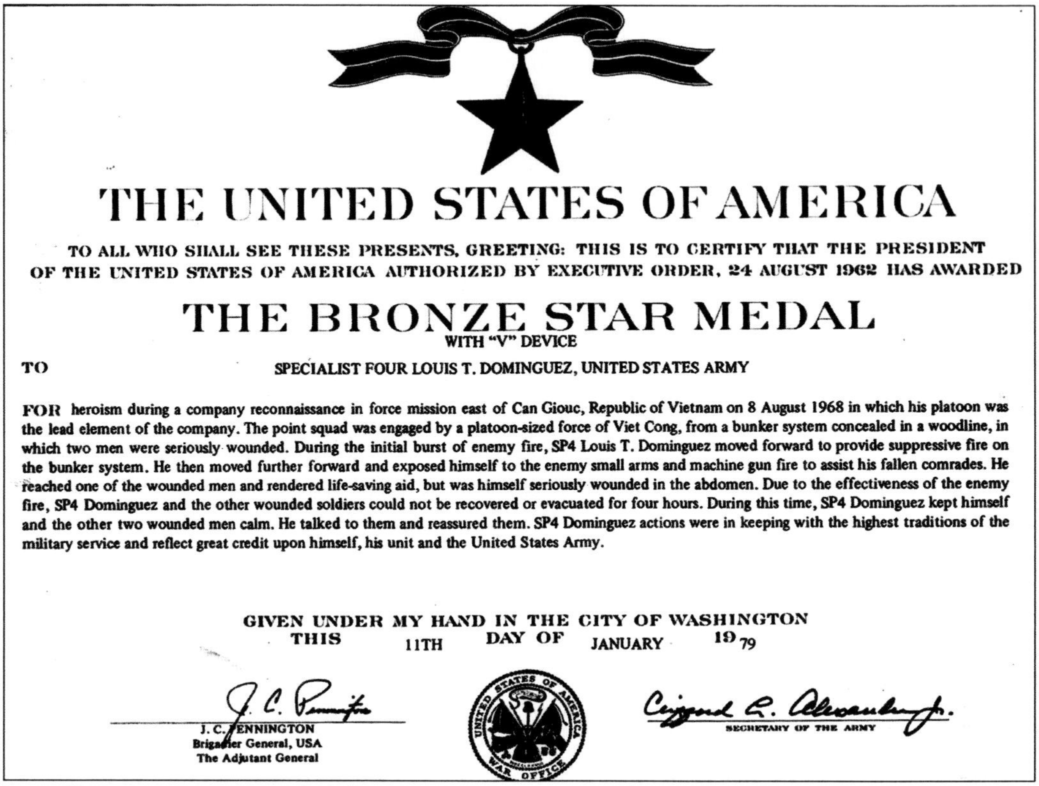

THE UNITED STATES OF AMERICA

TO ALL WHO SHALL SEE THESE PRESENTS, GREETING: THIS IS TO CERTIFY THAT THE PRESIDENT OF THE UNITED STATES OF AMERICA AUTHORIZED BY EXECUTIVE ORDER, 24 AUGUST 1962 HAS AWARDED

THE BRONZE STAR MEDAL

WITH "V" DEVICE

TO SPECIALIST FOUR LOUIS T. DOMINGUEZ, UNITED STATES ARMY

FOR heroism during a company reconnaissance in force mission east of Can Giouc, Republic of Vietnam on 8 August 1968 in which his platoon was the lead element of the company. The point squad was engaged by a platoon-sized force of Viet Cong, from a bunker system concealed in a woodline, in which two men were seriously wounded. During the initial burst of enemy fire, SP4 Louis T. Dominguez moved forward to provide suppressive fire on the bunker system. He then moved further forward and exposed himself to the enemy small arms and machine gun fire to assist his fallen comrades. He reached one of the wounded men and rendered life-saving aid, but was himself seriously wounded in the abdomen. Due to the effectiveness of the enemy fire, SP4 Dominguez and the other wounded soldiers could not be recovered or evacuated for four hours. During this time, SP4 Dominguez kept himself and the other two wounded men calm. He talked to them and reassured them. SP4 Dominguez actions were in keeping with the highest traditions of the military service and reflect great credit upon himself, his unit and the United States Army.

GIVEN UNDER MY HAND IN THE CITY OF WASHINGTON THIS 11TH DAY OF JANUARY 1979

J. C. PENNINGTON
Brigadier General, USA
The Adjutant General

SECRETARY OF THE ARMY

Louis Dominguez was awarded the army's Bronze Star with a V (valor) for aiding two wounded soldiers while waiting hours for medical help, after he, himself, had sustained serious abdominal wounds. After earning his college degree, he served as field deputy for state assemblyman Vincent Thomas and was instrumental in ultimately providing distinctive lighting for the Vincent Thomas Bridge. (Louis Dominguez.)

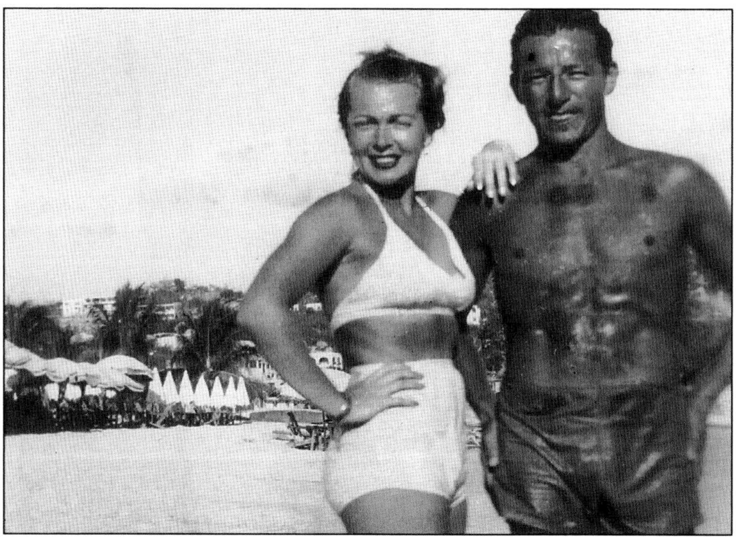

In this 1947 photograph, former World War II sergeant John Olguin poses with legendary 1940s Hollywood actress Lana Turner at an Acapulco, Mexico, resort where he was a temporary hotel lifeguard and Turner was filming a movie with actor Tyrone Power. After a brief stay in Mexico, he returned to the United States to marry the love of his life, Muriel. (John Olguin.)

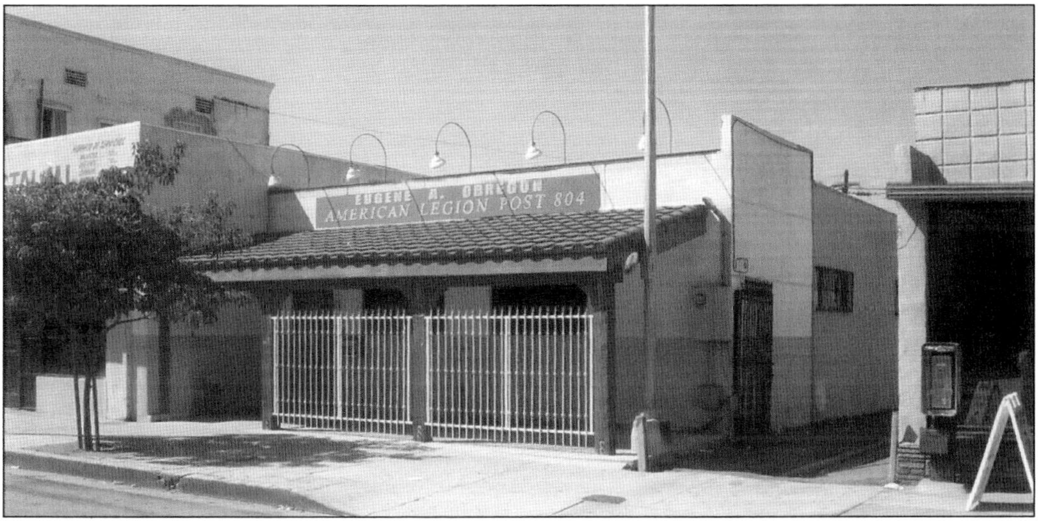

U.S. Marine Eugene Obregon, a Los Angeles native, was posthumously awarded the Congressional Medal of Honor in 1951 for using his body to shield another marine in Seoul, Korea, in 1950. This photograph is of the Eugene Obregon American Legion Post in East Los Angeles, which is named in his honor. Before receiving the Medal of Honor, he was awarded a Purple Heart and three Bronze Stars. (Author.)

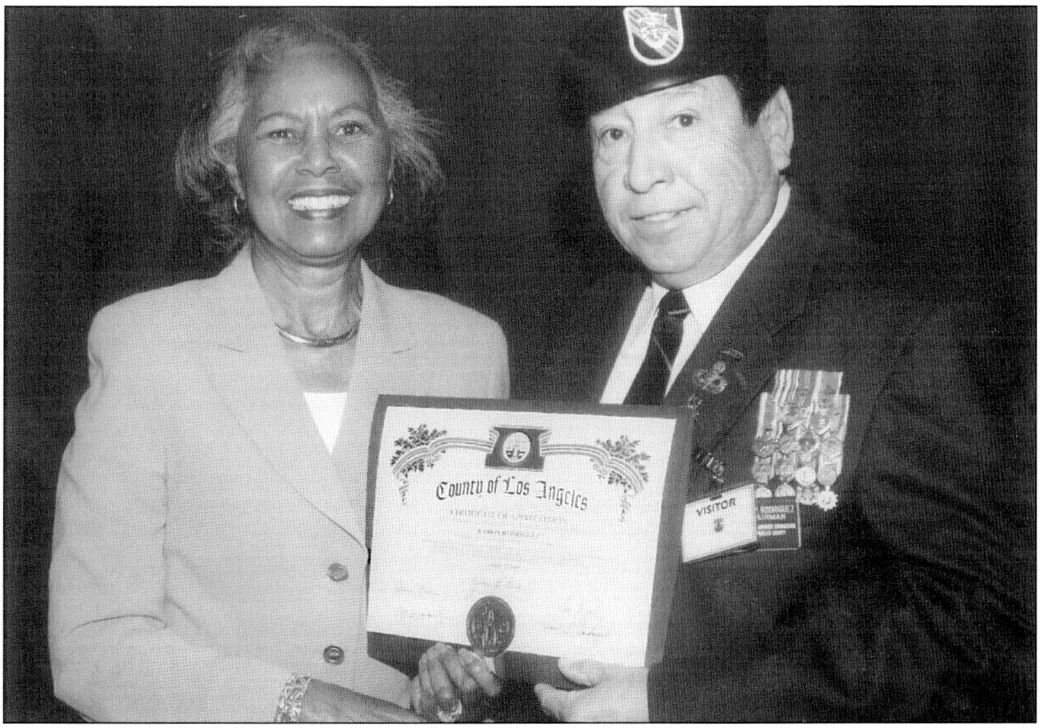

Sgt. Ramon Rodriguez was raised in Wilmington, California, and entered the army when he was 17. In this photograph, he is shown with California congresswoman Yvonne Burke, receiving a commendation for supporting Los Angeles veterans. Rodriguez is one of the most decorated soldiers of the Vietnam War, receiving five Purple Hearts, three Bronze Stars, and three Silver Stars. He is a candidate for the Congressional Medal of Honor. (Ramon Rodriguez.)

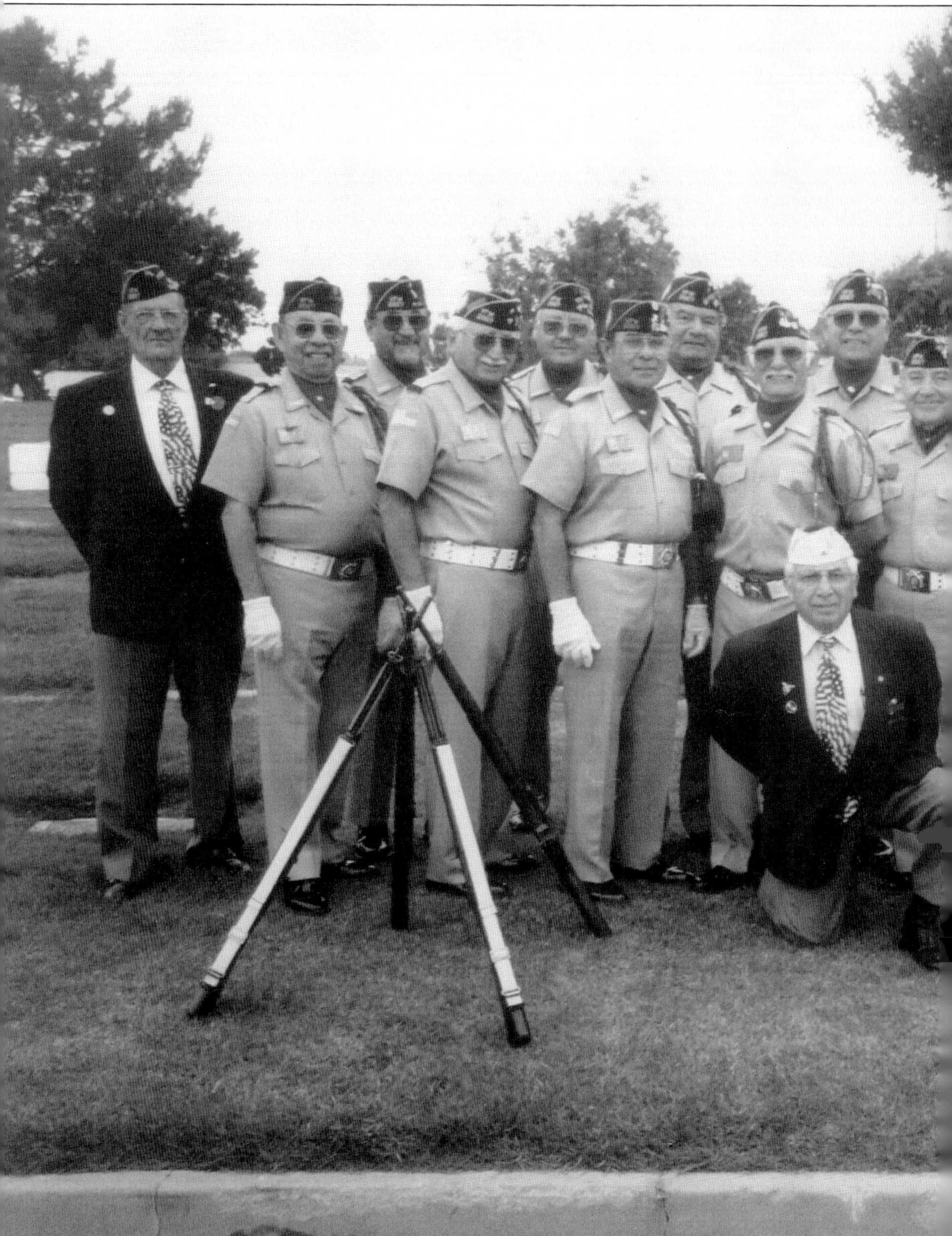

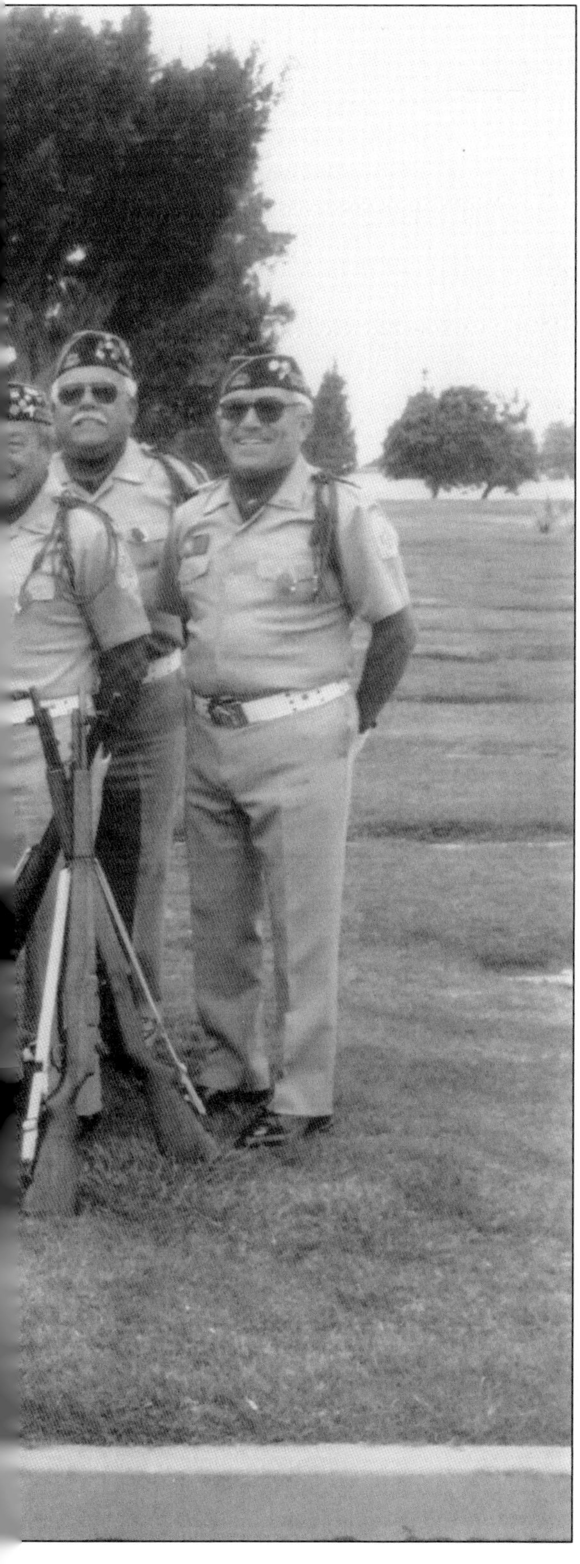

This 1990s photograph is of the Wilmington, California, Veterans of Foreign Wars, post No. 2967 Honor Guard and was taken at Green Hills Memorial Park in San Pedro. Pictured from left to right are Chaplain Cliff Perkins, Tino Martinez, Andrew Rodriguez, Gabby Mendoza, Billy Serrano, Julian Rodriguez, Chito Galvan, Rudy Gonzalez, Richard Rodriguez, Arnie Aranda, Louie Melendez, Jesus Madrigal, Bob Menes, and Ralph Mota. At the front is Efrain Ramirez, past commander. Many of the members are decorated veterans of World War II and Korea. Their present commander Martin Chacon is a Vietnam veteran. The post supports many activities in the community such as the Banning High School football program and children's Christmas parties. They are self-supporting and are frequently called upon for honor guard services for deceased veterans throughout Southern California. They are described as the best post on the coast. (Ralph Mota and Martin Chacon.)

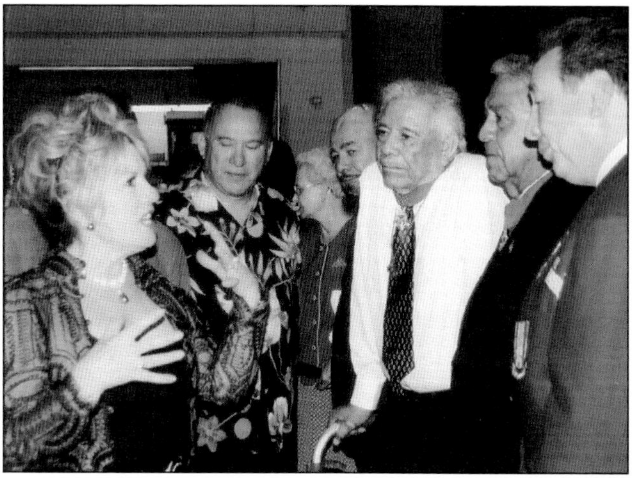

This photograph is from a Chicago League of United Latin American Citizens (LULAC) convention and shows a rare gathering of several living Mexican American Congressional Medal of Honor recipients being honored. From left to right are Mexican American singer Vicki Carr, unidentified, Rodolfo Hernandez, Silvestre Herrera, Joseph Rodriguez, and Ramon Rodriguez (not related), who was nominated for a Congressional Medal of Honor in 1982. (Ramon Rodriguez.)

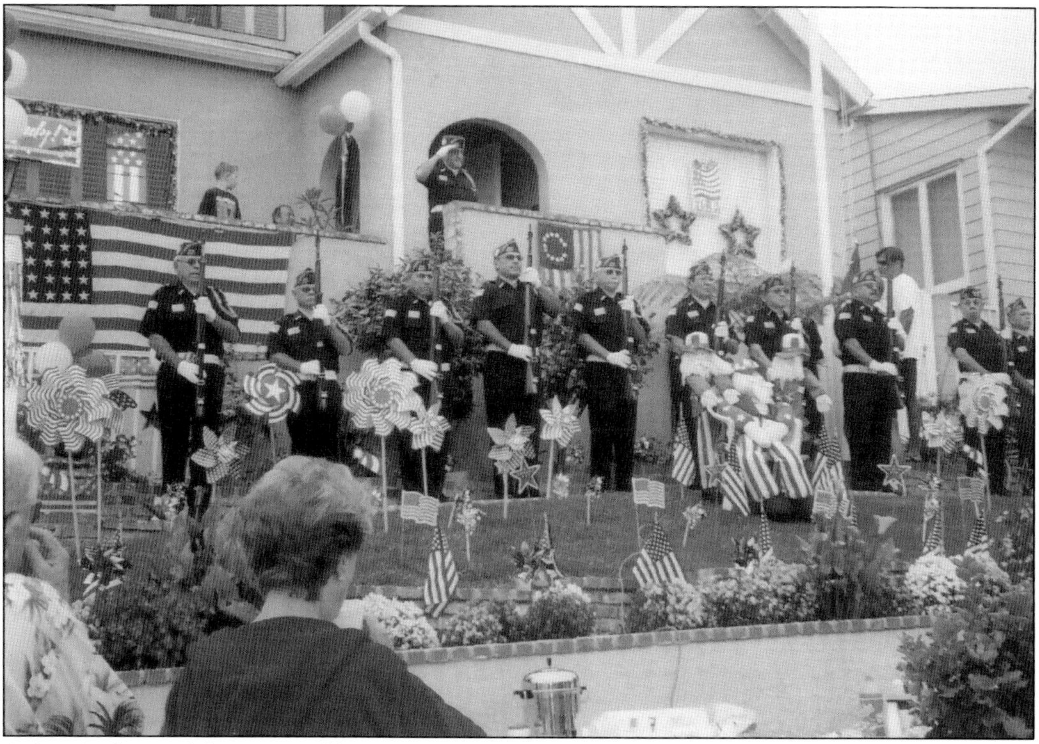

A San Pedro, California, neighborhood Veterans Day celebration is shown in this 2007 image. The honor guard for the celebration is provided by the Wilmington Veterans of Foreign Wars post No. 2967, under the leadership of Comdr. Martin Chacon. They provide the honor guard for many local celebrations and civic parades. One of their important activities is fund-raising for disabled veterans' families. (Ralph Mota.)

Eight

LANDMARKS

Landmarks are places, objects, boundaries, monuments, or areas that represent important themes in a city's history, culture, or development. Landmarks may be as evident as a building or structure, a cultural landscape, or a historical district. On the other hand, a landmark may exist only in the memory of those that remember it or as something captured in a photograph. Landmarks are often the evidence of the presence of a society, its culture, or its history.

Olvera Street, the birthplace of the city of Los Angeles, is one of the most important landmarks for Mexican Americans in Los Angeles. It evokes memories of ancestral beginnings and a past way of life, bringing back nostalgic thoughts of home and family. The bridges that cross over the Los Angeles River, connecting the east and west sections of the city, serve as landmarks reminding residents of past and present connections, linking the old with the new. On the east side of the river, the new Metro Gold Line Station at Mariachi Plaza, designed by Frank Villalobos, FAIA—a local architect—is a new landmark that instills pride in the Mexican American community.

Juanita's Food is an important landmark in the community of Wilmington, because the Mexican American–owned company put the town on the map as the canned *menudo* (Mexican tripe stew) capital of the world. San Pedro's old 1920s neighborhood nicknamed, "Mexican Hollywood," is a landmark that now exists only in nostalgic memories. Landmarks serve to create emotional, social, and cultural connections that provide the glue that further strengthens community bonds with time.

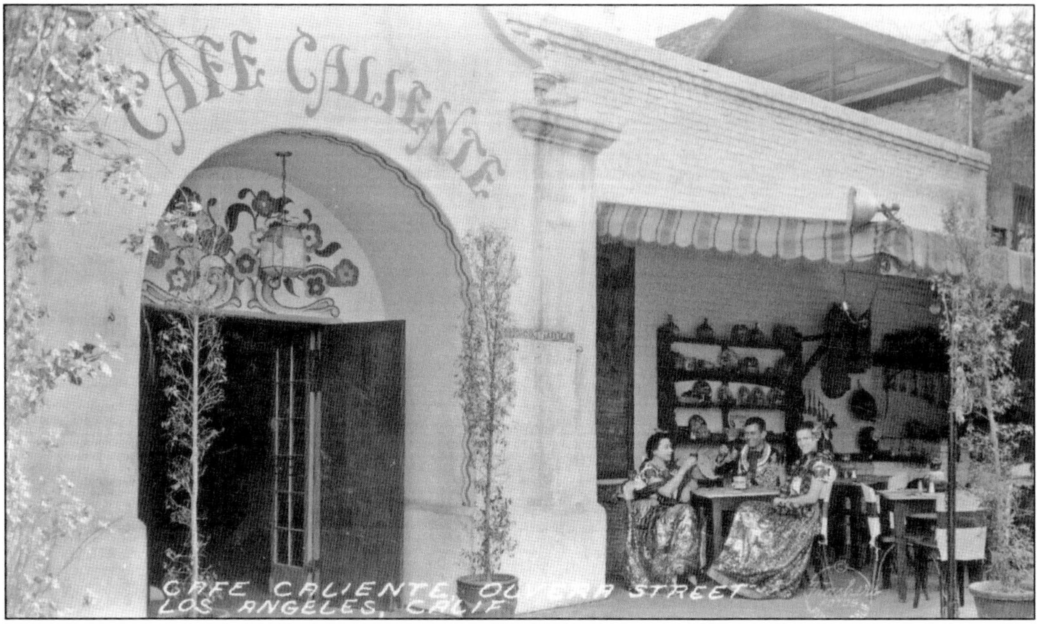

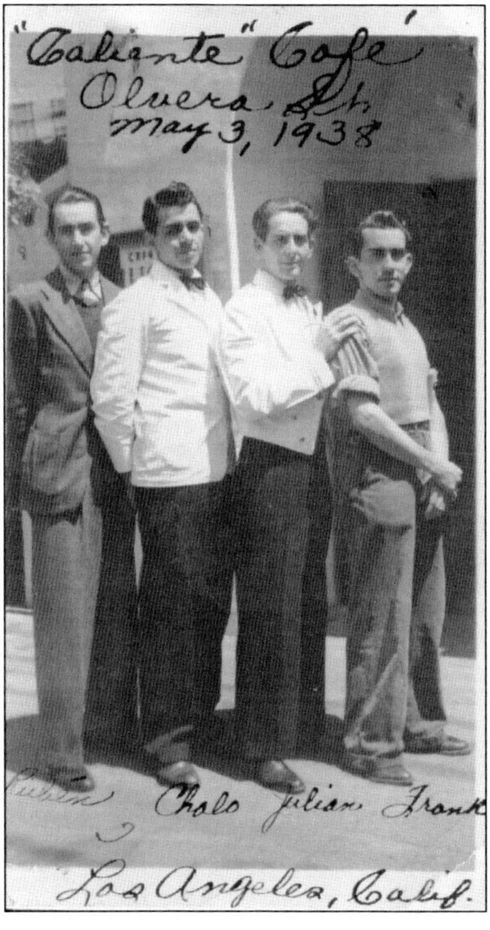

Before becoming the Café Caliente on Los Angeles' Olvera Street in the 1930s, this building above was used for wine-making. Later the café had a large dance floor and Latin orchestras. The café is now the Paseo Inn, operated by attorney Andy Camacho and his son Luis. It is considered one of the oldest bars in the city and has been designated a historical landmark of the city. (Ron Arias.)

This image shows some of the waitstaff at the Café Caliente. From left to right are Ruben ?, Chalo ?, Julian ?, and bartender Frankie Giner. The café was a popular nightspot for Hollywood celebrities, and according to Frankie's son Ron Arias, his father served many of Hollywood's stars of the 1940s. Rita Hayworth, Anthony Quinn, and Humphrey Bogart were all regular customers. (Ron Arias.)

This 1938 image shows two Café Caliente cigarette girls. Emma Estrada (right) is shown here with an unidentified coworker. The ladies would move among diners selling cigarettes from a specially designed wooden tray suspended by a large strap around the neck. Emma would later marry the café's bartender Frankie Giner, according to their son, journalist and author Ron Arias. (Ron Arias.)

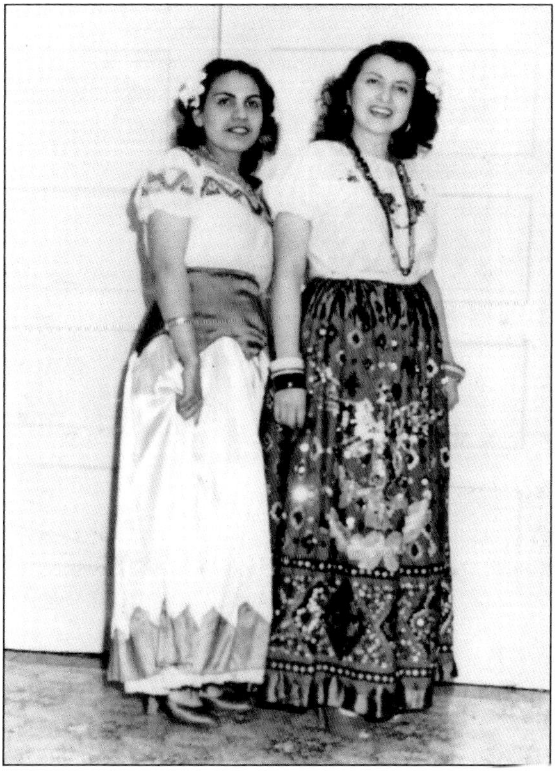

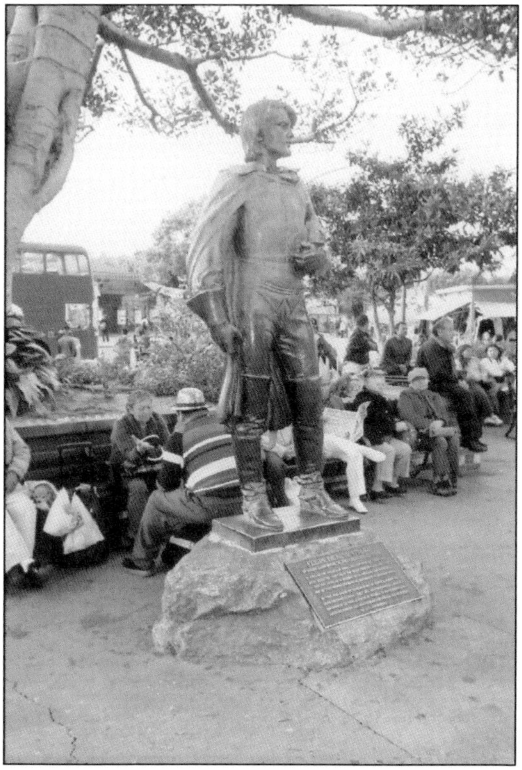

El Pueblo de Nuestra Señora La Reina de Los Angeles Del Rio Porciuncula was the formal name of Los Angeles, which was settled by 44 men, women, and children in 1771. This statue of governor Felipe de Neve, located in the circular plaza at the north end of Olvera Street, formally commemorates the birth of the city in 1781, some 10 years later. (Author.)

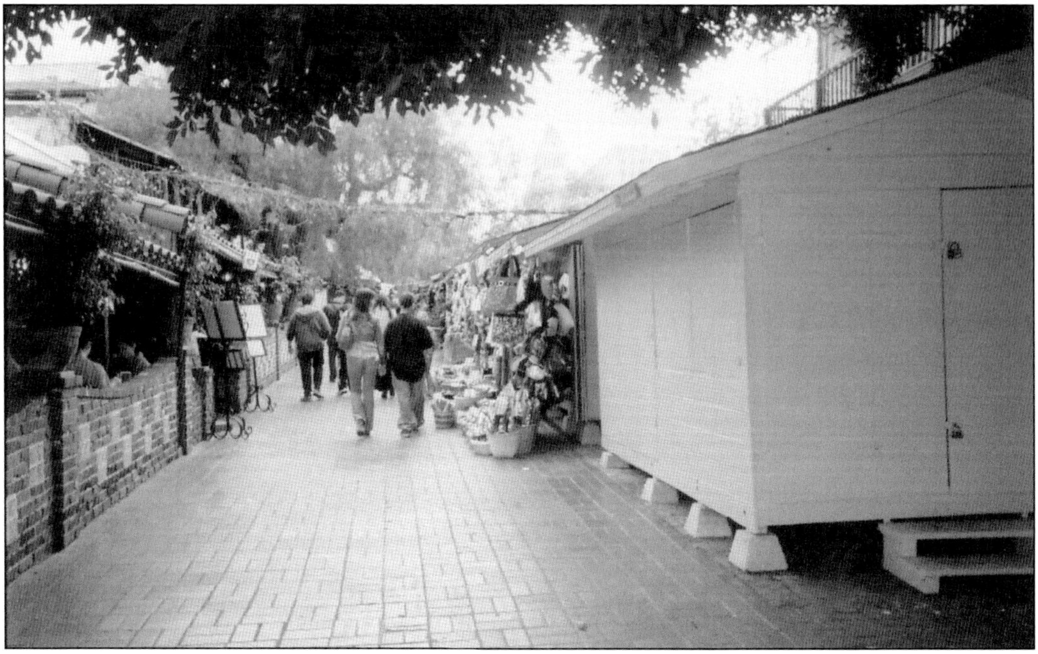

This photograph of Olvera Street looking to the south contrasts the oldest part of the city in the foreground with the modern city in the background, as seen in the early morning mist. The city's water supply was provided by the *Madre Zanja* (Mother Ditch), which ran under the steps of the vendor's booth at right, 225 years ago. (Author.)

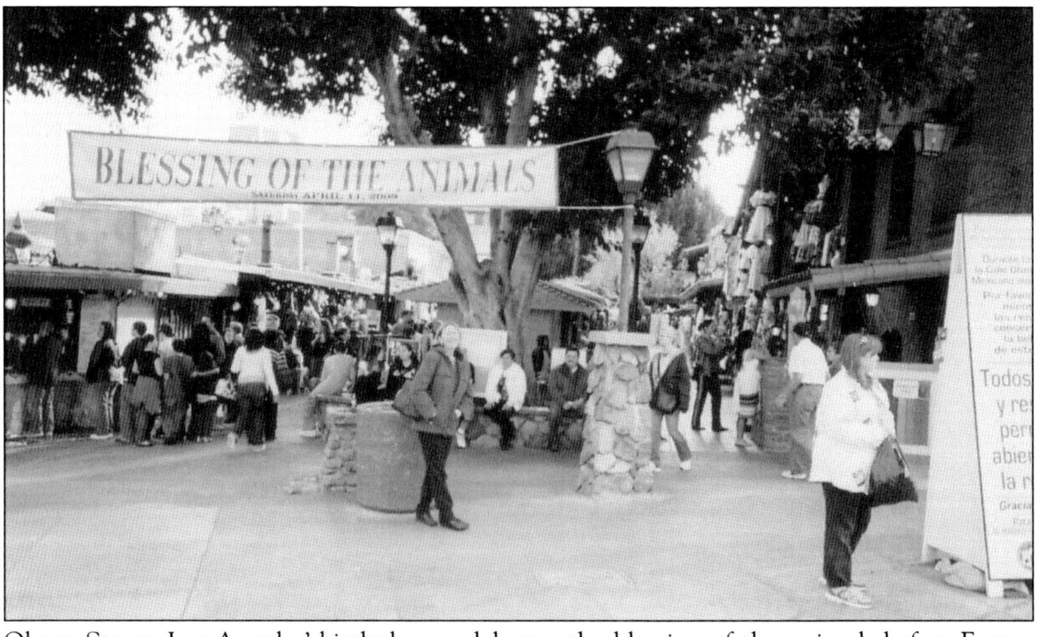

Olvera Street, Los Angeles' birthplace, celebrates the blessing of the animals before Easter. This tradition dates back to the third or fourth century in Europe. The blessing is performed in recognition of the useful service given to humans by animals. At the center of the photograph is Linda Areyan, who remembers this tradition being celebrated in Italy in honor of Saint Francis of Assisi. (Author.)

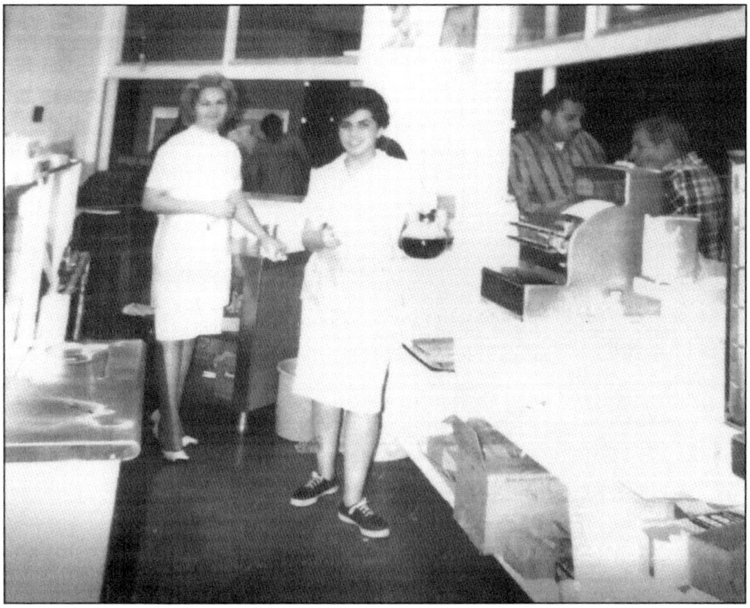

Garduno's restaurant in Montebello, California, was one of several popular landmark restaurants owned by the extended Garduno family. This 1958 photograph shows, from left to right, Christina Garduno and Alice Garduno busily waiting on customers at night. In the 1960s and 1970s, it was the place to go and be seen, and to find weekend parties. They were located next to Montebello High School. (Ron Garduno.)

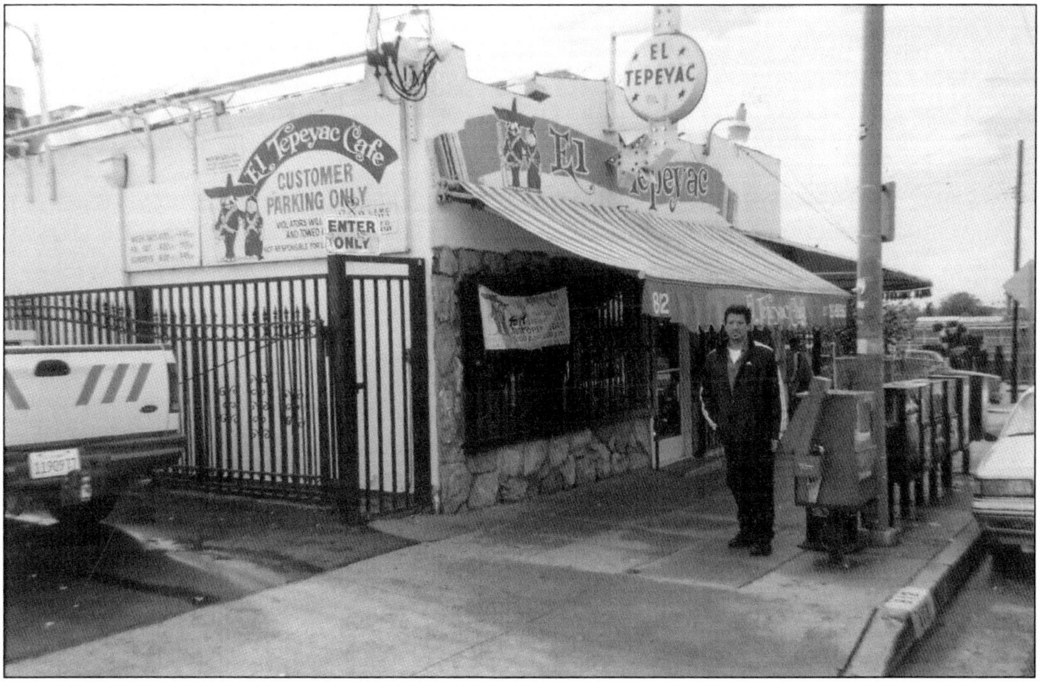

El Tepeyac, a landmark Mexican restaurant located on Evergreen Street in East Los Angeles, is a definite city marker. It has served generations of diners. Open seven day per week, it is known for the legendary Hollenbeck burrito. The small restaurant is frequented by Hollywood celebrities, politicians, office seekers, and policemen. Sal Rodriguez, a UCLA graduate who grew up nearby, is pictured outside the restaurant. (Author.)

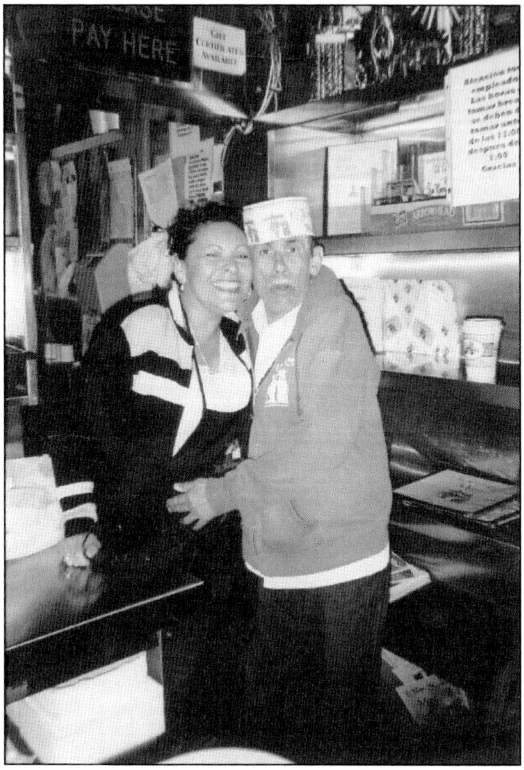

Manuel Rojas, right, is owner of El Tepeyac restaurant. Elena, his daughter, is seen working the counter of the landmark East Los Angeles restaurant. Manuel, who purchased the restaurant from his parents in 1951, still greets diners and jokes with them on the sidewalk, while they wait patiently for a seat. (Author.)

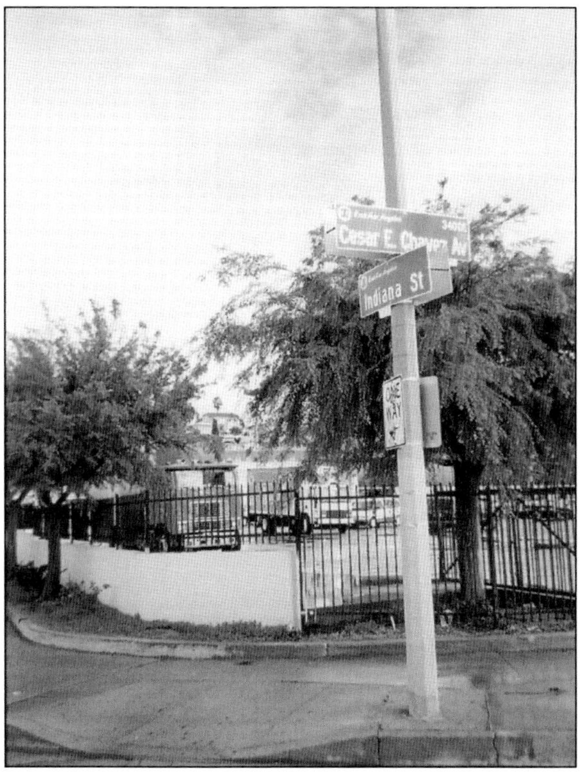

This street sign at the notable intersection of Cesar Chavez Avenue (formerly Brooklyn Avenue) and Indiana Street in the Boyle Heights neighborhood of East Los Angeles marks its eastern border. (Sal Rodriguez.)

This image of Los Cinco Puntos (Five Points) in East Los Angeles' Boyle Heights is an intersection where several streets connect. Nearby, the intersection of Cesar Chavez and Soto Avenues is known as the symbolic, social, and cultural center of East Los Angeles. (Author.)

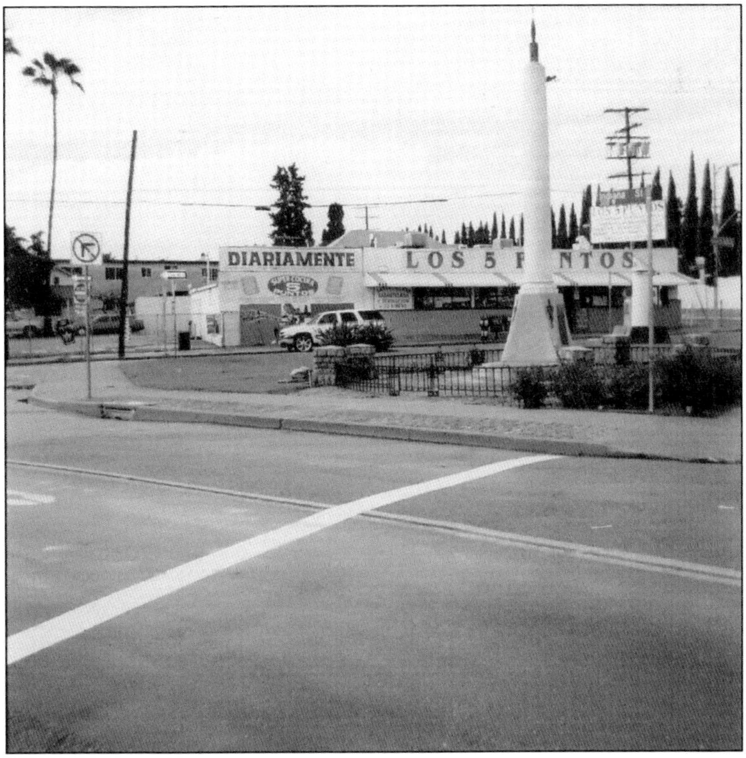

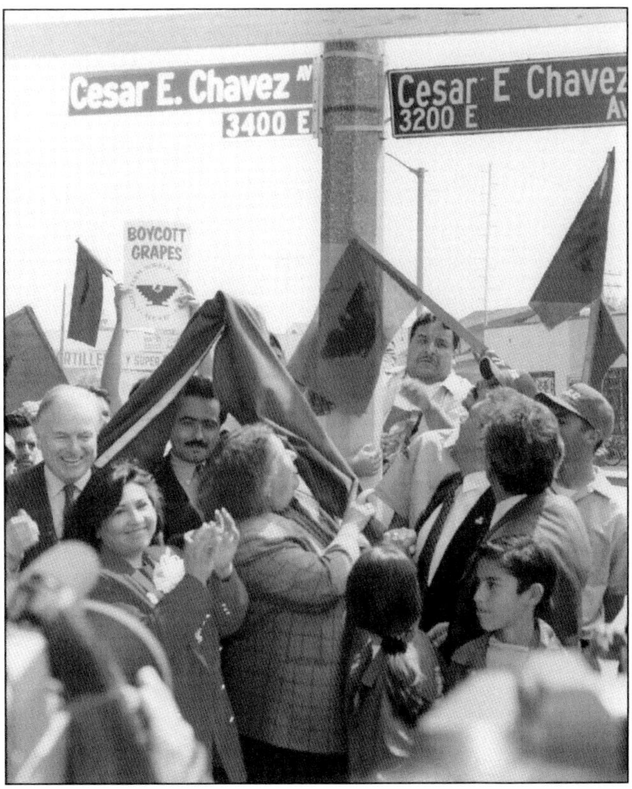

In 1995, the Los Angeles City Council voted to change the name of East Los Angeles' Brooklyn Avenue to Cesar Chavez Avenue in honor of the late farm worker and civil rights leader. Seen in this *c.* 1995 image are, from left to right, (first row) Los Angeles County supervisor Gloria Molina (left center); (second row) Mayor Richard Riordan; (third row, under flags) Councilman Richard Alarcon. (Alycia Enciso.)

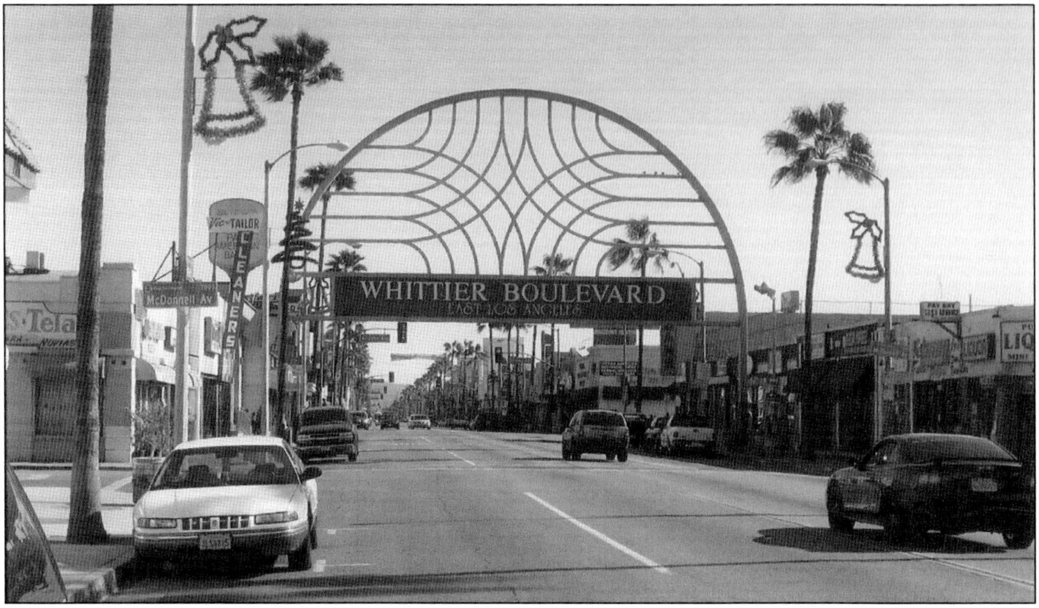

Whittier Boulevard in East Los Angeles has been called the Wall Street of the Eastside for the many businesses found there. The landmark Whittier Boulevard archway welcomes visitors and shoppers. Barrio Planners, the architectural firm of Frank Villalobos, FAIA, was responsible for its design and construction. (Sal Rodriguez.)

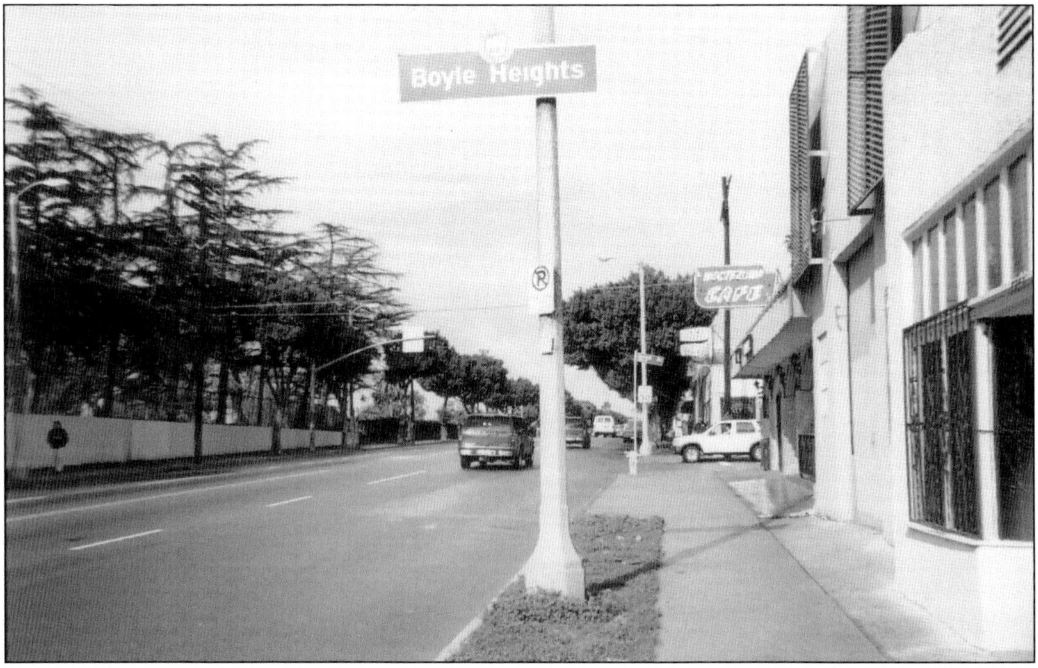

Some of the East Los Angeles landmark barrios are Boyle Heights, Lincoln Heights, City Terrace, an unincorporated area known as East Los Angeles, and El Sereno (the Calm). This photograph identifies the entrance to Boyle Heights, coming from east to west. Other major streets are First and Third. The tree line on the left is Evergreen Cemetery, the oldest in Los Angeles. (Author.)

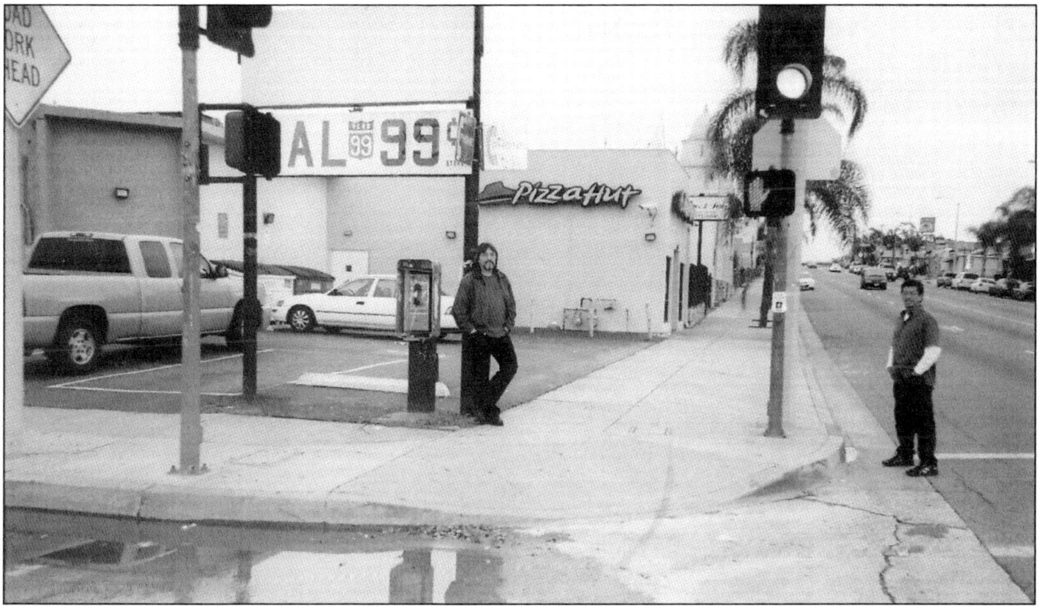

Lalo Guerrero, the legendary singer and composer, operated his nightclub Lalo's at the corner of Brooklyn Avenue and Marianna Street in East Los Angeles from 1962 to 1972. Guerrero, who also sang at the 1939 New York World's Fair, entertained thousands of his fans at this club. His songwriter son Mark, is in the center, and at right is Sal Rodriguez. The site is now a pizza restaurant. (Author.)

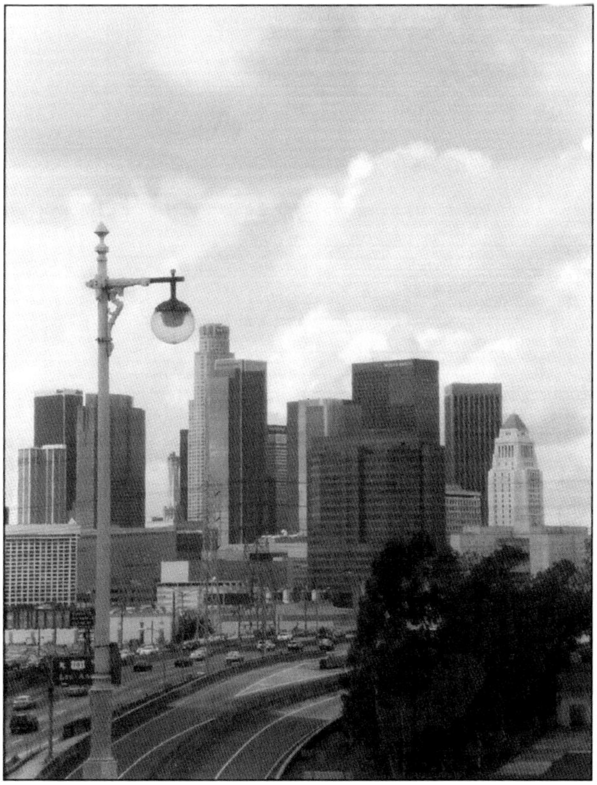

This landmark image of downtown Los Angeles is taken from a higher elevation in a residential area of Boyle Heights. The building at extreme right is Los Angeles City Hall. The current mayor is Antonio Villaraigosa. (Sal Rodriguez.)

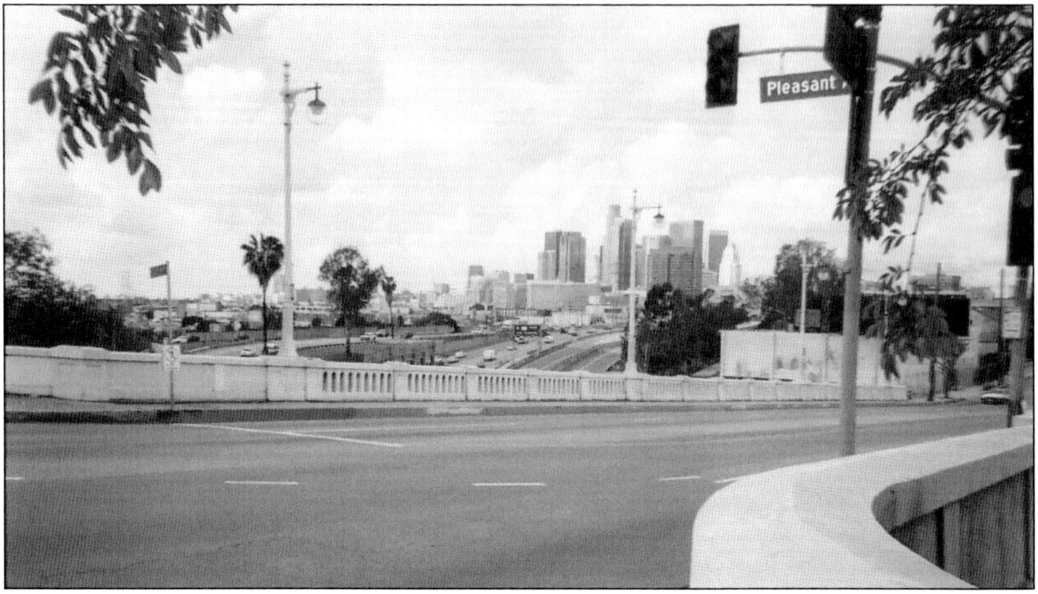

This photograph of downtown Los Angeles was taken looking west from a bridge at Cesar Chavez and Pleasant Avenues in East Los Angeles. This and several other bridges were built in the 1930s over the once-overflowing Los Angeles River, bringing pedestrian and automobile traffic into downtown. Today these bridges connect the old with the new. (Author.)

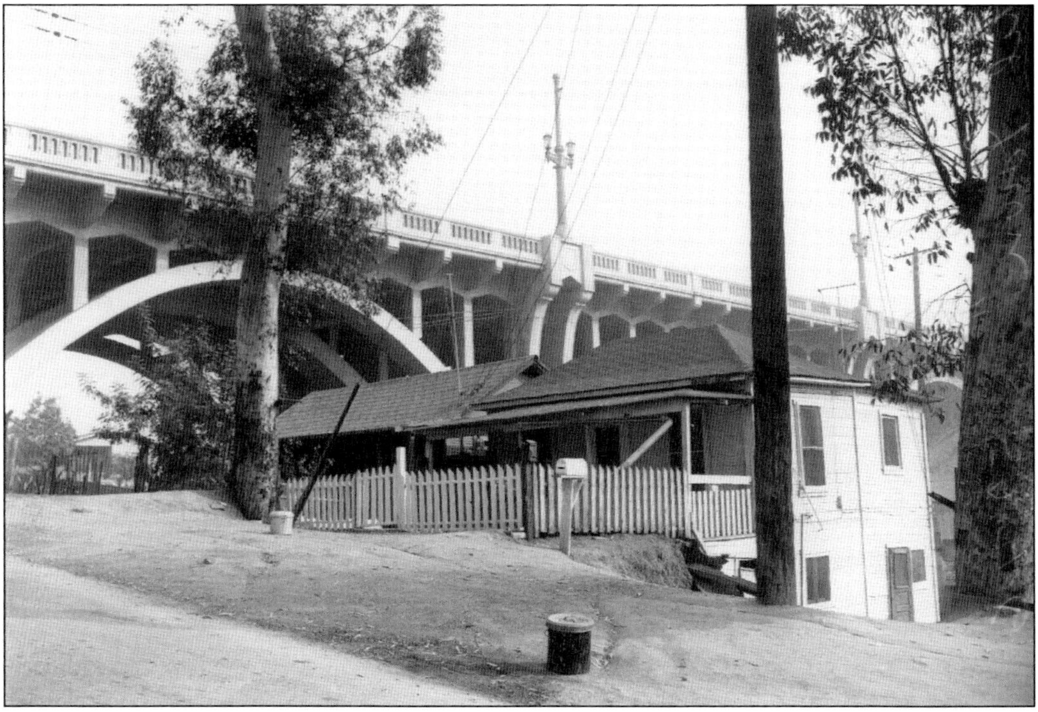

Between 1952 and 1953, by use of the law of eminent domain, Los Angeles' Chavez Ravine was the scene of the evacuation of an entire Mexican American hillside community, forced by city officials and the developers who built the Los Angeles Dodger's baseball stadium. The homes were all destroyed by 1953. This photograph shows one of the last homes to be bulldozed. (UCLA archives.)

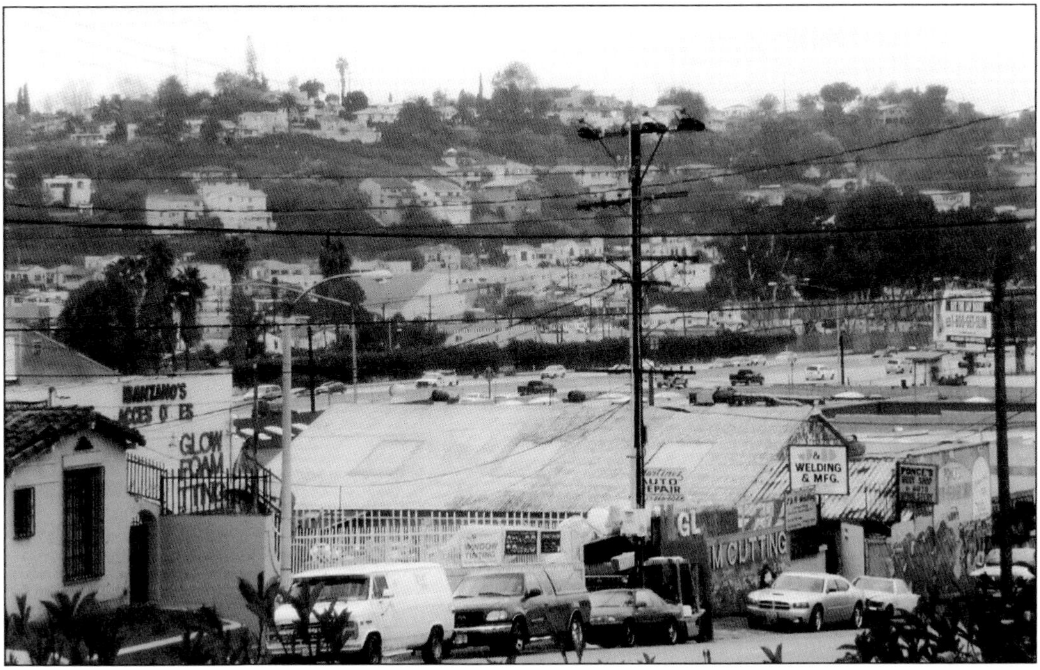

This image is a close-up view of City Terrace, another East Los Angeles neighborhood. Over several decades, the crisscrossing of freeways through the area has impacted the homogeneity of all Eastside communities. The Interstate 10 freeway is seen cutting through the center of this image. (Sal Rodriguez.)

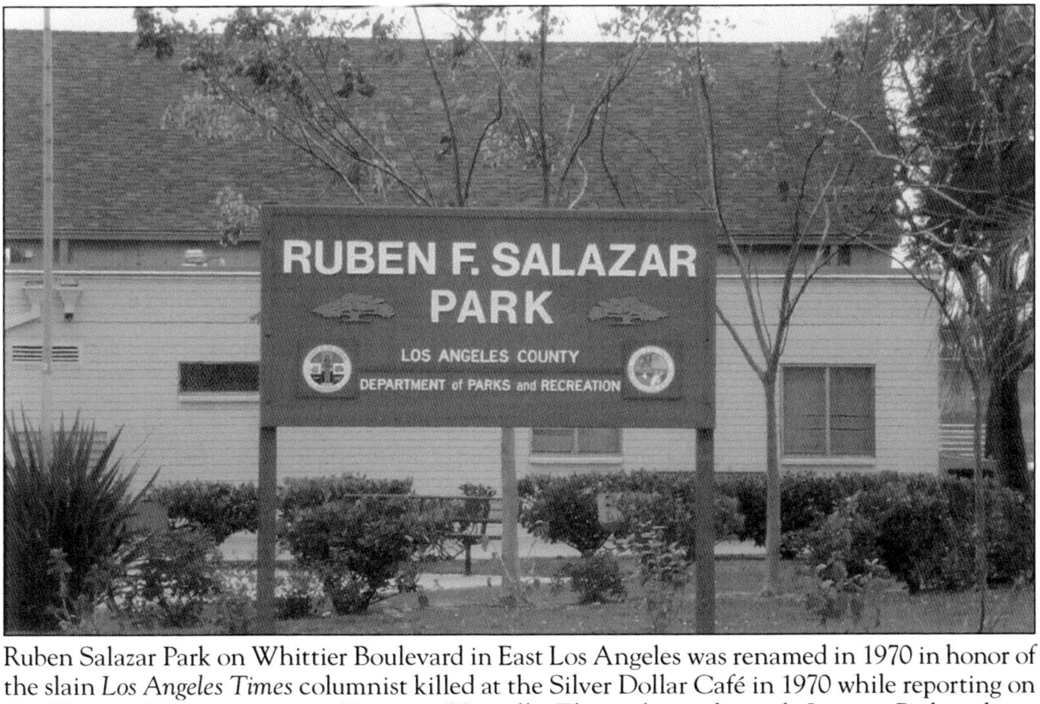

Ruben Salazar Park on Whittier Boulevard in East Los Angeles was renamed in 1970 in honor of the slain *Los Angeles Times* columnist killed at the Silver Dollar Café in 1970 while reporting on the Chicano Moratorium anti–Vietnam War rally. The park was formerly Laguna Park and was originally purchased from Cedars of Lebanon Hospital in 1938 for $15,000. (Sal Rodriguez.)

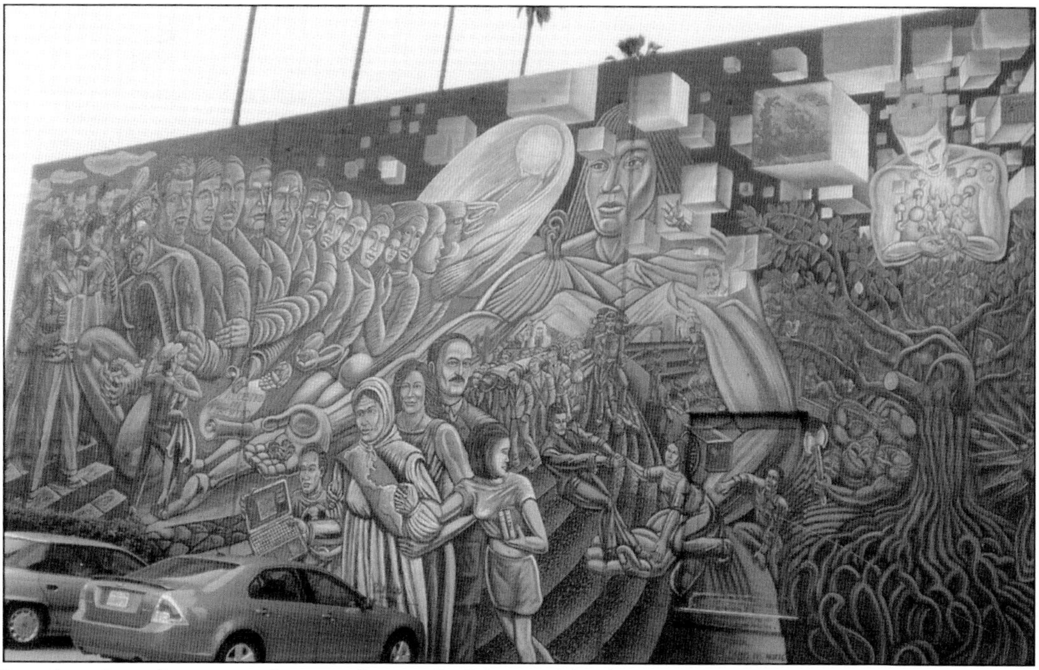

Los Angeles is known as the mural capital of the world. This mural appears on a building adjacent to Ruben Salazar Park in East Los Angeles. The work reveals the different historical journeys, from ancient to modern, taken by Mexican Americans in the United States. At extreme left, the Norteno music group Los Tigres Del Norte (Tigers of the North) appears to lead the musical journey. (Author.)

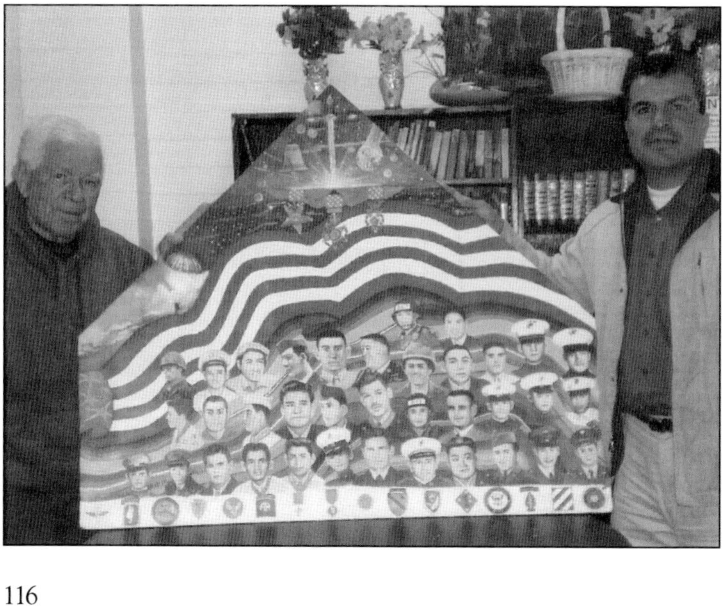

In this image, 36 Mexican American Congressional Medal of Honor recipients from all wars are captured in a proposed mural to be painted inside the senior center at Ruben Salazar Park in East Los Angeles. Framing the mural at left is Cris Mojica, recreation assistant. On the right is Mark Robles, recreation services supervisor. The proposed mural is the work of artist Richard Haro. (Author.)

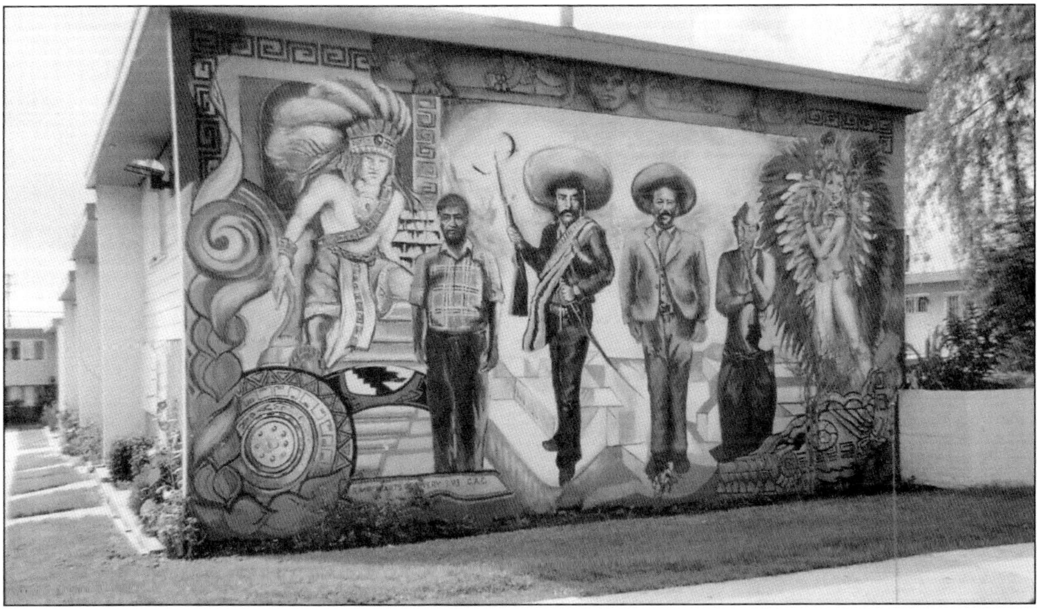

Murals such as the one in this photograph are found in Estrada Courts, a public housing project in East Los Angeles, and they are often painted by community artists and volunteers. From left to right are Mexican American labor leader and icon Cesar Chavez, Mexican revolutionaries Emiliano Zapata and Pancho Villa, and Mexican comedian Cantinflas. Murals often depict themes of social and political struggles for equality. (Author.)

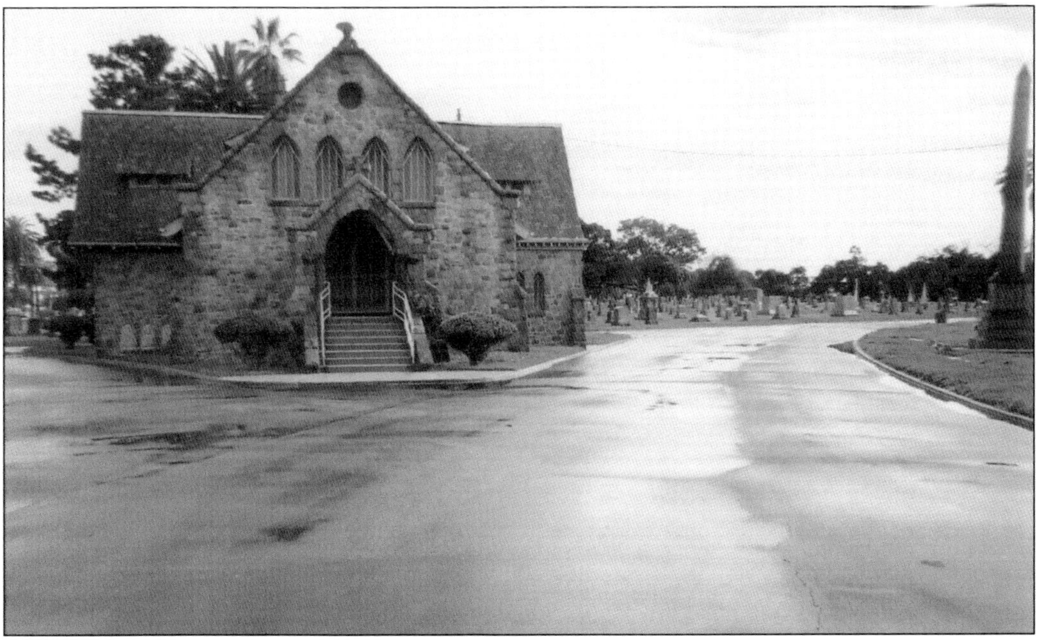

Evergreen Cemetery, a landmark established in 1877, is located at Cesar Chavez Avenue and Evergreen Street in East Los Angeles. It is the oldest cemetery in Los Angeles. Buried here are many members of the city's ethnicities: Hispanic, Armenian, Asian, African American, Jewish, and Caucasian, including names like Hollenbeck, Van Nuys, and Lankershim. Japanese American World War II Congressional Medal of Honor winners are also buried here. (Author.)

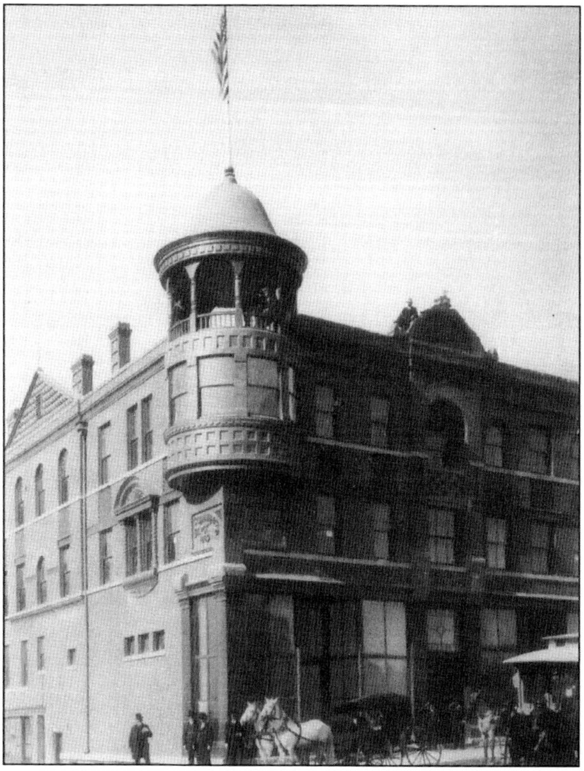

According to Diana Ybarra, president of the Boyle Heights Historical Society, George and Maria Sacramenta Cummings built the Boyle Hotel, originally known as the Cummings Hotel, at First Street and Boyle Avenue in East Los Angeles in 1809. Once a center of social and political life, it now houses many Mexican mariachi groups who play across the street at the Mariachi Plaza. (Lucy Delgado and the Boyle Heights Historical Society.)

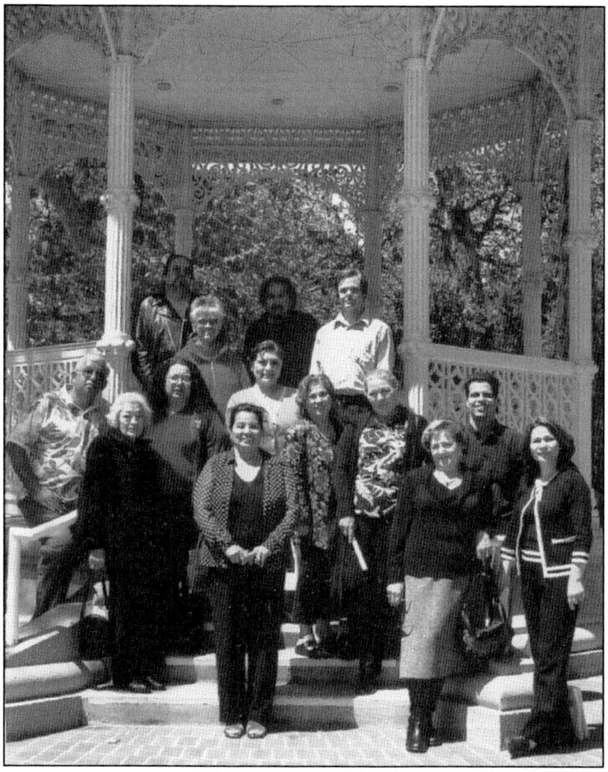

The Boyle Heights Historical Society preserves historical sites and information regarding their neighborhood. Pictured here are 14 members of the organization. From left to right are (first row) Terry Castaneda, Angela Bojorquez, and Felicia Acosta; (second row) Lucy Delgado, Rosalie Gurrola, Vicki Torres, and Paul Spitzerri; (third row) Joe Corral, Becky Delgado, and Diana Ybarra; (fourth row) Hortensia Corral, and Patrick Kolostyak; (fifth row) Victor Delgado and Alvaro Rodriguez. (Diana Ybarra.)

This colorful sign identifies the hillside barrio of City Terrace, northeast of downtown Los Angeles. California State University, Los Angeles, is located nearby with the largest enrollment of Mexican American students in southern California. Chicano muralist and artist Willie Herron's works are found throughout the area. (Sal Rodriguez.)

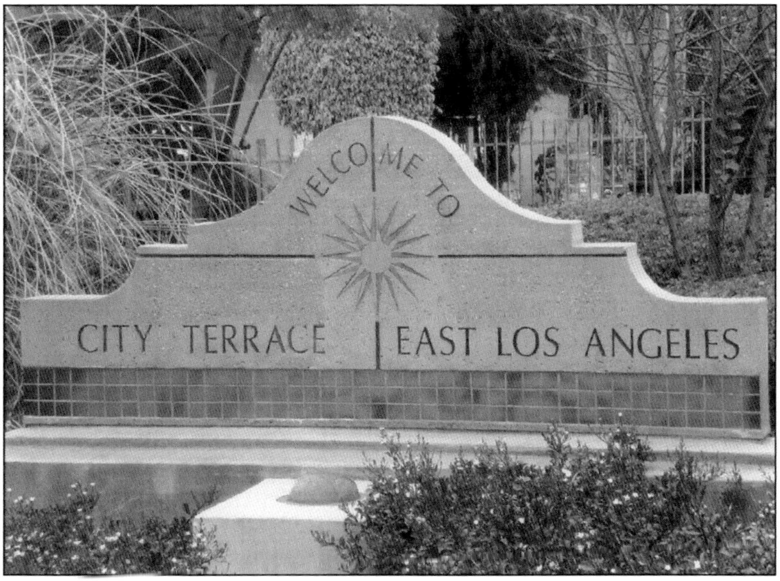

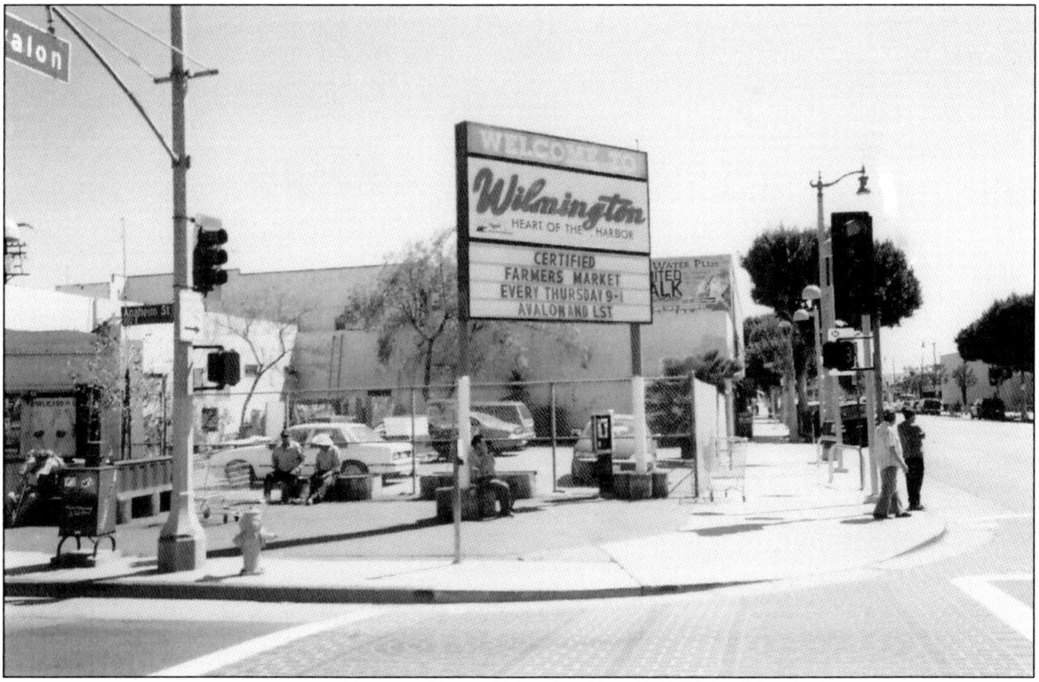

A landmark sign identifying downtown Wilmington, California, as the "Heart of the Harbor" is shown here. Wilmington is a port community of some 53,000 residents who are approximately 85 percent Mexican American. Its principal economic activity is tied to the port of Los Angeles. Many residents are proud members of the International Longshore and Warehouse Union (ILWU). It hosts the largest Labor Day parade on the West Coast. (Author.)

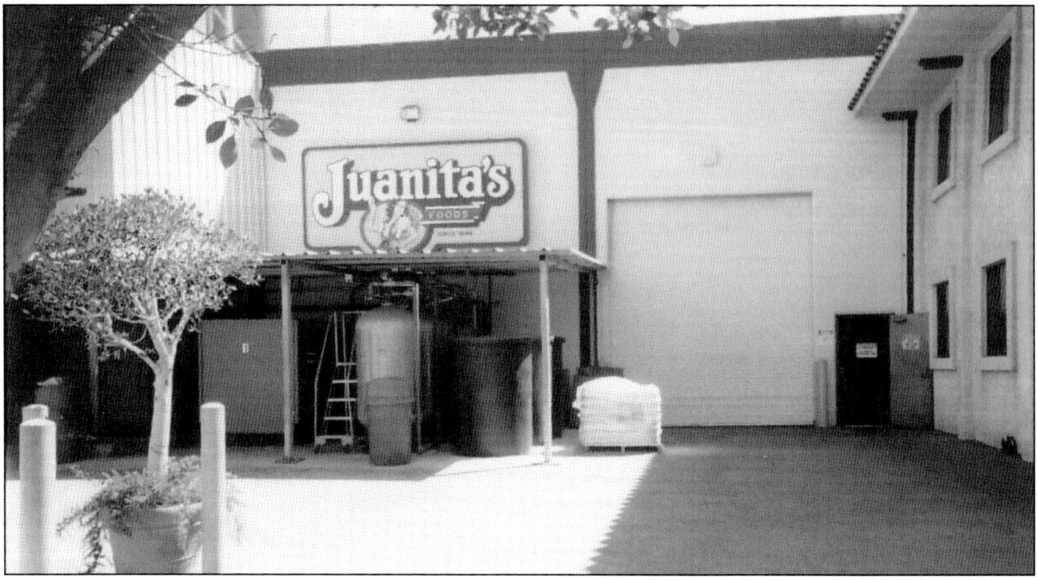

Juanita's Foods in Wilmington, California, founded by George De La Torre Sr., started as Harbor Canning Company in 1946, specializing in the canning of sport fishermen's catches. George De La Torre Jr. became president in 1968 and renamed it Juanita's Foods in 1986. The company pioneered the canning process for *menudo,* building a Mexican food business empire extending into Latin America. (Author.)

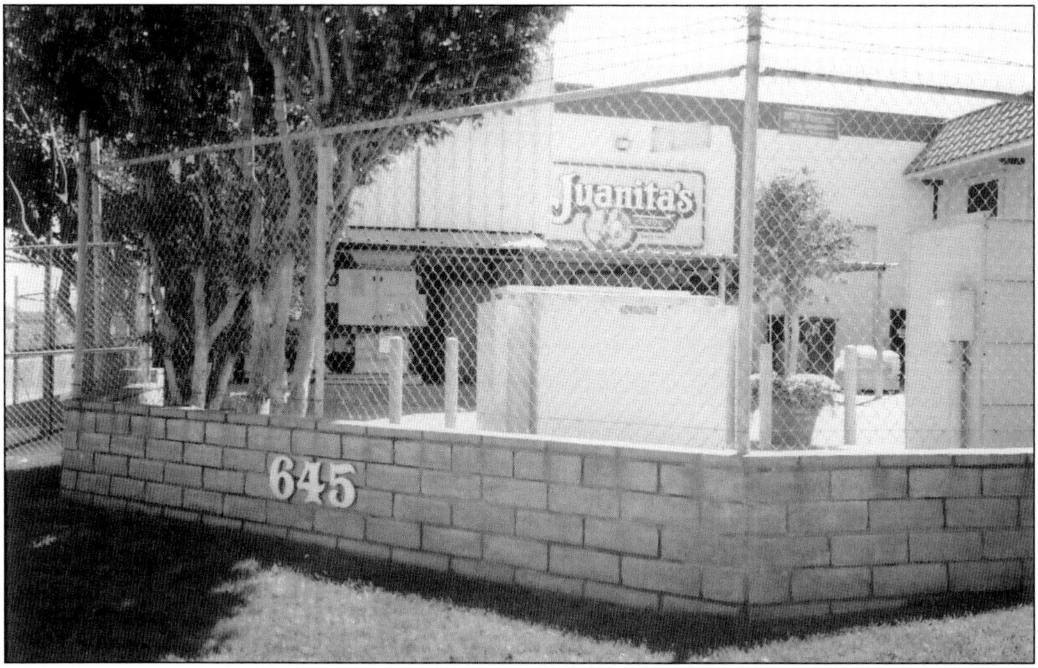

Juanita's Foods in Wilmington, California, shown here, put Wilmington on the map as the *menudo* capital of the world. George De La Torre Sr. was a native son of Wilmington and a leading philanthropist. He supported dozens of causes in the community, especially those involving youth and educational programs. He touched many lives. His passing in 2009 was a deep loss to the community. (Author.)

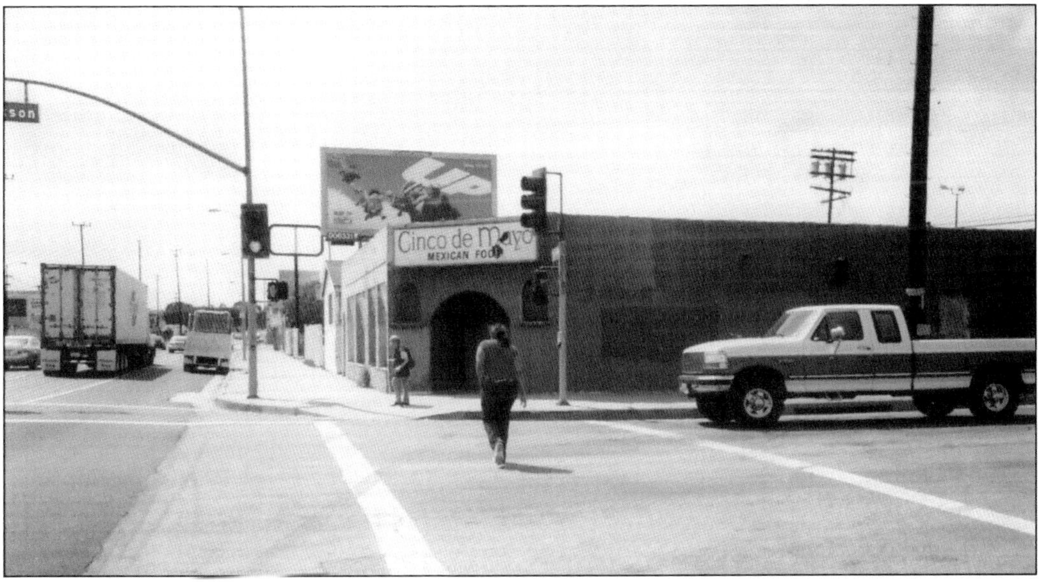

The iconic Cinco de Mayo restaurant, once operated by the Gonzalez family, though closed for many years, is still considered a Wilmington landmark. It opened in the late 1940s on Pacific Coast Highway and Watson Street and was the premier Mexican restaurant in the Los Angeles port area for years. Despite its closing, the sign above the door remains. (Author.)

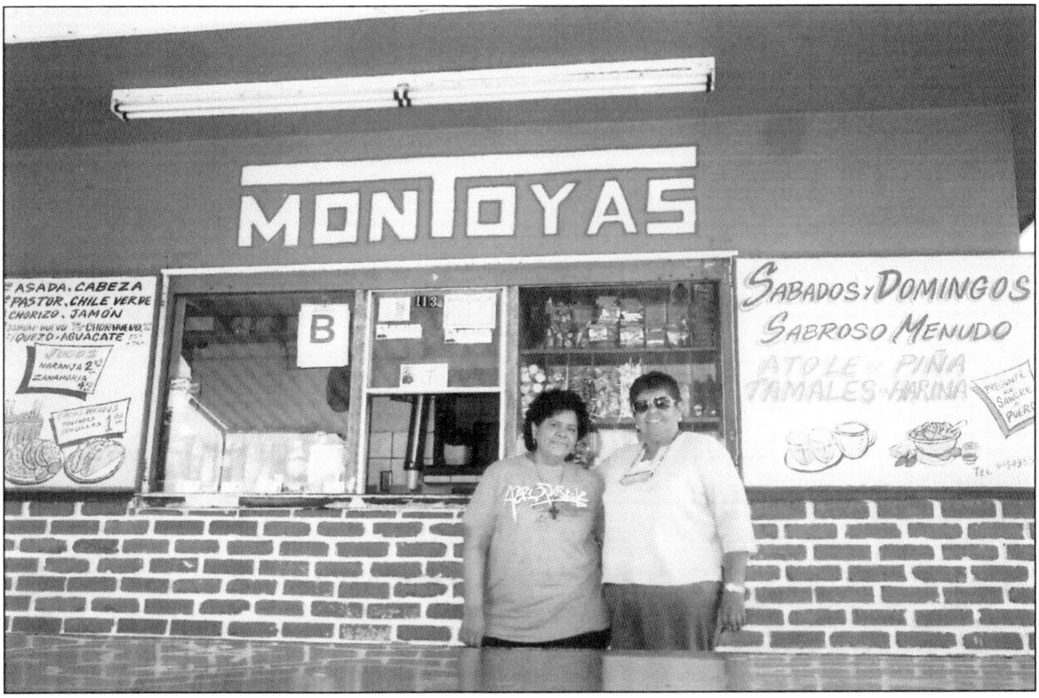

Another well-recognized restaurant and landmark in Wilmington, California, is Montoya's. With a menu serving homemade and largely traditional foods such as *menudo* (tripe stew), tortas (Mexican sandwiches), and atole (corn gruel), it is also known in the community as the place for burritos. Pictured from left to right are owner Evelia Rodriguez and community leader Connie Calderon. (Author.)

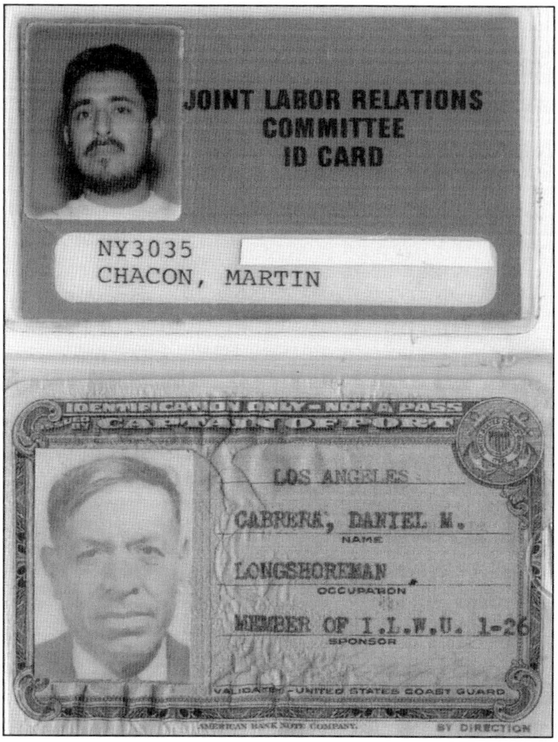

The International Longshore and Warehouse Union (ILWU) in Wilmington, California, forms the backbone of labor in the Port of Los Angeles. In this image at bottom is Daniel Cabrera's 1945 longshoreman's identification card. At left is the identification card of his grandson Martin Chacon, who has followed the longshoreman's tradition. Martin Chacon is a Vietnam veteran and commander of Wilmington's Veterans of Foreign Wars post No. 2967. (Martin Chacon.)

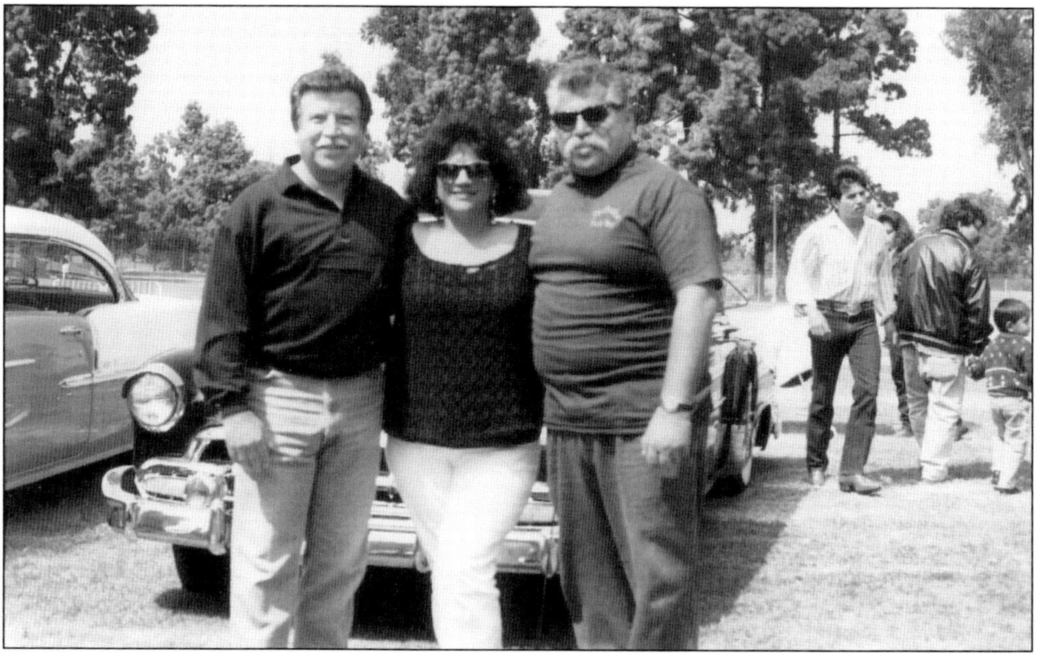

San Pedro, like Wilmington, is a port community of the city of Los Angeles, which has the busiest port in the nation. Its ethnically diverse population includes Croatian, Mexican, Italian, Portuguese, Greek, and Scandinavian residents. This image shows a distinct link between these groups and older classic cars. This *c.* 1989 photograph shows, from left to right, television newscaster Henry Alfaro and Diane and John Doyle (John Doyle.)

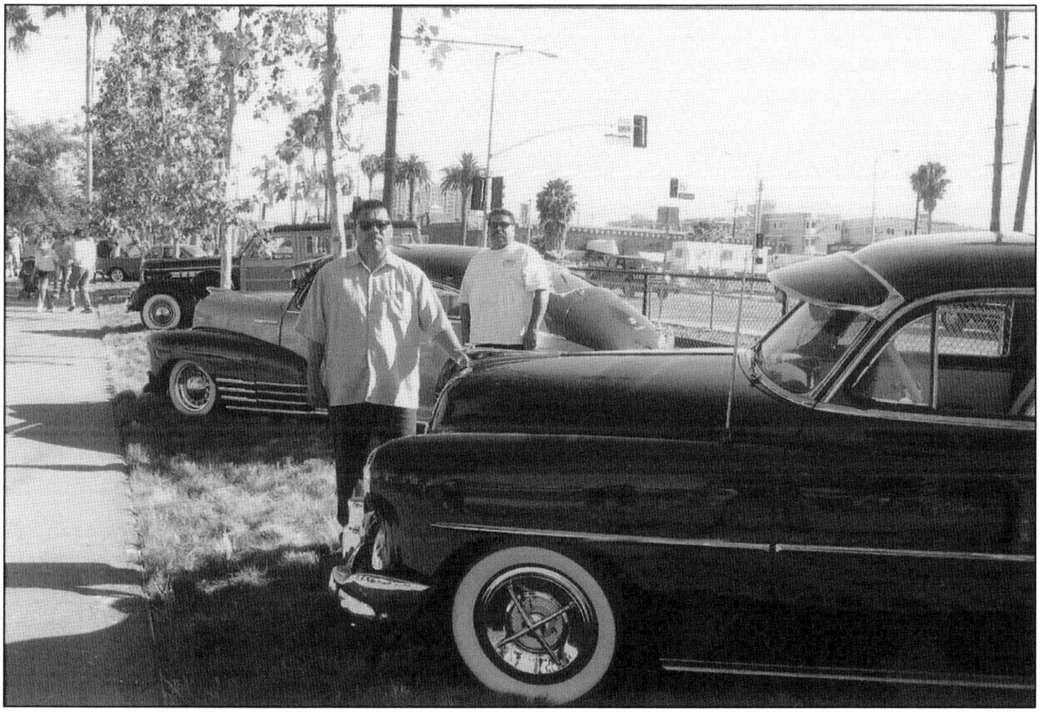

The community of San Pedro's love for classic cars is shown in this photograph. In front, posing with his 1952 Chevrolet is Eddie Bugarin, at center is Jess Reyes with his 1948 Chevrolet Fleetline, and at rear is Steve Kleinjan's rare 1938 Buick Roadmaster "Woody" station wagon. San Pedro is the site of the annual "Hot Pedro Nites" street cruise. (Author.)

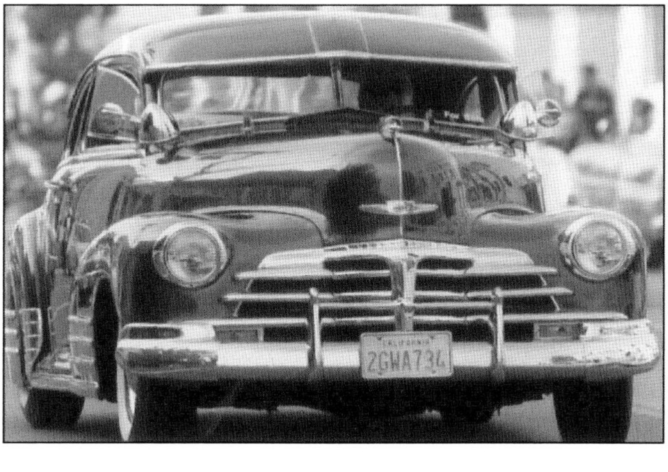

Classic car cruising in San Pedro, California, is a long-held tradition. Car clubs such as Los Reyes (the Kings), the Pharaohs, and the Legends are part of San Pedro and Wilmington, California, history. This 2008 image captures John Doyle's 1948 Chevrolet Fleetline sedan crusing Pacific Avenue, one of San Pedro's main thoroughfares. Classic cars date from the late 1930s to the late 1950s. (John Doyle.)

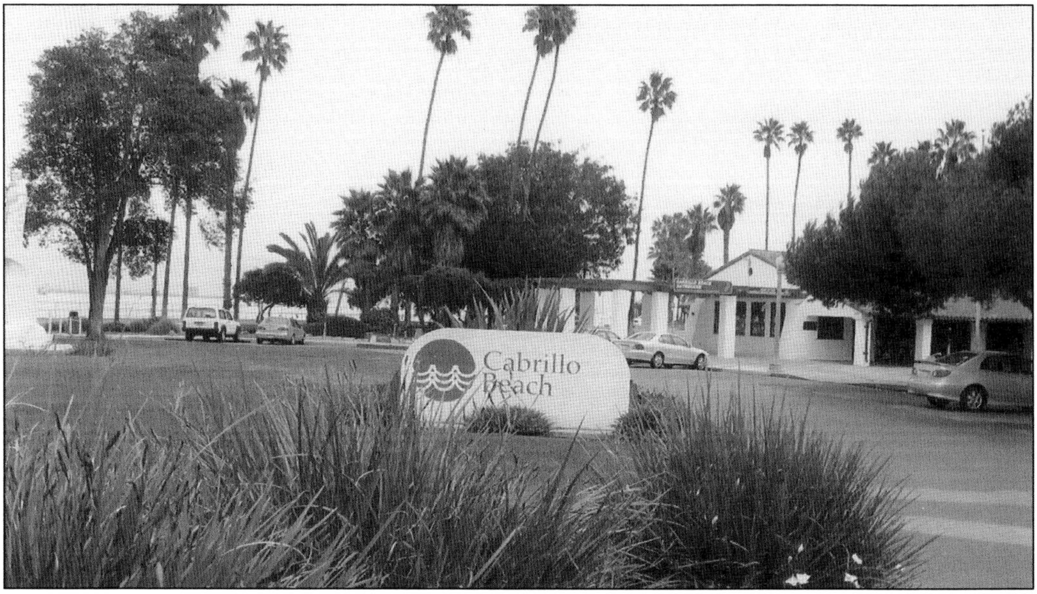

San Pedro's own secluded Cabrillo Beach is a source of strong community pride. Generations of Mexican American families have enjoyed swimming, sunbathing, fishing, sailing, water skiing, and grunion hunting here, together with San Pedro's diverse ethnic groups. One resident boasts, "We don't have to travel miles to other beaches; we have our own right here in our back yard." (Author.)

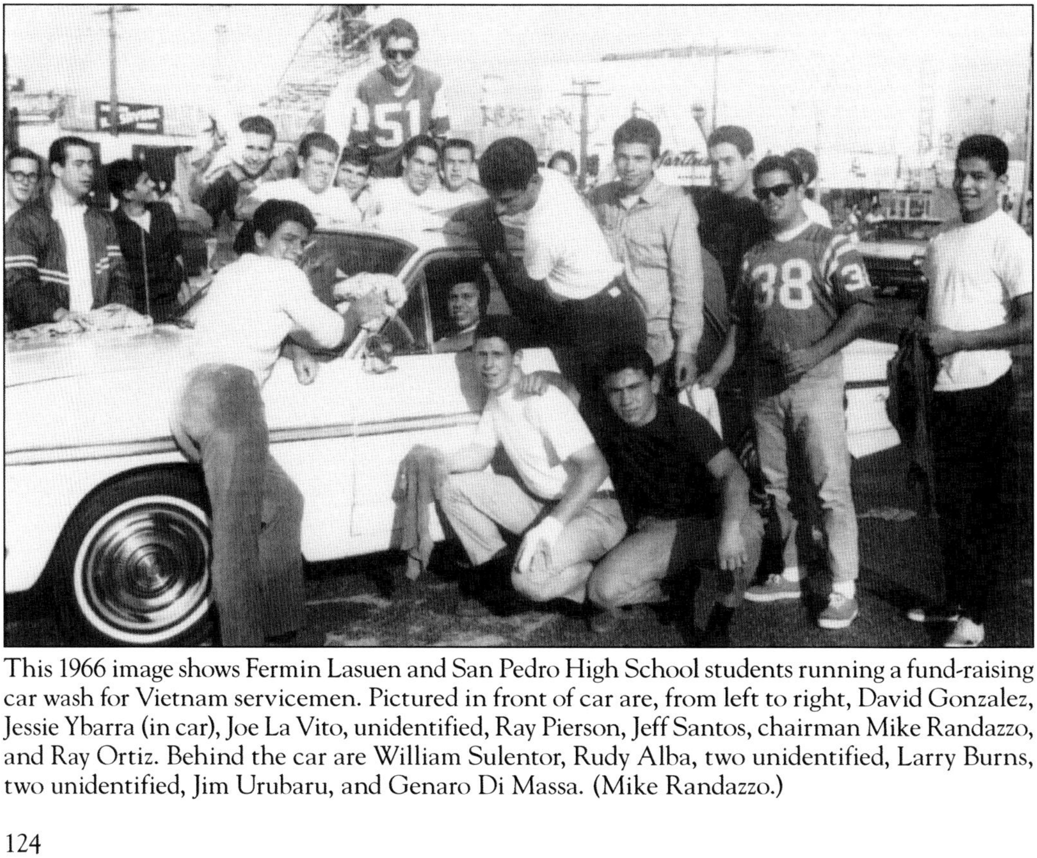

This 1966 image shows Fermin Lasuen and San Pedro High School students running a fund-raising car wash for Vietnam servicemen. Pictured in front of car are, from left to right, David Gonzalez, Jessie Ybarra (in car), Joe La Vito, unidentified, Ray Pierson, Jeff Santos, chairman Mike Randazzo, and Ray Ortiz. Behind the car are William Sulentor, Rudy Alba, two unidentified, Larry Burns, two unidentified, Jim Urubaru, and Genaro Di Massa. (Mike Randazzo.)

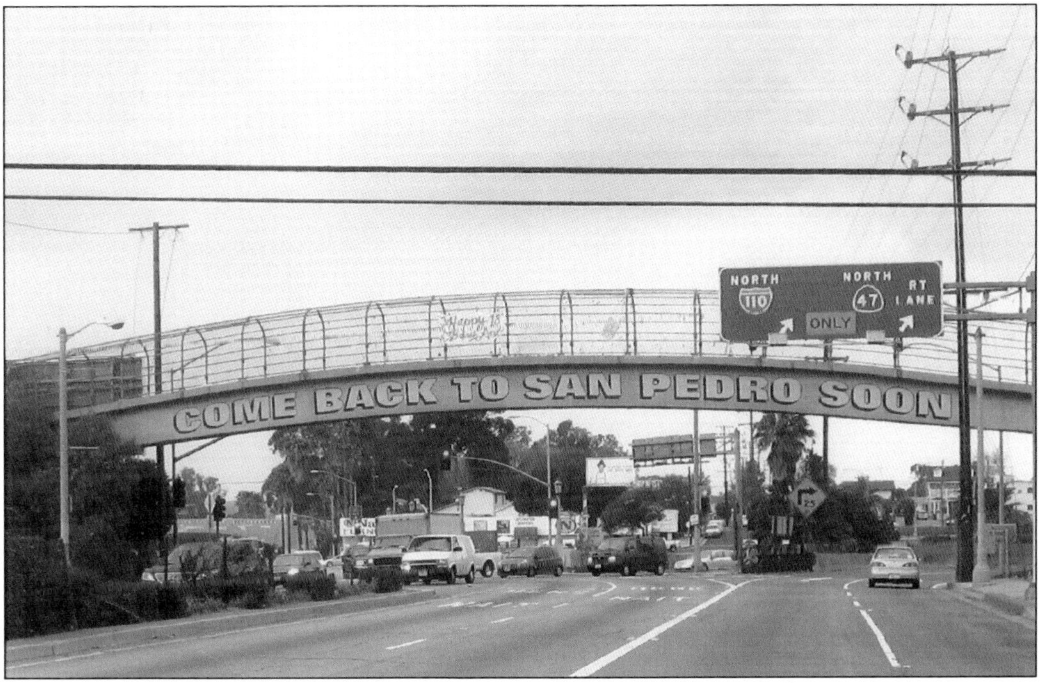

The unique friendliness of San Pedro is found on this Gaffey Street pedestrian overpass as you leave the city. On the opposite side of the overpass, the words, "Welcome to San Pedro," are seen. To the right of the overpass is the magnificent Vincent Thomas Bridge that welcomes thousands of ships and world visitors to San Pedro and the Port of Los Angeles, the nation's busiest port. (Author.)

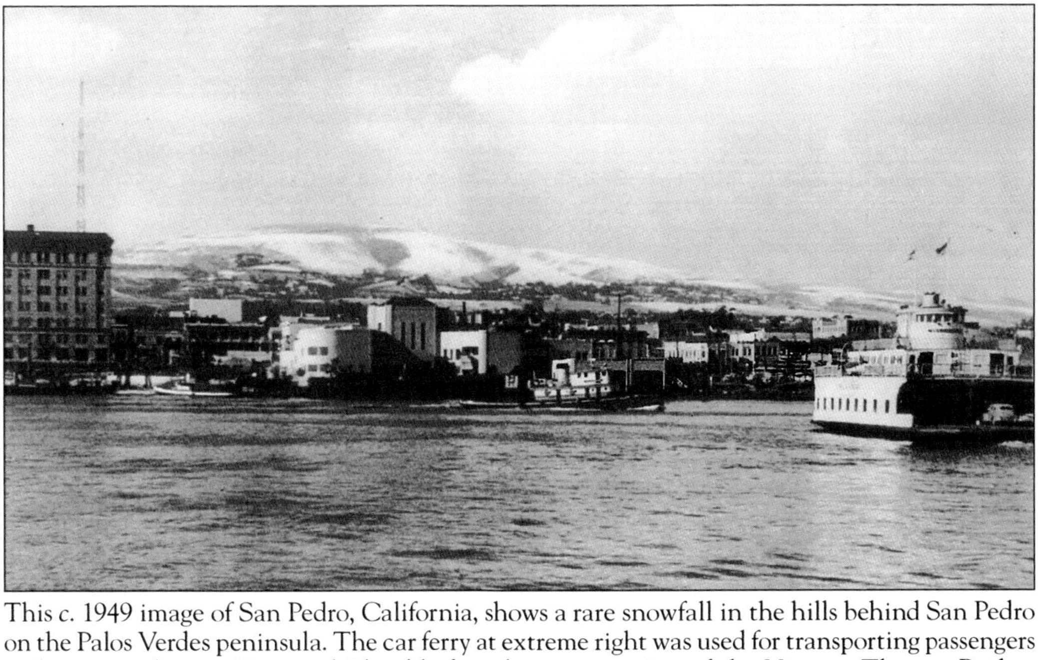

This c. 1949 image of San Pedro, California, shows a rare snowfall in the hills behind San Pedro on the Palos Verdes peninsula. The car ferry at extreme right was used for transporting passengers and cars to adjacent Terminal Island before the construction of the Vincent Thomas Bridge. (Ernie Martinez.)

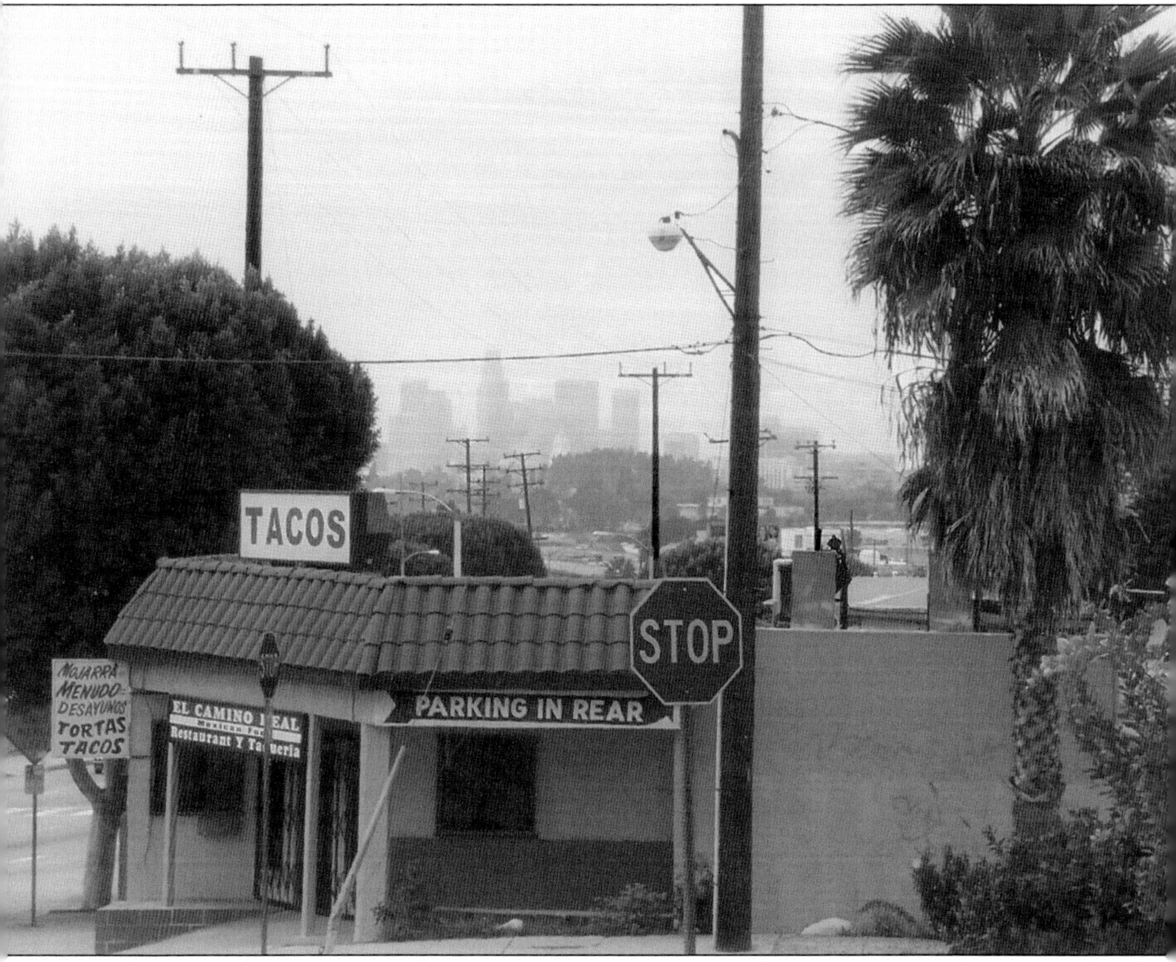

This 2009 photograph provides a distinct contrasting view of an East Los Angeles neighborhood with a typical Mexican family restaurant in the foreground and the skyscrapers of downtown Los Angeles in the background. This final image shows that, despite the modernization of downtown Los Angeles, the Eastside retains its local character.

Bibliography

Acuna, Rodolfo F. A *Community under Siege: A Chronicle of Chicanos East of the Los Angeles River.* Los Angles: UCLA Chicano Studies Research Center Publications, 1984.

Acuna, Rodolfo F. *Corridors of Migration*. Tucson: University of Arizona Press, 2007.

Catalano, Julie. *The Mexican Americans*. New York: Chelsea House Publishers, 1988.

Chabran, Richard, and Rafael Chabran. *The Latino Encyclopedia*. New York: Marshall Cavensish, 2006.

De La Pena, Abelardo. *Mi Barco*. Bloomington, Indiana: Author House, 2006.

Estrada, William D. *The Los Angeles Plaza*. Austin: University of Texas Press, 2006.

Garcia Berumen, Frank Javier. *The Chicano/Hispanic Image in American Film*. New York: Vantage Press, 2007.

Henry, Bill, and Patricia H. Yeoman. *An Approved History of the Olympic Games*. Sherman Oaks, California: Sherman Publishing, 1984.

Kanellos, Nicolas. *The Hispanic American Almanac: A Reference Book on Hispanics in the United States*. Detroit: Gale Research, 1984.

Meier, Matt. *Mexican American Biographies, a Historical Dictionary 1836–1987*. Westport, Connecticut: Greenwood Press, 2000.

Meier, Matt, and Margo Gutierrez. *Encyclopedia of the Mexican American Civil Rights Movement*. Westport, Connecticut: Greenwood Press, 2000.

Morin, Raul. *Among the Valiant, Mexican Americans in World War II and Korea*. Los Angeles: Valiant Press, 2002.